Selling Mothers' Milk

GEORGE D. SUSSMAN

Selling
Mothers' Milk

THE WET-NURSING BUSINESS
IN FRANCE

1715–1914

University of Illinois Press
URBANA   CHICAGO   LONDON

© 1982 by the Board of Trustees of the University of Illinois
Manufactured in the United States of America

This book is printed on acid-free paper.

Library of Congress Cataloging in Publication Data

Sussman, George D., 1943–
Selling mothers' milk.

Bibliography: p.
Includes index.
1. Wet-nurses—France—History—18th century.
2. Wet nurses—France—History—19th century.
3. France—Social conditions—18th century.
4. France—Social conditions—19th century.
I. Title.
RJ216.S9   338.4'76493   81-16277
ISBN 0-252-00919-3   AACR2

Philippe Ariès has insisted on the importance of distance and surprise in historical explanation: in the sixteenth century one comes up against a certain form of strangeness; strangeness especially for an observer from centuries away. How can we account for this discrepancy? That is the whole problem. What I want to say is that surprise and distance—those important aids to comprehension—are both equally necessary for an understanding of that which surrounds you—surrounds you so evidently that you can no longer see it clearly. Live in London for a year and you will not get to know much about England. But, through comparison, in the light of your surprise, you will suddenly come to understand some of the most profound and individual characteristics of France, which you did not previously understand because you knew them too well. The past likewise provides distance from the present.

FERNAND BRAUDEL, "History and the Social Sciences"

Contents

Preface

My interest in the wet nurses of France was piqued by a chance meeting, figuratively speaking, on the roads leading out of Paris during the cholera epidemic of 1832. In actuality the encounter occurred in the Archives Nationales in 1969 or 1970, when I was doing research for a study of French sanitary policy in the epidemics of the Restoration and July Monarchy. I was laboring through cartons of correspondence from local authorities to the minister of the interior reporting, at the minister's request, information on the first appearance of the cholera epidemic in their localities as the disease spread out of Paris. Again and again the mayors of small villages around Paris reported that the first case in their jurisdictions was either a wet nurse who had just returned from the capital with a baby or sometimes the baby.

As a reader of French history and literature, I had come across wet nurses before. But I had never bothered to question the alien and antiquated custom of wet-nursing. This time I began to wonder about it, perhaps because of the repetition of references and the difficulty of finding any other pattern for the spread of the disease in the endless cartons of disordered letters. How common was wet-nursing? Why did people send their babies away to the country to be nursed? One letter seemed particularly promising. It reported the case of a wet nurse who fell sick on the road between Auxerre and Vaux on her return from Paris, where she had spent eight days "living on only bread and water at the Bureau of Wet Nurses." The Bureau of Wet Nurses sounded like a public agency. If the government had been involved, a body of documentation lay somewhere in the public archives waiting to reveal the secrets of wet-nursing.[1]

ix

My quest for understanding of this phenomenon proceeded with the financial support of several grants, the assistance of many archivists and librarians, the encouragement and criticism of colleagues and friends, and the patience and support of my family. For financial support in the research and writing of this book and the articles that preceded it, I am grateful to the National Endowment for the Humanities (Summer Stipend for Younger Humanists, 1973), the American Council of Learned Societies (Grant-in-Aid of Research, 1975), the National Library of Medicine (NIH Grant LM 02331, 1975–77), and the Vanderbilt University Research Council (small grants in 1974 and 1976). Among the many colleagues and friends who have assisted me in various ways, I particularly thank Don Winters, who helped me learn to use the computer for the analysis of social data; Susan Wiltshire and Ned Newman, who plied me with citations, illustrations, and photocopies of material on wet-nursing; Robert R. Palmer, Dora Weiner, Charles F. Delzell, and others I am forgetting, who supported my applications for financial support with their letters of recommendation; Joan W. Scott and Louise A. Tilly, who prodded me toward a broader, more theoretical view of my subject; Marie-France Morel, who generously shared with me her knowledge and insight about eighteenth-century infant care in France; Sheila Murdick and Marion Peters, who cheerfully assisted me with the index; and my wife Sandy, who contributed much to this book.

Various historical associations and journals provided me with opportunities to develop and test the ideas and understanding presented in this book. For these opportunities I am grateful to my hosts and critics at the Western Society for French History (March 1974), the Washington Society of the History of Medicine (1975), the Corcoran Department of History at the University of Virginia (1975), and the Berkshire Conference on the History of Women (1978) and to the editors and readers of *French Historical Studies*, *The Journal of Interdisciplinary History*, and *The Journal of Family History*.[2]

I am responsible for all translations from French to English in quotations included in this book.

Notes

1. George D. Sussman, "Carriers of Cholera and Poison Rumors in France in 1832," *Societas*, 3 (Summer 1973), 233–51.
2. George D. Sussman, "The Wet-Nursing Business in Paris, 1769–1876," in *Proceedings of the First Annual Meeting of the Western Society for French History, March 14–15, 1974*, ed. by Edgar Leon Newman (Las Cruces: New Mexico State University Press, 1974), cols. 179–94; "The Wet-Nursing Business in Nineteenth-Century France," *French Historical Studies*, 9 (Fall 1975), 304–28; "Parisian Infants and Norman Wet Nurses in the Early Nineteenth Century: A Statistical Study," *Journal of Interdisciplinary History*, 7 (Spring 1977), 637–53; "The End of the Wet-Nursing Business in France, 1874–1914," *Journal of Family History*, 2 (Fall 1977), 237–58.

List of Abbreviations
Used in Citations

AAP Archives de l'Assistance publique, Paris

AC Archives communales, with name of commune
(AC Verneuil: Archives communales de Verneuil)

AD Archives départementales, with name of Department
(AD Eure: Archives départementales de l'Eure)

AN Archives nationales, Paris

APP Archives de la Préfecture de Police, Paris

BA Bibliothèque de l'Arsenal, Paris
Within the BA:
   AB   Archives de la Bastille

BN Bibliothèque nationale, Paris
Within the BN:
   CJdF   Collection Joly de Fleury
   MF   Manuscrits français
   NAF   Nouvelles acquisitions françaises

1

Introduction

IN A BOOK ABOUT the first generation of Pasteurian pediatricians in France, the French sociologist Luc Boltanski observed that infancy is an idea, a socially defined concept, only partially linked to the objective conditions of infant life. New theories of child-rearing may claim to break with earlier "prejudices" about childhood and to conform to the essential character of childhood. Yet, in elaborating new rules of child care immediately dependent upon the child's objective conditions of existence, even these theories, Boltanski contends, give rise to a new social definition of what childhood is and what it ought to be.[1]

At first sight, infancy and the care of newborns, among all human groups and activities, may appear to be particularly unsuitable to Boltanski's social and cultural approach. What could be more compelling or more universal than a baby's feeding requirements, the necessity of changing and bathing a baby and laundering its clothes, the baby's rashes and intestinal disorders, and the constant need to keep the baby in view and to intervene to prevent accidents. But Boltanski's point, supported by historical and contemporary evidence, is that, although the biology of infancy is universal in historical time, human perceptions of infancy and what it requires are socially conditioned and subject to historical change.

The historical and social character of infancy is manifest not only in the variety of theories and folk wisdom that have guided men and women caring for babies but also in the variety of social arrangements and agents employed in the activity. Historically, amid shifting household and social structures, the tasks of caring for newborn babies have been accomplished through various combinations of parents, family and kin, friends and neighbors, domestic servants, extramural sitters, wet nurses, professionals, industries such as diaper service and home-milk delivery, bureaucratic social agencies, and the product market (lest we forget our own debt to disposable paper diapers and plastic inserts for feeding bottles). In France during the eighteenth and nineteenth centuries the predominant pattern of infant care associated with larger, older cities like Paris and Lyon was rural wet-nursing.

Narrowly and literally defined, wet-nursing was the practice whereby a woman suckled another woman's child for pay. The wet nurse (*la nourrice* in French) may have suckled and cared for the baby either in her own home during the nursing period or in the baby's parents' home in which case she acted as sitter and nurse at the same time (the live-in nurse was called *la nourrice sur lieu* in French). In eighteenth-century France the wet nurses were almost always peasant women who took babies from the cities into their cottages in the country for the nursing period. In the nineteenth century well-to-do urban families preferred to recruit rural women as live-in nurses, although rural wet-nursing continued to flourish in the service of lower-middle and working-class families.

A peasant woman who kept a baby in her cottage many miles away from the city for a period of a year or more necessarily did much more for the baby than suckle it. Indeed, parents had little assurance that the nurse continued to suckle their baby at all once she carried it out of the city. Broadly conceived, wet-nursing was a form of infant care including much more than feeding. Sometimes the baby remained in the village beyond the acknowledged date of its weaning. Toward the end of the nineteenth century newborn babies were increasingly placed with rural nurses who, by agreement with the parents, did not breast-feed at all. This social pattern was called dry-nursing, *le nourrissage sec.*

Nonetheless, suckling was always central, if not to the reality of wet-nursing, then at least to the perception. Medical manuals suggested that it was the quality of the woman's milk that parents should investigate in selecting a wet nurse; the rest of the moral and physical environment in which the baby was to be placed was scarcely considered. The normal period that babies were left in the country (except in the case of foundlings) was likewise linked to contemporary medical opinion on the proper age for weaning, no matter when individual babies were actually weaned. Dry-nursing was a short epilogue at the end of the longer history of wet-nursing.

The custom of wet-nursing in the West is of classical descent. Favorinus of Arles, a second-century rhetorician who studied in Greece and settled in Rome, left a discourse arguing that a new mother of the senatorial class should suckle her baby rather than, as the grandmother argued, hire nurses to spare the mother's health. The discourse, preserved in the Latin translation of his disciple Aulus Gellius, makes many of the arguments against wet-nursing that were later picked up by moralists and physicians of the Renaissance and early modern period.[2] Another source from second-century Rome indicates that wet-nursing in the Imperial City was an organized, commercial activity. Festus, later epitomized by Paulus, wrote that certain columns in the Forum Holitorium ("vegetable market area") were called the Lactaria "because it was there they brought children who had to be nourished with milk."[3] If this reference does describe a placement center for wet nurses, then it would appear that second-century Rome adumbrates eighteenth-century Paris in the combination of upper-class reliance upon wet nurses, intellectual criticism of the custom, and a commercial organization for the placement of nurses, which may point to even broader social participation in the wet-nursing business.

The early history of wet-nursing in France is best documented in the royal line. All of the French royal children going back at least to the future St. Louis at the beginning of the thirteenth century were suckled by hired women, while many foreign princes and princesses (including the many children of the Habsburg Empress Maria Theresa) were nursed by their mothers. The royal nurse and several replacements who were kept in reserve were carefully selected six to eight weeks before the queen was expected to deliver. The royal babies were nursed for about two years. Their nurses were often changed, either because of lack of milk or as a result of court intrigue. The future Louis XIII had four nurses before he was weaned at the age of twenty-five months. One of the future Louis XIV's nurses was dismissed after she was denounced to the king by a Mousquetaire for talking with her husband in the garden of Saint Germain (the royal nurses were not supposed to see their husbands). After the weaning, the successful royal nurse was generally promoted to a permanent position in the court.[4]

At social levels below the royal line the evidence of wet-nursing in France goes back to the Middle Ages. The ordinance concerning police of the realm, issued by King John on January 30, 1350, contains a title devoted to the wages of wet nurses and of *recommandaresses*, "who are accustomed to hire out chambermaids and wet nurses." "Wet nurses nursing children outside the house of the children's father and mother," the ordinance declared, "shall earn and take one hundred *sols* a year, and no more." The *recommandaresse* who procured or hired out a wet nurse was entitled to two *sols* from the parents and the same sum from the nurse.[5]

Although a systematic survey of diaries, personal correspondence, and *livres de raison* has not been undertaken, selected sources of this sort suggest that wet-nursing was not generally practiced among the upper and official classes in the sixteenth century but became common in the seventeenth and especially the eighteenth centuries. The beginning of this evolution may be traced in the *livre de raison* of the Froissard-Broissia, a family of *parlementaires* from Dôle in the Jura region. Anatoille Froissard and his wife were married in 1532 and had five children. The only child about whom the nursing experience is recorded is the first, a son named Pierre: "The said Pierre was nursed and suckled [*nourry et alaité*] by my wife about eighteen months, until the fourteenth of April in the year 1535, after Easter, when he was weaned by my wife in the said place of Dôle, in the house of Mons. de Champvans, where I made my residence at the time of his birth."

In the next generation Jean Froissard, Anatoille's second son and *président* of the Parlement of Dôle, sired fourteen children between his marriage in 1572 and his death in 1595. With the earliest children the mother nursed and was either aided, or replaced after she became pregnant again, by hired women. For example, Claude, the second child and first son, born in October 1574, "was nursed by my wife and by a woman from Dôle, named Denise Vantesconet, who was hired as a servant in the house, to help my wife." At the end of July the mother, knowing that she was pregnant, stopped nursing the child, who was left in the country with the wife of the family's tenant farmer and Denise Vantesconet. A month later, with these two women ill, the baby boy was brought back to Dôle and given "for his sole nurse" Marguerite Baudier, a widow. A similar pattern was followed with the next children. But the later children were turned over to hired nurses from birth. Anne, born in 1581, was "nursed in the house" by a widow. Jehan Symon, born in 1587, was "put out to nurse at the farm of Vaucluse, where la Clauda, wife of Cl. Fontaine known as Mottet, nursed him for wages of 40 francs a year."[6]

In the seventeenth century the evidence of reliance on wet-nursing by the well-to-do and official class is widespread. Samuel Robert, a Huguenot and royal official in the Élection of Saintes, fathered six children between 1640 and 1649. The first, Jehan, "was given to nurse to Guillemette Audoüyn, wife of Gérosme Alayre, master carpenter of the said Sainct-Vivien, for the sum of sixty *livres* a year." Others were placed with the wives of a master mason, a sergeant, and a ploughman (*laboureur à boeufz*) in the country.[7] The bourgeois of Poitiers in the mid-seventeenth century placed their babies with tenants or former servants who were married and living in the country. The fee ranged from 35 to 45 *livres* a year, in addition to gifts (such as a pair of shoes), which were often specified in the contract.[8] A descriptive account of the Beauvais region, written by a lawyer and published in 1617, found it sufficiently unusual to remark that among the common people of the towns, the women were "for the most part doubly mothers: that is to say, nurses to their own children, which makes their beauty fade sooner, but also makes the children healthier."[9]

A *livre de raison* from the last quarter of the seventeenth century, that of Claude Le Doulx, counsellor in the Parlement of Paris, suggests the cost in human lives of the adoption of wet-nursing by the urban elite. The counsellor's wife gave birth to thirteen children between 1671 and 1695 and had at least one miscarriage. Only three of the children survived their first few years of life. The father recorded the facts of each successive death, embellished by a few medical details. But of one daughter, who died in 1677 after sixteen months of life, he wrote, "She died by the fault of the wet nurses, among others the last, who did not have enough milk."[10]

Upper-class reliance on wet-nursing as a mode of infant-feeding was not unique to France in the seventeenth century. An early contribution to the anti–wet-nursing literature is *The Countesse of*

Lincolnes Nurserie, published in Oxford in 1622. The work is dedicated to Briget, countesse of Lincolne, who nursed her own children, "wherein you have gone before the greatest number of honourable Ladies of your place, in these latter times." The author herself confesses that she hired wet nurses for her eighteen children, a decision that she later regretted. The refusal of mothers to nurse, "this unthankfulnesse, and unnaturalnesse," and the reliance on wet nurses instead were in Jacobean England, according to this witness, "oftener the sinne of the Higher, and the richer sort, than of the meaner, and poorer."[11]

The same pattern of maternal nursing by the lower class and wet-nursing by the upper class prevailed in the northern Italian states in the seventeenth century. Bernardino Ramazzini's classic of occupational medicine, *De Morbis Artificum,* published in Modena in 1700, includes a chapter on the diseases of wet nurses. Ramazzini's observations about the practice of wet-nursing in his own society are few and incidental to his medical purpose but nonetheless illuminating: "I observe that among the common people mothers always nurse their infants, unless prevented by some accident. . . . In this city very few of the nobility employ nurses in their houses. . . . They nearly always hand them over to nurses who rear them in their homes along with their own children, but they prefer to entrust them to country women rather than to women of the city."[12]

The distinctiveness of France with respect to wet-nursing and infant-feeding began to be noticed by some contemporaries in the eighteenth century. Antoine Deparcieux, in an early work on mortality statistics published in 1746, observed that outside of France upper-class women no longer relied on wet nurses. "In London most women nurse [their own babies], even the Princesses." Linked to this social observation was a moral judgment: "Are the duties of rank and reasons of interest so different in France, and especially in Paris, from what they are in Germany, in Holland, in England, etc., where almost all women nurse their babies, even women of the greatest distinction?" But another observation by Deparcieux suggests that it was not only the practice of the well-born and the well-to-do that set France apart: "In the large cities, at least in France, all the common people [*le menu peuple*] send their babies out to nurse six, eight, ten leagues away, and do not bring them back until three or four years of age." This practice, shared by the urban elite of Europe in the seventeenth century but practiced exclusively by their class, was disappearing in the eighteenth century everywhere but in France, and there it was expanding to new social groups in the cities. Deparcieux, despite his interest in vital statistics and his sensitivity to national differences in nursing practices, did not speculate on the impact of the differences in nursing practices on national mortality rates and population trends.[13]

The distinctiveness of France was still more pronounced in the nineteenth century. In the article "Wet Nurse," published in the *Dictionnaire encyclopédique des sciences médicales* in 1879, the Lyonnais physician Delore observed, "France is nearly the only country where the wet-nursing business [*l'industrie des nourrices*] is organized. Among all other nations, maternal nursing is the rule, even in the well-to-do classes." In England, Delore noted, "mothers who do not nurse generally prefer the bottle, and in cases where a wet nurse is indispensable, they bring her from France."[14]

From the time of the Franco-Prussian War a new kind of critical understanding of wet-nursing developed in France. Where earlier writers had recognized the custom as distinctively French and denounced it on moral grounds, social observers of the 1870s began to link wet-nursing with other unique characteristics of French family life and demography. Léon Lefort, writing in the *Revue des Deux Mondes* in March 1870, explored the relationship between national patterns of infant-feeding and infant mortality rates; he concluded that the principal reason for France's declining demographic position, in relation to her neighbors, was not wet-nursing but delayed marriage (attributed to conscription) and the practice of birth control within marriage.[15] In the early 1870s Louis-Adolphe Bertillon used statistics and cartography to demonstrate a direct causal relationship between wet-nursing, high infant mortality, and slow population growth in France.[16] Émile Zola's novel *Fécondité* (1899) is perhaps the most comprehensive view of the uniqueness of French wet-nursing. A moralistic and patriotic diatribe, the novel associates wet-nursing with high infant mortality, late marriage, birth control, and population decline in a sweeping imaginative synthesis of French demography and family life at the turn of the century.[17]

Certainly the French experience of wet-nursing was unique in Europe in the extent of mass participation, the high degree of social organization, and the long historical persistence of the custom. It is tempting, following Zola, to associate this practice with another feature of French demographic experience in the modern period—France's precocious decline in fertility. There are two ways in which this connection might have operated. First, breast-feeding nurslings might have reduced fertility by inhibiting new conceptions for the rural women who supplemented their income in this way (urban women practiced more deliberate family planning). Second, the same cultural attitudes—hostility to children or the woman's desire to spend her time at work or in the *salon* rather than in the nursery—may be behind the restriction of births and the practice of putting infants out to be nursed.[18] But such a direct relationship between the decline in fertility rates and wet-nursing is an oversimplification. The two phenomena were not necessarily congruent in France. The decline in fertility rates occurred first in the upper class, which was also the first to abandon wet-nursing. Moreover, the decline developed early in parts of rural France where mothers nursed their own children and, in some instances, where they did not also nurse urban infants.[19]

Whether from the comparative or the historical perspective, the central question about French wet-nursing of the eighteenth and nineteenth centuries is, why did it happen? Why did so many parents automatically place their newborn babies with previously unknown peasant women far from their homes for the first year or two of their lives? "How can we account for this discrepancy," this "strangeness," Braudel asked in the passage that I took as an epigraph for this book.

Observers in the past and recent historians have offered three different explanations, either singly or in combination, for the wet-nursing phenomenon. (1) Wet-nursing was a cultural artifact, the result of certain attitudes toward children and the family that we no longer share. (2) Wet-nursing was an adaptation to certain social and economic conditions, particularly female employment in an urban setting. (3) Wet-nursing was a material or technological necessity in the days before the germ theory and pasteurization simplified the problem of safe infant-feeding.

The cultural explanation of wet-nursing is related to Philippe

Ariès's idea of "the discovery of childhood."[20] The argument is that in the indefinite past adults were relatively indifferent to children. Children were so numerous and so many of them died before reaching maturity that parents could not afford to invest a great amount of effort, money, or affection in them. So parents neglected their children, or worse: they teased them, beat them, abandoned them, killed them, or put them out in the country to nurse. Any mother who could afford to hire a wet nurse would never sacrifice her sleep, her social life, her sexual pleasure (intercourse was supposed to interfere with lactation), or her small earnings in the store or shop in order to suckle and care for her own baby. This is how Jean Jacques Rousseau and other moralists and physicians, particularly in the eighteenth century, explained wet-nursing.[21] Several recent historians of the family adopt similar cultural explanations. Edward Shorter, for example, argues that "good mothering is an invention of modernization. In traditional society, mothers viewed the development and happiness of infants younger than two with indifference. In modern society, they place the welfare of their small children above all else." The resort to wet-nursing, for Shorter, is an instance of traditional indifference. "To the extent that [French mothers of the late eighteenth and nineteenth centuries] were willing to abandon mercenary nurses in favor of breastfeeding, they were placing the welfare of their infants above other criteria," that is, they were being modern.[22]

The eventual disappearance of wet-nursing, according to the cultural explanation, followed from a change in the culture's view of childhood—"the discovery of childhood," a revolution in child care. The educated upper classes began to abandon wet-nursing and adopt maternal feeding of infants in the late eighteenth century, when so many customs of child care and education came under attack from Enlightenment philosophers and physicians.[23] In the course of the nineteenth century maternal feeding spread progressively down the social scale along with the new view of childhood. "After 1800 a great decline in mercenary extramural wet-nursing took place," Shorter writes. "It was among the middle classes that the practice first came to a halt. Only later did the lower classes catch up."[24]

Most urban administrators in the eighteenth and nineteenth centuries who wrote on the subject and a few more socially conscious doctors advanced a socioeconomic explanation of wet-nursing for the urban populace who provided most of the babies concerned. The crucial element in this explanation, which has also been adopted by some recent historians, is women's work in certain urban settings.[25] In the late eighteenth and nineteenth centuries the increasing population and declining economic opportunities in the country produced a substantial stream of migrants to the cities, which grew rapidly as a result. In the new textile centers large numbers of women found work in the mills, but the immigrants also crowded into the older cities, where no revolutionary changes in the structure of the economy had yet occurred. In these cities women continued, in larger numbers, to fill traditional female roles in the urban economy. Unmarried women especially went into domestic service. Other women, married and single, worked for the most part in the garment industry or in retailing, either in their homes or in small, often family-run shops or stores.[26] Wages were low for men and women, rents were soaring, and fertility remained high (the birth rate of illegitimate children rose rapidly). Under these conditions all members of working-class families, including mothers of young children, had to make their contribution to the family's income. There was nothing new about mothers working, but many more of them were now working in urban shops and small apartments, that is, in settings where it was impossible for them to nurse their babies. Artificial methods of infant-feeding remained expensive, difficult, and extremely dangerous, especially in the city, through most of the nineteenth century. Thus, when even poorer peasant women offered to breast-feed and care for the urban women's babies in the country for very modest wages, a bargain was struck.

The constellation of social and economic circumstances that, according to this explanation, account for the wet-nursing phenomenon in France prevailed from the mid-eighteenth century to the early twentieth century. Around World War I there was a decline in the participation of women in the nonagricultural labor force, perhaps because of the increasing real wages of men or perhaps because of declining employment opportunities in the garment and textile industries.[27] Rising rural incomes and declining population simultaneously restricted the supply of wet nurses, while scientific discovery and technological development provided artificial alternatives to the wet nurse.

The third explanation of the wet-nursing business associates this phenomenon with the limited possibilities for safe infant-feeding in the past. Only in the late nineteenth century did the discovery of the germ theory and a technological revolution in the production and marketing of cows' milk make artificial or bottle-feeding a reasonable alternative to breast-feeding. Several recent historians have argued persuasively for the importance of these developments in setting off the great decline in infant mortality in the Western nations.[28] Applied to wet-nursing, this argument is generally combined with another explanation—the assumption that urban mothers refused to breast-feed their infants for either cultural or socioeconomic reasons. This left them no choice but the wet nurse, since artificial feeding was generally recognized to be difficult and dangerous. The revolutionary changes in artificial feeding in the late nineteenth century made it possible for the urban mother who was unwilling or unable to breast-feed to dispense with the wet nurse nonetheless, either by bottle-feeding her baby herself or by placing the baby in the city during working hours with a day nurse or in a nursery.

The marketing of fresh cows' milk, the understanding of the germ theory, and the invention of the modern feeding bottle and rubber nipple all developed in parallel in the nineteenth century and especially in the last quarter of that century. Sterilized milk first came on the market in the 1890s, and, simultaneously, doctors launched an international campaign to teach new mothers the techniques of sterilization. Several doctors who served as medical inspectors for wet nurses in the department of the Seine during the 1890s assumed that these developments would spell the end of wet-nursing. To Dr. Moutier, a partisan of the new technology of infant-feeding, this was an end to be desired. "Formerly," he wrote, "we made a major distinction between breast-feeding and bottle-feeding, and we preferred breast-feeding outside the home to bottle-feeding by the parents. Now, we think that a different distinction should be made: feeding at home and feeding away from home." Dr. Moutier explained that bottle-feeding with sterilized milk at home was to be preferred over any form of infant-feeding outside the home, although he still ranked bottle-feeding at home behind breast-feeding at home, either by the mother or by a live-in wet nurse. Another inspector, Dr. Curie, was more skeptical of the benefits of sterilized milk because of the careless way the nurses he had observed prepared it. More fearfully, then, he also predicted that sterilized milk would bring the wet-nursing business to an end. "Many mothers," Dr. Curie wrote, "have a repugnance for breast-feeding nurses [*nourrices au sein*], because of fear of contagious infections or of pregnancy, and especially, it must be said, because of jealousy. They are only looking for an excuse not to give their child to a nurse who breast-feeds. Feeding sterilized milk will furnish them that excuse."[29] By this theory, then, the emergence of a safe, artificial means of infant-feeding in the mid-1890s accounted for, or at least allowed for, the demise of wet-nursing.

These three basic explanations of wet-nursing provide the theoretical framework of the present book. I want to come to terms with the strange phenomenon of wet-nursing, to transform an antiquarian curiosity into an understandable historical fact. I try to view wet-nursing throughout France, but often the focus is Paris for two reasons: the importance of the capital in the wet-nursing business and the relatively good sources that survive there. The time-frame is from the beginning of the eighteenth century (1715) to World War I (1914), a period in which wet-nursing was closely policed in Paris, at least, and hence well documented. It is also the period in which rural wet-nursing was the predominant pattern of infant care for the artisans and shopkeepers of certain older French cities, including Paris, Lyon, and Marseille.

I have divided the period at the French Revolution. The Revolution made a significant difference in the legal and political framework of the wet-nursing business and in the infant-feeding practices of the educated elite, though not of the urban populace. Viewing the history of French wet-nursing in two periods also highlights certain recurring characteristics of organized wet-nursing—the dearth of nurses, middle-class hostility, intellectual criticism, the effects of political and military crises, and the problems of paying the nurses and of rural surveillance.

The eighteenth century was the classic age of French wet-nursing. During that period the practice was adopted by virtually all urban social classes and became a major cottage industry in the ·rural areas that maintained significant commercial contacts with the cities. About 1760 Enlightenment philosophers, physicians, and statesmen launched a broad critique of wet-nursing. The scrutiny and criticism of the Enlightenment had a limited impact on the nursing practices of upper-class families and a more significant impact on the development of the legislative and administrative framework in which the wet-nursing business operated. From the mid-eighteenth century class attitudes toward wet-nursing began to diverge, and tension developed between policy and practice.

During the first three quarters of the nineteenth century the proportion of urban families who resorted to wet-nursing was declining, but the number of babies and nurses involved in the business expanded with the urban population. The geographic scope of wet-nursing also expanded with the development of roads and railroads. Wet-nursing became a national business, symbolized by the passage in 1874 of the first national legislation for the protection of children placed with nurses (the Roussel Law) and the demise in 1876 of the Municipal Bureau of Wet Nurses of the City of Paris.

The last period of significant organized wet-nursing in France coincides with the first period for which national data are available. This period, extending from the mid-1870s to World War I, is also one of major changes in the theory and practice of infant-feeding. Thus, it is possible to follow with quantitative accuracy the shift from breast-feeding to bottle-feeding, the dissemination of Pasteurian techniques of sterilization, and, finally, the abrupt end of the wet-nursing business in France.

Notes

1. Luc Boltanski, *Prime éducation et morale de classe* (Paris-The Hague: Mouton, 1969), 133.
2. Aulus Gellius, *Noctes Atticae*, Book XII. I am grateful to Susan Wiltshire, associate professor of classics at Vanderbilt University, for this reference and the next.
3. See the 1913 edition of Paulus by W. M. Lindsay.
4. Pierre Louis Paul Balandra, *Les nourrices des rois dans l'ancienne France* (Paris: Librairie médicale Marcel Vigné, 1936); Alfred Franklin, *La vie privée d'autrefois: arts et métiers, modes, moeurs, usages des parisiens du XIIᵉ au XVIIIᵉ siècle*, vol. 19, *L'enfant* (Paris: Librairie Plon, 1896), 79–107; Jean Héroard, *Journal de Jean Héroard sur l'enfance et la jeunesse de Louis XIII (1601–1628), extrait des manuscrits originaux*, edited by

Eud. Soulié and Ed. de Barthélemy (Paris: Firmin-Didot frères, fils et Cie., 1868), vol. 1; P. Dionis, *Traité général des accouchemens . . .* (Paris, 1718), 462–65.

5. Decrusy, Isambert, and Jourdan, *Recueil général des anciennes lois françaises*, 4 (Paris: Belin-le-Prieur & Verdière, n.d.), 574, 610.

6. Froissard-Broissia, "Livre de raison de la famille de Froissard-Broissia de 1532 à 1701," *Mémoires de la Société d'émulation du Jura*, 4th ser., 2 (1886), 33–105.

7. Gaston Tortat, ed., *Un livre de raison au XVIIe siècle: journal de Samuel Robert, lieutenant particulier en l'élection de Saintes, 1639–1668* (Pons: Imprimerie de Noel Texier, 1883), 12–14.

8. Pierre Rambaud, *Les nourrices d'autrefois en Poitou* (Poitiers: G. Roy, 1915), 11, 13.

9. Antoine L'Oisel, *Memoires des pays, villes, comté et comtes, evesché et evesques, pairrie, commune, et personnes de renom de Beauvais et Beauvaisis* (Paris, 1617), 26.

10. AD Eure, E 3234, Livre de raison de Claude Le Doulx, conseiller au Parlement de Paris (1665–1712).

11. [Elizabeth Clinton], *The Countesse of Lincolnes Nurserie* (Oxford: John Lichfield & James Short, 1622), dedication, 15–16, 18, 11.

12. Ramazzini, *Diseases of Workers*, trans. by Wilmer Cave Wright (New York: Hafner Publishing Co., 1964), 177.

13. Deparcieux, *Essai sur les probabilités de la durée de la vie humaine* (Paris, 1746), 39, 41, 73.

14. Delore, "Nourrice," *Dictionnaire encyclopédique des sciences médicales*, ed. by A. Dechambre, 2nd ser., 13: 398, 395.

15. Lefort, "La mortalité des nouveaux-nés et l'industrie des nourrices en France," *Revue de deux mondes*, 86 (Mar. 15, 1870), 364–66.

16. Bertillon, *La démographie figurée de la France* (Paris: Masson, 1874).

17. Zola, *Les quatre évangiles, Fécondité* (Paris, 1899).

18. André Armengaud, "Les nourrices du Morvan au XIXe siècle," *Études et chroniques de démographie historique, 1964* (Paris, 1965), 139.

19. On the decline of fertility rates in France, see, among others, Louis Henry, "The Population of France in the Eighteenth Century," in *Population in History: Essays in Historical Demography*, ed. by D. V. Glass and D. E. C. Eversley (London: Edward Arnold, 1965), 434–56, and Étienne van de Walle, *The Female Population of France in the Nineteenth Century: A Reconstruction of 82 Départements* (Princeton: Princeton University Press, 1974).

20. Ariès, *L'enfant et la vie familiale sous l'ancien régime* (Paris: Librairie Plon, 1960). Ariès, however, does not share the cultural explanation of wet-nursing outlined here. In the few pages he devotes to the

subject (419–21) he argues that the Parisian custom of placing newborns with rural wet nurses, far from being an example of traditional parental indifference to children, arose in the seventeenth century as a "protective measure."

21. Rousseau, *Émile*, trans. by Barbara Foxley (New York: Dutton, 1911), 11, and Michael Bermingham, *Manière de bien nourrir et soigner les enfans nouveaux-nés* (Paris: Barrois, 1750), 7–8.

22. Shorter, *The Making of the Modern Family* (New York: Basic Books, 1975), 168, 175–90. See also Lloyd DeMause, "The Evolution of Childhood," in *The History of Childhood*, ed. by Lloyd DeMause (New York: Harper & Row, 1974), 34, and Jean-Louis Flandrin, "L'attitude à l'égard du petit enfant et les conduites sexuelles dans la civilisation occidentale: structures anciennes et évolution," *Annales de démographie historique*, 1973 (Paris-The Hague: Mouton, 1973), 177–79.

23. J. H. Plumb, "The New World of Children in Eighteenth-Century England," *Past and Present*, 67 (May 1975), 64–95, and J.-N. Biraben, "Le médecin et l'enfant au XVIIIe siècle (aperçu sur la pédiatrie au XVIIIe siècle)," *Annales de démographie historique*, *1973* (Paris-The Hague: Mouton, 1973), 215–23.

24. Shorter, *Modern Family*, 182, 184.

25. Antoine-François Prost de Royer, *Mémoire sur la conservation des enfants* (Lyon: Aimé Delaroche, 1778); Charles Mercier, *Les Petits-Paris, considérations sociologiques relatives à l'hygiène infantile* (Paris: G. Steinheil, 1894); Maurice Garden, *Lyon et les lyonnais au XVIIIe siècle* (Paris: Les Belles Lettres, 1970).

26. Joan W. Scott and Louise A. Tilly, "Women's Work and the Family in Nineteenth-Century Europe," *Comparative Studies in Society and History*, 17 (Jan. 1975), 36–64.

27. *Ibid.*, 39–40, and Peter N. Stearns, "Working-Class Women in Britain, 1890–1914," in *Suffer and Be Still: Women in the Victorian Age*, ed. by Martha Vicinus (Bloomington: Indiana University Press, 1972), 113–14.

28. M. W. Beaver, "Population, Infant Mortality and Milk," *Population Studies*, 27 (July 1973), 243–54, and Étienne van de Walle and Samuel H. Preston, "Mortalité de l'enfance au XIXe siècle à Paris et dans le département de la Seine," *Population*, 29 (Jan.–Feb. 1974), 89–107.

29. APP, D B/66. Préfecture de Police. *Protection des enfants du bas âge, rapport annuel, année 1896* (Paris, 1897), 92, 99–100.

PART I
The Eighteenth Century

2

Wet-Nursing and the Enlightenment

THE EIGHTEENTH CENTURY was the heyday of wet-nursing in France. Since the seventeenth century the practice had spread throughout the educated classes of city and town. But the most numerous consumers of wet-nursing services were the pre-industrial urban populace (artisans and shopkeepers) and foundlings, groups whose numbers were burgeoning in eighteenth-century France. Cities like Paris and Lyon sent nearly all their newborns to the suburbs and beyond for the nursing period. They were cities without babies. Nurses came and went, leaving faint traces (sentimental and hostile) in the imagination of the age—*Les adieux à la nourrice* (Aubry), *La visite à la nourrice* (Fragonard), *Le départ de la bercelonette, ou la privation sensible* (Greuze).[1]

The economic conditions of eighteenth-century France favored the expansion of the supply and demand for wet nurses. A population explosion resulted in rural overcrowding, urban growth (without any fundamental transformation of the means of production), extreme poverty in both city and country, and spiraling prices for food and housing. The same economic conditions also strained the capacity of the wet-nursing business to meet the demand. The soaring numbers of children abandoned at foundling institutions and the widespread delinquency of parents in paying nurses' wages, in particular, contributed to raising the price and lowering the quality of nursing services, especially in the last decades before the Revolution.

From mid-century new cultural forces and a revolution in medical thinking about the physical care of infants put additional strains on the practice of wet-nursing. Enlightened doctors, moralists, and statesmen, suddenly aware of and scandalized by excessive infant mortality, launched a general critique of wet-nursing from their different perspectives. Criticism and economic pressures together did not result in a wholesale return of urban mothers nursing their infants in late eighteenth-century France, but they did change the pattern of upper-class wet-nursing, and they provoked a significant intrusion by the state, or at least the city, into the operations of the wet-nursing business for the protection of the infants confided to it.

The Scope and Social Categories of Wet-Nursing

Perhaps the most comprehensive and the most accurate statistical description of infant-feeding for any population of newborn babies anywhere in the eighteenth century is that published by Jean-Charles-Pierre LeNoir, lieutenant-general of police of Paris, in 1780. LeNoir was in a position to know because in eighteenth-century Paris infant-feeding was not an intimate activity of family life but a vast public enterprise over which the municipal police had the most extensive (but not total) responsibility for surveillance. LeNoir wrote:

> We can estimate at 20,000 or 21,000 the number of babies born in Paris [each year]. One thirtieth at most sucks the mother's milk; an equal number is nursed in the mother's and father's home. Two or three thousand, belonging to the class of well-to-do citizens, are dispersed around the suburbs and environs with wet nurses of whom the parents assure themselves and whom they pay all the more because they are closer and more to their liking.
>
> But the least wealthy and consequently the most numerous class was necessarily forced to take wet nurses at more considerable distances and in some ways at random.[2]

Most of the "least wealthy" parents who placed their babies with distant wet nurses found these nurses through the four privileged *bureaux des recommandaresses* or placement bureaus for wet nurses, which were consolidated into one municipal Bureau des Nourrices in 1769. This was the enterprise over which the lieutenant-general of police exercised direct and increasing powers of surveillance during the eighteenth century. In the years 1733 to 1735 one of the four *recommandaresses*, whose register survives, placed a mean of 2,295 babies a year with wet nurses. If the other bureaus each placed an equal number (since 1727 the four bureaus had been required to divide their fees equally in order to avoid competition), 9,180 Parisian babies a year were placed with distant rural wet nurses in this way during the mid-1730s. The annual mean number of births in Paris in the same years was 18,841.[3] In 1751 a well-informed source stated that "around 11,000 to 12,000 wet nurses" came to the bureaus of the *recommandaresses* in Paris each year.[4]

Among the papers of the surgeon and hospital reformer Jacques Tenon are figures that he apparently transcribed from the registers of the Bureau of Wet Nurses for the years 1770 to 1776. During those years the mean number of babies placed by the bureau annually was 9,466. The mean annual total of births registered in Paris in the same years was 19,139. In other manuscripts related to his interest in foundling hospitals Tenon wrote that in 1792 Paris needed 5,000 new wet nurses for foundlings, 10,000 for the children of artisans and domestic servants placed by the Bureau of Wet Nurses, and about 5,000 whom the well-to-do would procure directly for their children. Confirming and supplementing LeNoir's breakdown of the wet-nursing business by social classes, Tenon explained, "[The children] of the rich people are placed by them in the neighborhood of Paris and watched over by their parents, who pay 24 or 30 *livres* a month and give in addition gifts, meat, wood, and money at the baptism and at the end of the nursing. Most of these very select nurses are in a position to entrust their own babies at less expense to other nurses and to provide their nursling with a new serous milk appropriate to a newborn, and these are no small advantages."

Tenon went on to explain that 9,000 to 10,000 children of bourgeois and artisans placed with wet nurses each year through the Bureau of Wet Nurses were under the surveillance of traveling inspectors (a short-lived arrangement). Their nurses were sure of receiving at least 9 *livres* a month (after 1769 the bureau guaranteed 8 and later 9 *livres*, whether or not the parents paid what they owed). "Most of [the bureau's] nurses received a few gratuities, at baptism and upon the return of their nurslings; they appreciated in addition the advantage for themselves and their family of nursing legitimate children, who were clean, strong, in good health and

viable." In these respects the babies to be procured at the Bureau
of Wet Nurses were preferable, from the nurses' point of view,
to the foundlings from the Maison de la Couche, who were generally weaker, sometimes infected by congenital syphilis, and never
supported by generous parents.[5]

The number of foundlings or, more accurately, children abandoned to the foundling administration of Paris soared through most
of the eighteenth century. The annual total rose from around 1,700
at the beginning of the eighteenth century to a peak of 7,676 in
1772, then settled around 5,800 in the 1780s. Much of the increase,
however, was attributable to the traffic in provincial babies brought
to the capital to be abandoned at the Foundling Hospital, until
the royal government began to restrict this flow in the 1770s. In
the last two decades of the Ancien Régime Parisian parents alone
abandoned about 4,500 children a year, about 22 percent of the
recorded baptisms. Abandoned children drew the poorest wet
nurses from the greatest distance, if they were fortunate enough
to be nursed at all. In 1788, when nearly 6,000 babies were abandoned in Paris, scarcely 1,500 wet nurses presented themselves
at the Maison de la Couche. The deficit was made up by long
delays in placement during which wet nurses attached to the institution suckled several babies at once (spreading infections), and
others struggled to keep the babies alive by artificial means of
feeding with various diets based on animal milk; many babies
died.[6]

LeNoir's estimates, then, can be restated this way: of approximately 20,000 babies born each year in Paris at the end of the
Ancien Régime, nearly one-half were placed in the country with
rural wet nurses procured through the municipal Bureau of Wet
Nurses, 20 to 25 percent from the wealthiest classes were placed
directly by their parents with more highly paid wet nurses closer
to Paris, 20 to 25 percent were abandoned with the foundling
administration to die early or to be nursed far from Paris by a
poorly paid woman, and a small remainder (a few thousand at
most) were nursed in their own homes either by their mothers or
by live-in wet nurses.

The social status of the Parisian parents who placed their babies
with wet nurses in the country during the eighteenth century can
be established somewhat more precisely from various surviving

documents that record the fathers' occupations. The principal source is the burial registers of rural parishes where the babies were nursed. For those who died there, the parish priest usually recorded their fathers' occupations and other information from the *certificat de renvoi* that each nurse was required to carry from Paris and deliver to her priest for this eventuality. Demographic and local historians who have worked with these burial registers have tried to classify the fathers' occupations and thereby characterize their social level. In addition, the surviving register of 1732 to 1736 from one of the four *bureaux des recommandaresses* also recorded fathers' occupations (as did the *certificats de renvoi*, should a large enough number of these be found in rural communal archives that are now being brought together).[7]

Dominique Risler examined the occupations of a sample of about 500 fathers who placed their babies through the bureau of the *recommandaresse* Anne Delaunay in the 1730s. Risler concluded that "all Paris, with the exception of nobility and beggars, participates in this migration of newborns toward the pure air of the country" but with "a strong predominance of artisanal society." About 60 percent of the sample were either master artisans or journeymen, 10 to 15 percent shopkeepers, about 10 percent domestic servants, 5 to 10 percent "Bourgeois de Paris," and the remainder were in various petty trades and occupations, including a few soldiers, farmers, and carters.[8]

Working with eighteenth-century burial registers, Jean Ganiage found 3,240 nurslings who died in fifteen tiny parishes in the Beauvaisis. None came from noble families, and only one came from the upper bourgeoisie (a banker's son). For the most part these nurslings, 90 percent of whom were born in Paris, belonged to families of artisans (45 percent) and families engaged in petty trade (over 25 percent) or service, especially domestic service (18 percent).[9] Three studies of village burial registers in different parts of Normandy in the eighteenth century show a similar predominance of shopkeepers and artisans among the fathers of deceased Parisian nurslings, generally with a smaller proportion of domestic servants than Ganiage found in the Beauvaisis, and perhaps a few more officeholders and liberal professionals, but never more than 10 percent from the upper classes even with the broadest definition of these categories. One of these studies concludes that "the place-

ment of these Parisian babies with wet nurses was not a matter
of fashion, but a response to compelling necessities," among which
the author lists the physical inability of some mothers to nurse,
the difficulty of artificial feeding in the city, and the mothers'
work.[10]

Two demographic studies of parish registers from more urbanized localities show a higher social level for the parents of nurslings
who died there. Marcel Lachiver found about 500 nurslings who
died between the mid-seventeenth and the mid-eighteenth centuries in Meulan, a town of 1,500 to 2,000 inhabitants in the
Beauvaisis. Shopkeepers and artisans still predominated among
their parents (42.7 percent plus 4 percent journeymen), but babies
from the upper classes were more common than in the villages
(8 percent bourgeois, 7.9 percent royal officials, and 6.5 percent
liberal professionals); those with parents in domestic service were
somewhat less common (4.8 percent).[11] Paul Galliano examined
the social status of the parents of 644 babies who died in nineteen
parishes of the southern *banlieue* immediately adjacent to Paris in
the years from 1774 to 1794. These parents found their babies'
wet nurses through personal contacts (the municipal bureau did
not make placements so close to Paris) and paid a premium to have
their babies nursed close to home, where they could supervise the
nursing personally. Six percent of the parents in Galliano's sample
were nobles, and 15.5 percent were civil officials or liberal professionals. But even here 44 percent of the parents were master
artisans and tradesmen, 24 percent were journeymen or workers
of various kinds, and 6 percent were domestic servants.[12]

In all the rural and suburban parishes where Parisian babies
were placed with wet nurses, with the possible exception of the
most distant parishes where the foundlings were placed, the children of artisans and shopkeepers outnumbered all others. The
children of nobles, royal officials, liberal professionals, and the
upper bourgeoisie were a significant minority in the suburban
parishes closest to the capital and in the market towns of the Île-
de-France. Children of domestic servants were a more prominent
minority in smaller, more remote villages. But the majority everywhere came from the pre-industrial urban class of independent
artisans and shopkeepers, for whom the cost of wet-nursing was
a significant sacrifice, but not to be compared with the loss of the

woman's contribution to the family workshop or retail establishment.[13]

Trends

Although the social pattern of infant-feeding in Paris presented above in cross-section appears to have been fairly stable from the beginning of Louis XV's reign until the Revolution, nevertheless, important changes were occurring. The major trends during the eighteenth century were a rising demand for wet nurses, the emergence of widespread criticism of wet-nursing as a way of raising babies, and increasing intervention by social agencies in the activity of infant care. These three trends were interconnected.

A complete statistical series, except for abandoned children, is lacking. It is, therefore, not possible to determine whether the proportion of Parisian parents resorting to rural wet nurses to feed their babies rose in the eighteenth century. It seems likely that the number of wet nurses required by the city increased, as the annual number of births rose slowly over the century and the number of children abandoned each year in Paris increased sharply. Even if the components of an increasing demand cannot be determined, the effects of a probable increase are apparent: the rising cost of wet-nursing, the increasing distance from Paris at which babies were placed, frequent shortages in the supply of wet nurses, and a deterioration in the quality of available wet nurses. In eighteenth-century Paris the rising demand that produced these effects was embodied in the competition between the foundling hospital and wet-nursing bureaus for the limited supply of rural wet nurses. At the end of the seventeenth century the foundling hospital recruited its wet nurses in Normandy, Picardy, and the Beauvaisis and paid them 5 *livres* a month during the baby's first eighteen months of life. Because of shortages of nurses, wages had to be raised in 1694 and 1728, while the recruitment of wet nurses extended out as far as the Nord and Burgundy by 1750. In 1765 the hospital once again raised the monthly wages paid wet nurses during the first year of the baby's life, from 6 to 7 *livres*. This increase, together with the irregularity of payments by hard-pressed Parisian parents, apparently drew a large number of nurses (or of the *meneurs* who led them to the capital) from the four *bureaux des recommandaresses* to the Maison de la Couche, where the foundlings awaited placement.[14]

Alarmed by a new dearth of nurses for the legitimate children of working families, the police authorities of Paris carried out a major reorganization of the wet-nursing business outlined in a royal declaration of July 24, 1769. "We noticed day by day," the declaration's preamble observed, "the diminution in the number of women who were accustomed to coming and taking nurslings." To attract these wet nurses back, the police consolidated the four *bureaux des recommandaresses* into a new Bureau of Wet Nurses, which guaranteed the nurses' wages of 8 *livres* a month with eventual recourse by the bureau against parents who failed to pay it.[15] These changes succeeded in shifting the surplus of wet nurses back to the placement bureau and the shortage back to the foundling hospital. One year after the new bureau's organization its directors boasted, "The flow of wet nurses to the Bureau des Recommandaresses is increasing day by day" and, indeed, had become so great "that most of them returned home without nurslings; or else, tired of waiting their turn, went to pick up nurslings at the foundling hospital, where there has been a dearth of wet nurses, because those who would have gone there found it more advantageous to hire themselves out at the Bureau des Recommandaresses."[16]

From the other side, the hospital authorities complained in 1773, "Those *meneurs* who in the preceding years brought 20 or 30 nurses on each trip they made to Paris, bring only 7 or 8. Other *meneurs* bring only 2 or 3, and others none, asserting that they found none who wanted to hire themselves out for the Foundlings."[17] Another increase in the wages paid by the hospital in 1773 did not attract the required number of wet nurses. The desperate foundling administration was reduced to dangerous expedients, even allowing *meneurs* to take babies "by commission" for distant rural wet nurses who refused to come to Paris to pick up the babies themselves. All such practices reduced the hospital's control over the quality of wet-nursing—and reduced the babies' chances of survival.[18]

Maurice Garden noted similar trends in eighteenth-century Lyon, where the wet-nursing business was unregulated and not organized in placement bureaus. There, too, as the number of babies to be placed increased, the distances at which they, especially the foundlings, were placed increased as well. But the farther away the placement, the longer the journey, the less effective the surveillance, and the higher the mortality. In Lyon, Garden shows, the deterioration of wet-nursing services had two effects. First, it contributed to a *prise de conscience*, an awareness even among the working class of the high cost of wet-nursing in human lives and a protest against the practice, but a protest that was bound to fail because the necessity for women to work made wet-nursing unavoidable. Second, the crisis was the impulse to reform the wet-nursing industry, to bring it under police and professional surveillance and to subsidize at least a few working women who wanted to nurse their own babies.[19] The same causes produced similar effects in Paris, although a temporary imbalance between the supply and demand for wet nurses was not, of course, the only reason for the general polemical attack launched against wet-nursing beginning in the middle of the eighteenth century.

The Enlightenment Critique of Wet-Nursing

Rousseau's famous plea for maternal nursing in Book I of *Émile* (1762)—the mother is the baby's natural nurse, as the father is the child's natural tutor—is the *locus classicus* of the eighteenth-century campaign against wet-nursing. Writers commenting a generation after the appearance of *Émile* on Rousseau's impact on infant care exclaimed at how the Genevan Philosophe had somehow succeeded in persuading mothers to nurse their children where so many physicians and moralists before him had failed. The success they spoke of, however, was obviously limited to a small circle of the social and cultural elite in France. It was further limited, according to these writers, in being confined to a single element of Rousseau's educational program and in being short-lived in its impact.[20] Already in 1783 Louis-Sébastien Mercier declared that the fashion of maternal nursing among Parisian women had passed.[21]

These reflections of near contemporaries on Rousseau's influence on nursing patterns in France exaggerate his individual importance in this instance and underestimate the scope and impact of the infant welfare movement, which was the context of his remarks. Recent historians have shown that none of the individual reforms in infant care advocated by Rousseau—including maternal breast-feeding, light and loose clothing instead of swaddling, frequent baths in progressively colder water—were original with him.[22] The same constellation of proposals appeared in a spate of books on infant care and the preservation of children, which began to come out around 1760. It was almost an organized campaign to reform cultural patterns of infant care. In 1760 King Louis XV is supposed to have asked physicians for works on the causes, prevention, and cure of children's diseases.[23] One of the first in the field, even anticipating the king's invitation, was the *Traité de l'éducation corporelle des enfans en bas âge, ou Réflexions pratiques sur les moyens de procurer une meilleure constitution aux citoyens* (1760) by Jean-Charles Des Essartz. Some of Rousseau's enemies and Des Essartz himself, in his preface to the second edition, suggested that Rousseau drew all his ideas on infant care from this source alone.[24] In 1761 the clothing, feeding, and exercise of infants was the subject of an essay contest sponsored by a scientific society in Haarlem. The prize went to the Genevan Jacques Ballexserd, whose *Dissertation sur l'éducation physique des enfants* was published in 1762, the same year as his more famous compatriot's treatise on education. Another contestant, Joseph Raulin, published his three-volume *De la conservation des enfants* in 1768–69. The fashionable Parisian midwife Madame Marie-Angélique Anel Le Rebours contributed the *Avis aux mères qui veulent nourrir leurs enfants* in 1767. The second edition in 1770 carried endorsements from the popular Swiss physician Samuel Tissot and the Faculty of Medicine of Paris. Swedish, English, German, and Italian works critical of wet-nursing and favorable to maternal feeding were translated and published in France in the 1760s and the two succeeding decades.[25] Thus, Rousseau's remarks on infant care in *Émile* were only the most prominent instance of a more general polemical campaign against wet-nursing and for a radical reform in the way babies were brought up in eighteenth-century France.

Although medical works formed the core of the campaign against wet-nursing, laymen, particularly political writers and government officials, also made significant contributions. Indeed, political and moral arguments had a prominent place even in the medical works. Doctors, as well as government officials, wrote as if their goal were not to preserve individual lives but to reduce infant mortality of the population as a whole, to reverse the depopulation which they perceived to be the trend of their time, and thereby to promote the economic and military strength of the nation.[26]

Underlying the campaign against wet-nursing were the complexities of the relationship between rural and urban society as that relationship was viewed by the generation that also produced the major works of Physiocratic theory and Enlightenment humanitarianism. The country, this generation recognized, was where the great majority of the nation's population lived. The Physiocrats taught that agriculture was the basis of the state's economic activity and tax revenue. Statesmen and patriots looked to the peasantry to fill the ranks of the army and militia. Philosophers and many physicians still idealized the simple rural life as more natural, less corrupt, and more healthy than urban, especially upper-class, life. On the other hand, urban intellectuals of this generation discovered in the reality of rural life unhealthy conditions—a medical desert unserved by professionals, extreme poverty, and a thriving culture of traditional routine, prejudice, and superstition, notably in matters relating to health and hygiene.[27] Both the moral critique of urban life and the discovery of the reality of rural life contributed to the animus of the attack against the custom of urban parents leaving their children with rural wet nurses for the first year or more of life.

The Effects of the Enlightenment Critique

The primary effect of the campaign against wet-nursing upon the well-to-do, in addition to a short-lived fashion of maternal nursing around Paris and the court, was probably to encourage parents to choose their babies' wet nurses more carefully and to keep them under closer surveillance. In the nineteenth century bourgeois parents usually brought the wet nurse from the country to live in their homes in the city where they could supervise their baby's care directly in accordance with the latest professional advice (see chapters 5–7). Since neither the suburban wet nurses who served the well-to-do in the eighteenth century nor the live-in nurses of the nineteenth century were procured through public agencies or registered with the authorities (at least until the late nineteenth century), the exact years when the transition occurred can only be guessed at on the basis of such qualitative sources as letters, memoirs, and medical manuals.

Foundlings were a special object of concern for late eighteenth-century reformers because of their soaring numbers and their very high mortality. Since maternal feeding was, by definition, out of the question for this group and the number and quality of available wet nurses were diminishing, reformers looked desperately but unsuccessfully for ways of feeding abandoned newborns artificially.[28] Probably more successful in preserving foundlings' lives were the royal decrees of the 1770s, which required provincial hospitals to care for infants abandoned in their regions instead of transporting them to Paris to be left at the foundling hospital there. Whereas 90 percent of the newborn foundlings from the provinces had died on the trip to Paris before the reform, infant mortality for foundlings of Reims fell to about 46 percent after 1779 when the Hôtel-Dieu of that city began to place them directly with wet nurses of the surrounding countryside.[29]

The polemical campaign against wet-nursing that began about 1760 probably had its most significant impact on the largest group that depended upon rural wet-nursing: the poor but not indigent families of urban artisans and tradesmen. In the mid-1780s several private philanthropists who understood the economic reasons for the resort to rural wet-nursing by this group organized charities to aid poor mothers who would agree to nurse their own babies at the sacrifice of some of their normal earnings. The playwright Pierre de Beaumarchais proposed such a charity in 1784 and offered to contribute the profits from *The Marriage of Figaro*. The archbishop of Lyon took up the offer and founded the Institut de bienfaisance en faveur des pauvres mères-nourrices, which aided 475 Lyonnais mothers in the years 1785 to 1788.[30] In Paris Madame d'Oultremont-Fougeret, wife of a royal financial official, founded the Société de charité maternelle for the same purpose in 1786. The society, which enjoyed official patronage, lasted throughout the nineteenth century and was the model for similar organizations in many provincial cities.[31]

Such private efforts were obviously inadequate to reduce significantly the number of babies placed with rural wet nurses, and public authorities were generally not prepared in the late eighteenth century (and even less through most of the nineteenth century) to assist urban working families with the costs of nursing.[32] An exception was the Hospital of Rouen, which offered one year of assistance to newborns in poor families with three or more children. This program, which aided several hundred "enfants de la ville" every year in the period from 1741 to 1790, antedated the campaign against wet-nursing and did not require the mothers to nurse their babies. The mid-eighteenth-century movement of opinion may help to explain, however, the growing proportion of "enfants de la ville" of Rouen who were nursed by their own mothers rather than placed with wet nurses: less than 1 percent in the 1740s, over 50 percent by 1765, and over 70 percent by 1789.[33]

The new system of paying wet nurses introduced by the police authorities in Paris in 1769 was a measure of infant protection that did not burden the city with a direct subsidy to the working poor for their nursing expenses. Under this system the new Bureau of Wet Nurses tried to assure an adequate supply of wet nurses for the capital and to prevent the nurses from neglecting or returning their nurslings prematurely by advancing the nurses their monthly wages on a regular basis, then strictly collecting these debts from the fathers (who were often slow and irregular payers), even imprisoning the debtors who fell too far behind. In one sense, the guarantee of wet nurses' wages was a creative and realistic response to the neglect and abuses that the critics of wet-nursing were bringing attention to in the 1760s. The measure was also intended, as noted above, to overcome the dearth of nurses that developed in that decade as a result of rising demand.

But the guarantee of wet nurses' wages and the general reorganization of the wet-nursing business in Paris in 1769, which will be discussed more extensively later, should not be viewed only as the result of conditions specific to the 1760s. These reforms were also the culmination of a series of police regulations of wet-nursing dating back to the royal declaration of January 29, 1715. The preamble of that declaration identified the reason for all of the eighteenth-century legislation (and what distinguished it from earlier legislation to protect the trade privileges of licensed *recommandaresses des nourrices*): the state's interest in "the preservation and raising of children."[34] In Paris police regulation and surveillance of rural wet-nursing developed before the Enlightenment campaign against this mode of infant-feeding and provided a way of at least mitigating the worst abuses of a system that was too well integrated with the needs of urban working families and of peasant women from the surrounding country to dispense with entirely. Thus the major effect of the mid-eighteenth-century campaign against wet-nursing on the children of working families in the capital was a significant development of police regulation and surveillance over their wet-nursing. At the same time other French cities, particularly Lyon, tried to introduce police regulations on the Parisian model, without lasting success.[35] The extension of police regulation in Paris may have contributed incidentally to the abandonment of rural wet-nursing by upper-class parents, who eschewed any association with the police and hospital agencies that increasingly dominated the business.[36]

Notes

1. Étienne Aubry (1745–81), *Les adieux à la nourrice,* painting in the Sterling and Francine Clark Art Institute, Williamstown, Mass.; Jean-Louis Fragonard, *La visite à la nourrice,* wash drawing in the Armand Hammer Collection; Jean-Baptiste Greuze, *Le départ de la bercelonette, ou la privation sensible,* from the series of drawings entitled *Bazile et Thibault, ou les deux éducations* (see Anita Brookner, *Greuze: The Rise and Fall of an Eighteenth-Century Phenomenon* [Greenwich, Conn.: New York Graphic Society Ltd., 1972], 111, 136, 156).

2. [Jean-Charles-Pierre] LeNoir, *Détail sur quelques établissemens de la ville de Paris, demandé par sa majesté impériale la reine de Hongrie . . .* (Paris, 1780), 63.

3. AAP, 283, Registre pour Anne Françoise Yon Delaunay, l'une des quatres Recommandaresses de la Ville et fauxbourgs de Paris, and Dominique Risler, "Nourrices et meneurs de Paris au XVIIIe siècle" (Mémoire de maîtrise d'histoire, Faculté des Lettres et Sciences humaines de Nanterre, June 1971), 38–39. For the number of births in Paris in the eighteenth century, see Département de la Seine, *Recherches statistiques sur la ville de Paris et le département de la Seine, Année 1823,* 2d ed. (Paris: Imprimerie royale, 1834), table 53.

4. AN, H 1461, annotations evidently written by a police official on a memoir dated Mar. 1751, proposing that a single wet-nursing bureau be created in Paris.

5. BN, NAF, 22,746, Papiers du chirurgien Jacques Tenon (1724–1816) sur les hôpitaux pour enfants-trouvés, fols. 254, 154–55, 27; A. Chamoux, ed., "Mise en nourrice et mortalité des enfants légitimes," *Annales de démographie historique, 1973* (Paris-The Hague: Mouton, 1973), 418–22; Louis S. Greenbaum, " 'Measure of Civilization': The Hospital Thought of Jacques Tenon on the Eve of the French Revolution," *Bulletin of the History of Medicine,* 49 (Spring 1975), 43–56.

6. Claude Delasselle, "Les enfants abandonnés à Paris au XVIIIᵉ siècle," *Annales: économies, sociétés, civilisations,* 30 (Jan.-Feb. 1975), 187–218, and Albert Dupoux, *Sur les pas de Monsieur Vincent: Trois cents ans d'histoire parisienne de l'enfance abandonnée* (Paris: Revue de l'assistance publique, 1958), ch. 7.

7. I found fifteen *certificats de renvoi* in the communal archives of Beaubray (5 Q 4) and sixty-one in the communal archives of Verneuil (5 Q 9), both recently deposited at the Archives Départementales de l'Eure. All of these, however, date from the period between the Revolution, when the mayors took over civil registration from the priests, and the early Restoration, when administrative procedures associated with wet-nursing were significantly modified.

8. Risler, "Nourrices et meneurs," 39–41.

9. Jean Ganiage, "Nourrissons parisiens en Beauvaisis," in *Hommage à Marcel Reinhard: Sur la population française au XVIIIᵉ et au XIXᵉ siècles* (Paris: Société de démographie historique, 1973), 283.

10. Étienne Gautier and Louis Henry, *La population de Crulai, paroisse normande. Étude historique* (Paris: Presses universitaires de France, 1958), 68; A. Goubert, "Le placement et la mortalité des enfants de Paris dans les paroisses du Vieux-Rouen et de Bouafles de 1686 à 1824," *Bulletin de la Société des études locales dans l'enseignement public. Groupe de la Seine-inférieure* (1935–36), 63; Michel Le Pesant, "Les nourrissons parisiens dans les campagnes de l'Eure sous l'Ancien Régime," *Cahiers Léopold Delisle,* 6 (1957), 139–41. The quotation is from Le Pesant, 140.

11. Marcel Lachiver, *La population de Meulan du XVIIᵉ au XIXᵉ siècle (vers 1600–1870). Étude de démographie historique* (Paris: S.E.V.P.E.N., 1969), 127–28.

12. Paul Galliano, "La mortalité infantile (indigènes et nourrissons) dans la banlieue sud de Paris à la fin du XVIIIᵉ siècle (1774–1794)," *Annales de démographie historique, 1966* (Paris: Éditions Sirey, 1967), 170–71.

13. Garden, *Lyon et les lyonnais,* 116–40, especially 137–38 on women's work and the resort to wet-nursing. In Lyon parents who put their

infants out to nurse worked predominantly in the food trades and silk manufacturing, occupations that paid enough to enable them to afford the nurse's monthly wages and in which the women worked alongside their husbands, whether in stores or workshops. Day laborers, shoemakers, construction workers—those engaged in low-paying occupations or occupations where the man worked alone—generally did not put their children out to nurse in eighteenth-century Lyon.

14. Dupoux, *Sur les pas de Monsieur Vincent*, 92, 97–99, and BN, NAF, 22,746, Papiers de Tenon, fol. 168.

15. *Le Code des nourrices, ou recueil des déclarations du roi, arrêts du Parlement, ordonnances et sentences de police; concernant les nourrices, les recommandaresses, les meneurs & meneuses* (Paris: P. D. Pierres, 1781), 50–57.

16. BN, MF, 14,300, Extraits des lettres écrites par les curés de l'arrondissement de nourrices à M. de Sartine, Conseiller d'État Lieutenant général de Police de la Ville de Paris, à l'occasion de son nouvel établissement concernant les nourrices et observations des directeurs aux réflexions contenues aux dits extraits, fols. 4, 43.

17. Quoted in Dupoux, *Sur les pas de Monsieur Vincent*, 99.

18. BN, CJdF, 2425, Observations sur les plaintes adressées par le Procureur du Roi de la Ville d'Aire en Artois à M. le Procureur général, contre une femme nommée Constance Mantel, accusée de faire commerce d'enfans-trouvés, fols. 312–15.

19. Garden, *Lyon et les lyonnais*, 116–40.

20. Mme. la comtesse de Genlis, "Allaitement," in *Dictionnaire critique et raisonné des étiquettes de la Cour . . .* , 1 (Paris, 1818), 17–18; [Rétif de la Bretonne], *Les contemporaines, ou avantures des plus jolies femmes de l'âge présent*, 6 (Leipzig, 1780), 437–39; Roze de l'Épinoy, *Avis aux mères qui veulent allaiter . . .* (Paris: P. F. Didot, 1785), i–ii, 1–3.

21. [Louis-Sébastien Mercier], *Tableau de Paris*, new ed. (Amsterdam, 1782–83), 6:30.

22. Roger Mercier, *L'enfant dans la société du XVIIIe siècle (avant L'EMILE)* (Thèse complémentaire pour le doctorat ès lettres, Université de Paris, Faculté des Lettres et Sciences humaines, Paris, 1961), and Marie-France Morel, "Théories et pratiques de l'allaitement en France au XVIIIème siècle," *Annales de démographie historique, 1976* (Paris-The Hague: Mouton, 1977), 393–427.

23. J. E. G. [Jean-Emmanuel Gilibert], "Dissertation sur la dépopulation causée par les vices, les préjugés et les erreurs des nourrices mercenaires . . . ," in *Les chefs-d'oeuvres de Monsieur de Sauvages*, ed. by J. E. G., 2 (Lyon, 1770), 250–52.

24. Mercier, *L'enfant dans la société du XVIIIe siècle*, 7–9.

25. *Ibid.*, 146–47, and bibliography, esp. 194–98.
26. Morel, "Théories et pratiques de l'allaitement."
27. Marie-France Morel, "Ville et campagne dans le discours médical sur la petite enfance au XVIIIe siècle," *Annales: économies, sociétés, civilisations*, 32 (Sept.-Oct. 1977), 1007–24; and Marie-France Morel and F. Loux, "Prime éducation, savoirs populaires et pouvoir médical: XVIIIe–XXe siècles," *Politique aujourd'hui* (May-June 1976), 87–103.
28. Dupoux, *Sur les pas de Monsieur Vincent*, 118–22; and Morel, "Théories et pratiques de l'allaitement," 418–25.
29. Delasselle, "Les enfants abandonnés," 188; Antoinette Chamoux, "L'enfance abandonnée à Reims à la fin du XVIIIe siècle," *Annales de démographie historique, 1973* (Paris-The Hague: Mouton, 1973), 263–85.
30. Marcel Fosseyeux, "Sages-femmes et nourrices à Paris au XVIIe siècle," *Revue de Paris* (Oct. 1, 1921), 549–50, and Garden, *Lyon et les lyonnais*, 125.
31. Morel, "Théorics et pratiqucs d'allaitcmcnt," 408.
32. Jules Renault and G. Labeaume, "L'évolution de la Protection de l'enfance," *Bulletin de l'Académie de Médecine*, series III, 117 (1937), 763–77.
33. Jean-Pierre Bardet, "Enfants abandonnés et enfants assistés à Rouen dans la seconde moîtié du XVIIIe siècle," in *Hommage à Marcel Reinhard. Sur la population française au XVIIIe et au XIXe siecles* (Paris: Société de démographie historique, 1973), 19–47, esp. 23–24.
34. *Code des nourrices*, 1.
35. Garden, *Lyon et les lyonnais*, 124; Camille Bloch, *L'assistance et l'état en France à la veille de la Révolution. Généralités de Paris, Rouen, Alençon, Orléans, Chalons, Soissons, Amiens. 1764–1790* (Paris: Librairie Alphonse Picard et Fils, 1908), 108.
36. The directors of the new Bureau of Wet Nurses commented in 1771, "How do you oblige a comfortable bourgeois, a man of rank, a gentleman to have his wet nurse report to any kind of police bureau? He will say that he needs no one but himself, his family, or friends to supervise the care due in raising his child." BN, MF, 14,300, fol. 18.

3

The Wet-Nursing Business

Wealthy families in the eighteenth century found wet nurses through personal contacts—friends, relatives, rural tenants, or servants—and maintained personal contact with the nurse during the period the baby remained with her through correspondence and frequent visits. Although the wealthy used rural wet nurses, they did not participate in the organized wet-nursing business, which was a complex social and economic activity, subject to police regulation, but also autonomous, spontaneous, and defiant of any controls. The wet-nursing business fell into two parts: first, the part (approximately two-thirds) that was organized through the *bureaux des recommandaresses* and later the Bureau des Nourrices to serve the needs of families, primarily of artisans and tradesmen; and, second, the wet-nursing of foundlings, which was organized in a somewhat similar fashion except that the hospital took the place of parents and placement bureau. This chapter focuses on that part of the wet-nursing business organized through the placement bureaus.

In its simplest form the organization of the wet-nursing business consisted of parents in the city who paid for a service, country women who provided the service, and intermediaries called *meneurs* or *meneuses* who provided the essential communication between parents and nurses, including the initial introduction, the transportation of nurses and babies when necessary, and the transmission of payments, packages of clothing, and messages at regular intervals. Some French cities such as Lyon and Bordeaux with significant populations of artisans and tradesmen served by rural wet nurses possessed no more complex organization than those three basic elements.[1] In Paris an additional element of formal organization, which existed since at least the fourteenth century, was the placement bureaus of the *recommandaresses* to which the *meneurs* led the rural women seeking nurslings to meet parents who were seeking nurses.[2]

Jean-Charles-Pierre LeNoir, the lieutenant-general of police of Paris, summarized the three major problems associated with this basic organization of the wet-nursing business: first, abuses of the confidence of parents and wet nurses by the *meneurs*; second, the difficulty of compelling poor parents to pay the wet nurses and the consequent neglect of their children by unpaid nurses; and, third, the absence of surveillance over the wet nurses.[3] Police regulation of the wet-nursing business developed over the eighteenth century in Paris (but in no other French city) to deal with these basic problems. This chapter examines the developing body of regulations, then the participation of the principal groups involved in the wet-nursing business—*meneurs* and *meneuses*, nurses, parish priests and mayors who provided surveillance of the nurses in the villages, parents, and nurslings.

Regulation

Most of the Parisian regulation concerning the wet-nursing business before 1715, especially that of the seventeenth century, was issued by judicial authorities on behalf of the two or four licensed *recommandaresses* to enforce their exclusive right to lodge and place both rural wet nurses and servant girls in Paris. An unusual regulation by the provost of Paris on August 17, 1685, focused on "disorders and abuses which have been discovered to be committed daily both by wet nurses from villages far from this city who come here to pick up babies, as by certain women called *Meneuses de Nourrices* who lead them here." The language of this act suggests that the organization of the wet-nursing business in the country by the *meneuses* might have developed not long before the late seventeenth century, about the time the foundling hospital also began to place babies with rural wet nurses, though the Parisian placement bureaus for wet nurses and servant girls had operated since the Middle Ages. The regulation of 1685, in addition to the usual reiteration of the privilege of the *recommandaresses*, specifically required that a woman coming to Paris to take a nursling must bring a certificate from the *curé* of her parish giving her name, moral character, marital situation, and the number and ages of her children. On her return to her parish the wet nurse was to bring the *curé* a copy of her registration at the bureau of the *recommandaresse*. The act did not state the purpose or purposes of this twofold certification—whether to protect the lives of babies placed with these nurses, to protect the monopoly of the licensed *recommandaresses*, or to ensure that *curés* be able to record nurslings' burials correctly and completely.[4]

The declaration of the king of January 29, 1715, opened a new era in the organization of wet-nursing services for the city of Paris. It was the first regulation to declare the protection of children to be its objective, and it brought the *recommandaresses*, who were from then on exclusively concerned with procuring babies for rural wet nurses, into the jurisdiction of the lieutenant-general of police rather than that of the lieutenant-criminal of the Châtelet, where "the former usage, . . . without any other title than possession," had placed them. The declaration of 1715 created four *bureaux des recommandaresses* in place of the preexisting two and required each to keep careful registers, which would be inspected monthly by a *commissaire* of the Châtelet and quarterly by the lieutenant-general of police. It prescribed three certificates to be carried back and forth between the nurse's parish and Paris: the certificate of the *curé* with information about the nurse; the *certificat de renvoi*, which recorded information from the register of the *recommandaresse* concerning the nurse and nursling (baby's name and age and father's name, address, and occupation) and which the nurse was required to carry back from Paris to her parish priest; and a receipt by which the rural *curé* indicated to the lieutenant-general of police of Paris that the nurse had delivered the *certificat de renvoi*.

The royal declaration followed the tradition of seventeenth-century legislation in reiterating the monopolistic privilege belonging to the *recommandaresses*, but it broke new ground in a series of regulations designed to protect the lives of nurslings in the country. Thus, under severe penalties, nurses were forbidden to take two babies at once and were required to inform the parents within two months if they became pregnant. Nurses were also forbidden to return the babies to Paris, "even for absence of payment," without the express orders of the parents or the lieutenant-general of police. The lieutenant-general had the power to condemn parents who failed to pay the wet nurse, including the power to imprison debtors with no judicial procedure beyond a simple verification of the debt.[5]

After a dozen years of experience of the new organization of the wet-nursing business in Paris a second royal declaration, issued on March 1, 1727, extended the control exercised by the lieutenant-general of police. To prevent any destructive competition among the four *recommandaresses* this declaration created a common treasury in which the *recommandaresses* were to deposit all the fees they collected from the parents to be evenly divided among the four. Their fee was set at 30 *sols* for each nursling. The major innovation of the declaration of 1727 was to extend police regulation to the *meneurs* and *meneuses* who brought the nurses to Paris. Henceforth, these peripatetic entrepreneurs would be required to deposit a certificate of character from their parish priest at the bureau of one *recommandaresse*, with whom they would register and deal exclusively. The *meneurs* and *meneuses* were also required to keep a register of payments received from parents and remit these to the nurses within two weeks. One historian has suggested that the requirement of keeping a register opened this profession for the first time to men, "too few women being capable of keeping account books."[6] The declaration of 1727 specified that the *meneurs* and *meneuses* take as their fee 1 *sol* per *livre* (5 percent) collected from the parents, "in accordance with custom," but did not refer to the fees they collected for transporting nurses and packages. The declaration also developed further the responsibility of the nurses before the law: they were required to come to Paris personally to pick up a nursling; they had to return a baby within two weeks of the time its parents or guardian requested the return, and to inform the parents and return the baby's personal effects within two weeks of its death; and they were warned in a general way that they would be "punished according to the rigor of our ordinances" if they were responsible for the baby's death.[7]

After 1727 there was no significant reorganization of the wet-nursing business in Paris until 1769, but a series of police ordinances gradually extended the lieutenant-general's protective jurisdiction and, especially from the mid-1750s, increasingly sought to prescribe the quality of care that nurses provided to the children of Paris. A police ordinance of June 23, 1747, specified that rural women who came to Paris with a *meneur* or *meneuse* were subject to all the requirements of registration at the bureau of a *recommandaresse* and with their *curé*, even if the baby they picked up was to be nursed in some other manner than breast-feeding.[8] A police ordinance of May 9, 1749, stated that nurses from the suburbs and environs of Paris who procured babies directly from the parents without using the bureau of a *recommandaresse* would be required to deliver to their parish priests a certificate from the parents with all the details about the baby and its parents normally included on the *certificat de renvoi*.[9] Thus babies from well-to-do families would be registered in the country, if not in the city, in the same way as the children of artisans and tradesmen. But the purpose of this act was probably more administrative—to help *curés* fill out their burial registers accurately—than protective. A police ordinance of May 25, 1753, requiring that *meneurs* or *meneuses* remit payments to rural wet nurses in the presence of the *curé* or a substitute, who must certify the payment in the *meneur*'s register, was evidently designed to protect the nurses from unscrupulous *meneurs*.[10]

Another purpose, possibly related to the new humanitarian interest in the welfare of children, is suggested by a decision of the Chamber of Police of the Châtelet of June 1, 1756, that required wet nurses not sleep in the same bed with their nurslings, lest they suffocate the babies, but place them in a separate cradle. In the future no nurse was to be entrusted with a nursling by a *recommandaresse* unless the certificate from her parish priest stated that she possessed a cradle.[11] On this subject the secular authorities were taking over a position long advocated by the French bishops, who, seeing a disguised form of infanticide in the frequent cases of overlaying, had prohibited parents and nurses from sleeping in the same bed with babies under one year of age on penalty of excommunication.[12] A police ordinance of December 17, 1762, certainly reflected the new professional interest in and knowledge of infant care. Although the certificate from the nurse's *curé* had always recorded the date of her last birth, the ordinance of 1762 for the first time set limits on the "age" of a nurse's milk: it could be no less than seven months old, for the protection of the nurse's own baby (unless it had died or been placed with another wet nurse), and no more than two years old, for the nursling's protection. These limits represented the best compromise to maximize both babies' chances of survival according to the lights of contemporary medical theory, which favored matching the baby's age with the age of his nurse's milk and prolonging nursing until the appearance of all the baby teeth, or for at least a full year.[13] The ordinance of 1762 brought medical professionals directly into the Parisian wet-nursing business for the first time. It provided for free examinations of wet nurses by a physician or surgeon, who was evidently salaried by the police, whenever the parents, *recommandaresse*, or police inspector requested; a nurse who refused to be examined would not be allowed to take a nursling. Nurses or their *meneurs* also had the right to demand a free medical examination of a baby presented to them (a precaution against congenital syphilis), as did the parents with a baby returned to them after nursing. Finally, the ordinance of 1762 faintly adumbrated a system of surveillance of the wet nurses in the country by the requirement that the *meneurs* or *meneuses* should supervise their nurses and inform the *curés* of any circumstances that would prevent the nurses from continuing to nurse or of any ill-treatment of the nurslings.[14]

The last major reorganization of the wet-nursing business in Paris before the Revolution was effected by the king's declaration of July 24, 1769.[15] According to its preamble, the problems that this act sought to resolve were overcrowded and unhealthy conditions in the four existing placement bureaus, long delays in parents' payments of nurses' wages, which were discouraging potential nurses from coming to Paris and creating a dearth of such nurses, and poor or irregular communication of the babies' needs to the parents. The declaration of 1769 abolished the four existing bureaus of the *recommandaresses* as of January 1, 1770, and replaced them with a single large bureau under the supervision of two *recommandaresses*. Over the bureau it created a new level of administration, the Direction des Nourrices, consisting of two directors appointed by the lieutenant-general of police. The directors replaced police officials (indeed, they were former police officials) in assuring communications between Parisian parents and rural wet nurses and in enforcing the payment of nurses' wages by the parents, and they supervised new functions introduced by the declaration of 1769. An additional fee of 1 *sol* per *livre* (5 percent) was deducted from the parents' pay to the nurses to cover the costs of this new layer of administration. Both parents and nurses complained of this new charge and tried to shift the burden to the other party.[16]

To overcome the deleterious effect of the slow payment of nurses' wages by the poor families of Paris, the declaration of 1769 separated the two functions of collection from the parents and payment to the wet nurses. One employee was to be appointed in each quarter of Paris and its suburbs (twenty-two in all) to collect the nurses' wages each month on behalf of the direction. These employees enjoyed all the powers formerly vested in the police to collect this privileged debt. The directors, on the other hand, would pay the *meneurs* and *meneuses*, on each trip they made to Paris, their fees and wages to distribute to the wet nurses they handled in the country, whether or not the parents who had contracted with those specific nurses were up to date in their payments.

The system of collecting from the parents by special employees replacing the *meneurs* in this function did not work out in practice and was quickly abandoned. The *meneurs* and *meneuses*, without the obligation to collect wages nor the prospect of tips, neglected to visit the parents with news of their babies. Parents were not satisfied with the scrappy notes of the *meneurs* on each baby, which were communicated to them in writing by collectors who never saw the babies themselves. Within a year of the reform the *meneurs* and *meneuses* were once again collecting the nurses' wages directly from the parents.[17] But the other half of the reform, by which the payment of nurses' wages was guaranteed whether or not the parents paid, remained in force. This was probably the most important change effected in 1769. Its consequences were debated for a century—particularly whether it encouraged the nurses to take better care of the babies and whether it was to blame for the degeneration of the wet-nursing bureau into a public charity.

The declaration of 1769 also made a valiant but ultimately unsuccessful effort to enforce systematic surveillance of the care dispensed by wet nurses to their nurslings in the country. The principal burden had to remain with the *meneurs* and *meneuses*, who were supposed to visit the widely scattered nurses on each trip in order to pay them. The declaration of 1769 prescribed a new, thirteen-column table, in which the *meneurs* were to record the details of each visit they made to each nurse, including the payment made and the signature of the *curé* to verify it, notes on the baby's condition, parents' messages to convey to the nurse and the nurse's messages for the parents.[18] The *meneurs* were required to present this table to the directors for inspection on their next visit to Paris.

In addition to the *meneurs*, the declaration created the new position of *Inspecteur de tournée* or traveling inspector to assure the surveillance of wet nurses in the villages. The lieutenant-general of police was to appoint one or more inspectors to visit the locations where nurslings from Paris were placed. This innovation proved to be too expensive. Antoine de Sartine, the lieutenant-general of police responsible for the declaration of 1769, was slow to appoint inspectors for this reason.[19] For a brief period around 1773 it appears that four inspectors, each paid 3,000 *livres* a year plus the cost of a horse, were appointed to inspect the babies placed both by the Bureau of Wet Nurses and by the foundling hospital. The task was too great for four men, and the cost was too high. Albert, Sartine's successor, tried a new system of surgeon-inspectors appointed in towns throughout the nursing districts. For an annual fee of 5 *sols* per parish and 2 *sols* 6 *deniers* per child, the surgeons were required to visit and report on each nursling in their jurisdiction every three months and to provide free care to those they found sick (but not to prescribe any remedies without the permission of the parents or parish priest).[20] The scarcity of evidence suggests that the system of surgeon-inspectors did not function very long and was no more successful than several other efforts in the eighteenth and nineteenth centuries to provide effective surveillance over the care provided to Parisian infants by wet nurses in remote rural hamlets.

The last in the series of pre-Revolutionary regulations of the wet-nursing business in Paris published in the *Code des nourrices* of 1781 was a police ordinance of November 19, 1773, which tried to extend administrative discipline over the *meneurs* and *meneuses* for the safety of the babies under their control. The *meneurs* were required to maintain according to certain specifications the wagons in which they transported babies. They were not allowed to transport babies on the straw in these covered wagons unless nurses sat on suspended front and back benches to watch the babies.

They were forbidden to carry any baggage or merchandise in their wagons other than the babies' effects and feed for the horses. In Paris, where the *meneurs* were accused of entrusting babies and their layettes to people selected indiscriminately, henceforth anyone performing a professional errand for the *meneurs* and *meneuses* would have to register with the direction and the Bureau of Wet Nurses. The *meneurs* themselves were required to register their lodgings in Paris and the place where they kept their horses and wagons.[21]

The Meneurs and Meneuses

Throughout the eighteenth century the police administration of Paris tried to organize the wet-nursing business in a bureaucratic manner for the protection of the thousands of infant lives that were entrusted to rural wet nurses every year. The police tried to centralize the business, to differentiate the various functions involved (placement, transport, communications, collections, payment, and surveillance), to prescribe uniform minimal standards of performance for each function, to assign each function and responsibility for its performance to specific individuals, and to enforce careful accounting and written records at every stage. But the wet-nursing business resisted police regulation and regimentation. Neither the independent artisans and tradesmen who put their babies out to nurse nor the poor peasant women from isolated villages who nursed the babies were accustomed to dealing with organizations of such scale, complexity, and impersonality as the Direction of Wet Nurses. For them, all aspects of the complex exchange in which they were involved had to be embodied in a single individual, a familiar face, a live voice. That individual was the *meneur* or *meneuse*, who represents the irremediably archaic character of the wet-nursing business, involving as it did an exchange between two premodern populations.

In the mid-1730s fifty and sixty-three different *meneurs* or *meneuses* were counted in two different months in the register of the *recommandaresse* Anne Delaunay. If the three other *recommandaresses* each had a similar number bringing nurses to their bureaus, the total number of *meneurs* and *meneuses* serving the families of Paris (that is, excluding the foundling hospital) may have numbered 200 to 250.[22] In 1776 Framboisier de Beaunay, the director of the Bureau of Wet Nurses, listed 177 registered *meneurs*.[23] A majority of those listed in the register of the *recommandaresse* were women. Only the surnames, with no indication of sex, appear on Framboisier's list; however, the list does indicate beside each name the *meneur*'s residence and its distance from Paris. The distances range from seven to sixty leagues, with a mean of 19.33 leagues (approximately seventy-seven kilometers or forty-eight miles). Eighty percent of the *meneurs* in 1776 lived between seven and twenty-five leagues from Paris.

From the *recommandaresse*'s register of the 1730s it appears that most of the *meneurs* and *meneuses* came to Paris at least once a month and brought with them a certain number of wet nurses each month.[24] The number of nurses they brought varied considerably from month to month and from one *meneur* to another. Dividing the number of babies placed in two different months by the number of *meneurs* visiting the bureau during those months, it appears that on the average each *meneur* brought between four and five nurses to Paris each month. A similar figure is obtained for the year 1776 by dividing the number of babies placed through the Bureau of Wet Nurses that year (9,528) first by the number of registered *meneurs* (177), then by twelve for the months.

To recruit these nurses some *meneurs* ranged widely over many different parishes, often competing with several other *meneurs* in the same villages, while others concentrated their efforts. In the year from July 1, 1732, to June 30, 1733, Margueritte Cappe brought only twenty-two wet nurses from two different parishes in the diocese of Soissons to the bureau of the *recommandaresse* Delaunay. In the same year a *meneur* registered only by the name (ironic in this context) Jean-Jacques brought eighty-five wet nurses from thirty-seven different parishes in the three dioceses of Amiens, Beauvais, and Noyon. Some *meneurs* were said to recruit from over fifty parishes.[25]

But the *meneur* not only had to recruit nurses and bring them to Paris, he also had to visit them periodically with their pay and packages, to return babies to Paris, and to visit parents periodically in Paris to collect the nurses' wages and report on the babies. Considering that at the beginning of 1776 there were 12,719 nurslings from Paris registered at the Bureau of Wet Nurses living in the country[26] and 177 registered *meneurs*, the average *meneur* would have handled about seventy accounts at one time. Obviously, most *meneurs* could not possibly have visited all the rural nurses and all the Parisian families listed in their books on each of their monthly trips.

Enlightened police officials sometimes expressed a strong prejudice against the *meneurs* and *meneuses*, itinerant entrepreneurs whom they could neither govern nor do without. Prost de Royer, the lieutenant-general of police in Lyon, offers an extreme example of these feelings in a memoir he wrote in 1778 pleading for the introduction of legislation similar to that of Paris to regulate the wet-nursing business of Lyon. The *meneuses* of Lyon, called *messageres*, according to Prost, were found in the markets and public squares,

> a kind of go-betweens without name, without domicile, without property. They attend the Baptism, collect the gifts, carry off the baby, place it at a discount, exchange it or give it to the first person who comes along.
>
> Do we even know them? They have clothing, a face and a surname common to so many others. They do not give the wet nurse the child's name, which they have not learned from the family. They certainly do not give the family the name of a nurse, whom they do not yet have and whom they only hope to find later. . . .
>
> [The baby's] condition and its life are in an obscure labyrinth, whose thread is held by this go-between who has no register at all and who does not know how to read. If she disappears or if she dies, all the babies under her charge are lost with her. Most [of the babies] die, without the priests, who did not know of their existence until they buried them, being able to register them: how many death certificates without names or with disfigured names! The remainder, children returned to the city after vain searches, increase the number of foundlings.
>
> This picture is not exaggerated: it is a fact.

The lieutenant-general of police offered an example of a *messagere* from Bresse, a nursing region north of Lyon. "Known only by a surname and for appearing at the Marché des Carmes," she was arrested after several mothers brought complaints against her. "The *messagere* said that she operated like all the other *messageres d'enfants*; that she had done her best; that she had been deceived herself;

that she had no registers; that she did not know how to read; but that if she were given the time, she would find everything in her head; that she carried on this trade to support herself, and she asked to be pardoned."[27]

Prost's account, based on the worst cases who were brought before the police courts and reflecting the great social distance between enlightened urban magistrate and illiterate rural women, was probably an exaggeration, even of the unpoliced wet-nursing business in Lyon. In Paris the police magistrates appear to have succeeded during the eighteenth century in compelling the *meneurs* and *meneuses* to register, to keep records of their transactions, and to accept a degree of responsibility for the babies, sums of money, and packages of clothing entrusted to them. But the Parisian authorities usually exercised caution in imposing new controls on the *meneurs* and *meneuses* because they recognized that the placement bureaus depended upon their good will to provide the wet nurses who were essential to the city year after year and in all seasons, including the months when the labor requirements of agriculture made it especially difficult to induce peasant women to come to Paris. This was the reason the directors of the new Bureau of Wet Nurses gave in 1771 for resisting the idea of assigning each *meneur* a compact jurisdiction of several specific parishes in the country where he would have the exclusive right and obligation of recruiting and supervising wet nurses. The fear of creating a dearth of nurses by alienating the *meneurs* and *meneuses* must have figured also in the directors' decision to abandon the plan of having salaried employees collect the nurses' wages from the parents in Paris. At the same time (1771) the directors were reluctant to interfere with the *meneurs'* custom of collecting the nurses' first and last months' wages to pay for their transportation to and from Paris, and they hesitated (until 1773) to forbid the *meneurs* to carry merchandise unrelated to wet-nursing in their wagons, despite the danger these bundles posed for the babies lying in the straw on the floor of the wagons.[28] When the authorities finally did try in 1821 to replace the *meneurs* altogether, substituting several different kinds of salaried employees, they only succeeded at making outlaws of the *meneurs*, weakening official control of much of the wet-nursing business, and losing the patronage of many parents as well (see chapter 5).

Surviving disciplinary records from the eighteenth century do not give evidence of much tension between the *meneurs* and *meneuses*, on the one hand, and police, on the other, over technical violations of ordinances regulating registration, recordkeeping, surveillance, or the condition of wagons. Most of the *meneurs* and *meneuses* who were punished were guilty of withholding from wet nurses money that they had received for them from parents. Parents usually brought the offense to the attention of police officials after the wet nurse wrote directly to them to complain of their failure to pay her. In August 1729, for example, François Poirier, who kept a wineshop on the Rue Saint-Martin, received a letter (phonetically spelled and loosely constructed with no punctuation) from his baby's wet nurse, who lived in a village near Mantes-sur-Seine (Mantes-la-Jolie?). She asked him to pay the *meneuse* "because I am very surprised that since I have your baby I have received only two months' wages [paid in advance], yet I know well that you can afford to pay your baby's months." Poirier, who maintained that he had paid the *meneuse* Marie Royer three months more (and still owed two), was afraid that the nurse might slacken off in the care she gave his son because of her belief that he had not paid anything. Poirier brought his complaint to the police, who had already received other complaints against Royer. The previous spring the same *meneuse* had collected 24 *livres* from a mason's wife in Paris for three months but had paid the nurse only 9 *livres*. The nurse wrote to the mother threatening to return the child, and the mother replied to the nurse's *curé* explaining that she had paid 24 *livres* to the *meneuse*. On the basis of these two complaints Royer was fined 50 *livres* and imprisoned in Paris for a short period during the fall of 1729, until the money she had withheld from the nurses was reimbursed.[29]

The *meneur* Blaise Morel was guilty of a more elaborate fraud— or of much greater negligence. One of the complaints against Morel involved a master engraver of the Rue Saint-Louis named Santigny, whose child spent nearly six years in the Beauvaisis with a wet nurse and her husband, Pierre Mabillot. Mabillot claimed that he had received 22 *livres* 10 *sous* directly from the father for the first three months, 30 *livres* from the *meneur* in one single payment, and nothing more. The *meneur* told Mabillot the parents had moved to a new address in Paris, but Mabillot was unable to locate them there. Then the *meneur* told the nurse's husband that the father had died and that he should turn the child over to the foundling hospital. After more than five years the nurse herself went to Paris and found the parents at their original address, from which they had never moved. Santigny thought his child had died and cautiously insisted on a certificate from the nurse's *curé* testifying to the fact that his child had remained at her house all the time. Santigny also produced receipts for 110 *livres* that he had paid the *meneur*. Morel insisted in his defense that he had paid Mabillot more than 30 *livres* but admitted that he kept no records. The police inspector arranged a financial settlement among the three parties, but Morel and his seventeen-year-old son were also imprisoned for two months and fined for this and other offenses related to their profession. In a petition for his release Morel volunteered the information that he was collector of the *taille* in his village, and, since he was the only one of the collectors who could read and write, his confinement delayed the collection of royal taxes.[30]

Another example of a more elaborate fraud, in which the wet nurse might have been a co-conspirator, was the case of the *meneuse* Leroy, who collected the nurse's wages from the parents until April 1, 1730, and even asked them for clothing in progressively larger sizes, although the baby had died the previous October 16. Leroy was fined 100 *livres* and forbidden to exercise the profession of *meneuse* again.[31]

The *meneurs* and *meneuses* who were disciplined for extorting money from parents and withholding it from wet nurses were often also accused of violating other police regulations of the wet-nursing business. The two kinds of offense, fraud and indiscipline, usually went together, perhaps because the police only began investigations when parents or wet nurses brought complaints. Morel and his son, in addition to defrauding several parents and nurses, were also accused of placing two babies with the same wet nurse, who was moreover pregnant at the time, and of procuring a baby for another wet nurse outside the bureau of his *recommandaresse*. Royer, notorious for her slow payment or nonpayment of nurses' wages, was also accused of switching a baby from one nurse to another, despite the parents' satisfaction with the first nurse, for no other reason than that the second nurse was a relative of the *meneuse* who had given birth two weeks before and who would, therefore, be nursing two babies at once. Michelle Housseau, who called herself "*meneuse d'enfans* and wet nurse for the past thirty years with no reproach," was arrested in 1731 for not registering the wet nurses she brought to Paris at the bureau of the *recommandaresse* and other "knavery." The other accusations included one from a dissatisfied parent who complained to the *recommandaresse* that Housseau returned her child with the wrong blanket. The initiative for the *meneuse*'s arrest came from the *recommandaresse*. The imprisoned woman seemed most concerned about "a very bad horse" which the authorities had impounded and "which is her only resource for earning a living."[32]

Overall, the two hundred or so *meneurs* and *meneuses* who served Paris in the early eighteenth century were neither the meticulous and responsible bureaucrats envisaged by the police regulations nor the ignorant and careless ogresses whom Prost de Royer described for Lyon. They were, it appears, small independent entrepreneurs competing with others and occasionally cheating and probably only a notch above their rural neighbors in capital, level of instruction, and resourcefulness. Over the course of the eighteenth century increasing police regulation and subsidization of wet-nursing may have reduced their numbers, raised somewhat their standards of honesty and professionalism and their income, and made it more difficult for former wet nurses to move up into the more lucrative business of recruiting nurses. But the *meneurs* and *meneuses* remained a popular profession, for their essential asset was the ability to communicate with peasants, on the one hand, and urban artisans and tradesmen, on the other, about matters that were of great financial and personal significance to both groups. Sophisticated urban magistrates may not always have given this ability due credit. Nevertheless, eighteenth-century Paris depended upon the *meneurs* and *meneuses* for a resource that was essential to its large working population, and many poor remote villages were equally dependent on them for the cash they distributed which the villages had no other way of earning.

The Wet Nurses

The wet nurses who served eighteenth-century Paris came for the most part from the provinces to the north and west of the capital, particularly Normandy and Picardy. Wet nurses from Champagne and especially Burgundy, who were to become so common in nineteenth-century Paris after the development of the railroad, were less conspicuous in the eighteenth century, not only because of the distance of these provinces from the capital, but also because of the relative underdevelopment of roads to the east and south. Wet nurses from the southeast generally traveled to Paris by riverboats (*coches d'eau*) at a cost that put them at a competitive disadvantage with the nurses who came to the capital by road from other directions.[33]

To the complaint of a rural priest that the wet nurses were "ordinarily very poor," the directors of the Bureau of Wet Nurses replied, "It is always true that the indigence of women of the country is the only reason they come to Paris [to take nurslings]."[34] This simplest social characterization of the wet nurses could be misleading. Wet nurses did not come from the poorest stratum of every village around Paris but from all or nearly all strata of specific poor villages that had discovered the wet-nursing business (probably through specific *meneurs* or *meneuses*) as a means of supplementing declining incomes in a period of population growth. The pattern is apparent in fifteen parishes of the Pays de Thelle, 60 kilometers to the northwest of Paris, between Beauvais and Gisors. The total population of these villages, studied by Jean Ganiage, rose from about 4,000 in 1715 to 5,171 in 1791. To provide for their growing numbers the villagers turned to an array of new industries—working wood, bone, and horn into tableware, buttons, and fans, lace-making, and wet-nursing. Ganiage asserts that the total number of urban babies nursed in these five villages over the eighteenth century (estimated at 12,000 to 14,000) nearly equalled the number of babies born to the women of the villages in the same period (fewer than 17,000). In other words, nearly all women who had the capacity to nurse profited from the opportunity. The parish burial registers confirm this statistical inference. They show nurses from nearly all professional and social categories of the villages, including the families of day laborers, artisans, and peasant-proprietors, some of whom paid as much as 40 to 50 *livres* in *taille*. Only the narrow circle of large tenant farmers and estate managers did not take in nurslings but probably placed their own children with wet nurses.[35] For the other families wet-nursing provided a supplemental resource, small but nevertheless important, in part because it was so secure (after the guarantee of 1769) that the nurses could borrow money from their *curé*, the *meneurs*, or others against their future wages.[36]

However poor individual nurses may have been, few appear to have sacrificed their own babies' lives for the opportunity to sell their milk. Eighteenth-century wet nurses suckled their own babies exclusively for six to ten months, when they survived, before taking a nursling. Certificates from the nurses' parish priests copied verbatim into the register of the *recommandaresse* Delaunay indicate the age of the nurse's milk and, usually, whether her last child was living or dead. In a sample of 416 nurses who took babies from this bureau between July and September 1732, in 323 cases the nurse's last baby was still living and in sixty-eight cases it had died (in the remaining twenty-five cases the priest only recorded the age of the nurse's milk without specifying whether her baby survived). For the 323 wet nurses whose own babies survived, the mean age of their babies at the time that the mothers contracted to nurse another baby (and presumably weaned their own) was between ten and eleven months; the median and modal ages were between nine and ten months. Only four of the 323 mothers took a nursling before their own babies had reached six months of age; 218 (two-thirds of the total) waited until their babies were six to eleven months old, and the remainder waited even longer (unless those with especially old milk were only replacing other nurslings who had died). Thus, even before the police ordinance of 1762 made it mandatory, the overwhelming majority of wet nurses did wait until their own babies were seven months old before selling their milk to raise other babies. The mothers whose babies had died could provide younger milk, since they evidently took nurslings immediately after their babies died, generally in the first few months of life. One-third of the nurses in the sample whose babies had died had given birth in the past two months, two-thirds in the past six months.[37]

Ganiage, in a demographic study of three villages in the Beauvaisis, was able to link ninety-two nurslings whose names he found in the burial registers with the family histories of their wet nurses. Only five of the ninety-two nurslings replaced babies who had died. The others were on the average eight-and-one-half months younger than their *frère* or *soeur de lait*. In one-half of the cases the nurse's baby was six to nine months older than the nursling. Ganiage concluded, "It was when their babies were at the age to be weaned that the village women went to Paris to take a nursling." He also found that when the nursling died early, the women returned to Paris for a second or third one to replace it.[38]

The trips to Paris were the most difficult and costly part of the wet nurse's career. Most nurses would make this trip twice with each nursling, to pick up and to return the baby. By custom the nurses paid the *meneurs* all of their first and last months' wages to cover the cost of their transportation, while the parents paid for the baby's transportation and for the nurse's only if they summoned her to bring the baby back to the city on short notice, requiring her to travel by public carriage rather than with the *meneur*. The trip probably took two or three days each way over the normal distance of about twenty leagues from the *meneur's* residence to Paris, plus the time it took the nurse to walk (carrying a baby and layette) from her hamlet to the *meneur's* residence. The babies and their belongings were carried in the *meneur's* wagon over the major part of the journey, but some of the nurses might have to walk beside the wagon if there was not enough room inside.[39]

In Paris at the beginning of the 1770s the wet nurses waited for the parents to come and hire them at the new Bureau des Nourrices, from which the *meneurs* and *meneuses* were excluded so as to protect the parents from undue pressure. Fifty to one hundred and often even more wet nurses waited at the new bureau at any one time. Delays of one to two weeks before a woman was hired were not uncommon. The wait was costly. "Most of the nurses, until they are hired, live only on bread and water, or bad fruit when the season permits."[40]

The principal source of knowledge on the quality of infant care provided by the wet nurses in the country is the testimony of those urban doctors and administrators of the late eighteenth century who wrote on the preservation of children in a spirit of reform. In their campaign to promote maternal nursing they naturally denigrated the wet nurses, whom they criticized for following traditional routines that Enlightenment medical theory had only recently turned against. The reformers, however, ignored the roots of these practices in medical history and popular culture and

attributed them instead to the wet nurses' ignorance and superstition or, worse, their laziness and greed.[41]

Feeding and dressing the infant were two areas of concern. The
wet nurses, according to the medical reformers, overfed the babies,
first by suckling them whenever the babies cried and so not giving
the babies a chance to digest their previous feeding, then by weaning the babies prematurely and plying them with a thick indiges-
tible porridge (*bouillie*). The peasant women hoped by these feeding
practices to give their babies the chubby appearance that they
associated with good health. The doctors accused the nurses of
laziness and insensitivity in trying to stifle the baby's every cry
with the breast and of covering up their own lack of milk by
premature weaning and hand-feeding. With respect to the baby's
dress, the enlightened reformers vehemently denounced the wet
nurses for another practice which medical theory had only recently
turned against. Swaddling, the doctors now argued, was unnatural
and pernicious for the baby's health and development. Rural wet
nurses only bound up their nurslings, the doctors charged, to give
themselves less trouble about watching and changing the babies.
Frequent changes, baths, and exposure to air and fire were considered essential in the new theory of infant hygiene to protect
the baby from internal and external diseases caused by prolonged
contact with dirt, urine, and excrement. The nurses neglected
these precautions not only out of laziness but also out of a positive
prejudice in favor of cradle cap and of human wastes, which were
thought to have therapeutic value in some circumstances. Enlightened observers further accused the wet nurses of rocking the babies
excessively to quiet their crying and of bringing the babies into
their bed at night for feedings, during which the nurse risked
falling asleep and smothering the baby.

One does not need to concur in all the moral and medical
judgments of the eighteenth-century reformers nor in their blanket
condemnation of all wet nurses in order to accept the general
picture of the infant care provided by wet nurses that these wit-
nesses project: a relatively short and intensive period of breast-
feeding (significantly shorter than the twelve to eighteen months
prescribed by contemporary medical manuals) followed by a staple
diet of porridge; swaddling, infrequent changes or baths, a general

attitude of indifference to bodily hygiene and even a superstitious inclination against it; an overall deportment that aimed at keeping the baby content and quiet with a minimum of effort.

Beyond this traditional pattern of infant care, for which reformers condemned the wet nurses, were individual instances of gross negligence, which critics also tended to regard as characteristic of all wet nurses. The worst time for such neglect was the month of August, when wet nurses helping with the harvest were supposed to leave the babies bound up in their cradles or out in the field, either unattended or watched only by small children. Babies left unsupervised in the country were especially subject to two serious accidents: crawling or falling into the fire and being attacked by animals, especially pigs. The royal declaration of 1727 warned wet nurses that they would be prosecuted if they were responsible for a baby's death. In the margins of a draft of the declaration a police official wrote, "This article is important. The accidents which occur as a result of the nurses' negligence are too frequent not to remedy. I had the experience four days ago of a rural wet nurse who left her baby swaddled in a bed and found him dead on her return from the fields. Others leave them in their cradles everywhere and expose them to being devoured by pigs. There are many examples of this."[42]

But the resulting prosecutions do not appear to have been particularly frequent or severe. A stocking-maker of the Faubourg Saint-Denis complained to the police in 1736 that his daughter's wet nurse had negligently caused the baby to be fatally burned. Furthermore, he added, the nurse refused to return the baby's belongings on the pretext that two months of her wages were still due. The stocking-maker asked for the immediate return of the baby's belongings and damages. The *meneuse* confirmed that the wet nurse had left the baby alone near the fire, which it fell into, sustaining burns from which it died twenty-four hours later. The police arrested the nurse but released her after only two weeks. The same punishment was meted out to another wet nurse at the same time for a similar accident that, however, resulted only in the baby's being disfigured by burns. Again, it was the father, a master shoemaker of the Place Saint-Martin, who brought the complaint. The nurse's *curé* pleaded for her release: "The accident was very grievous for her and her husband, who are very poor people, but very good Christians and who are burdened with three small children."[43]

These two cases from the first half of the eighteenth century suggest a certain attitude of tolerance or resignation on the part of magistrates, clergy, and perhaps even some parents toward the accidental injury or death of babies left with wet nurses. Maurice Garden contends that in Lyon this acceptance of the wet nurses' negligence disappeared in a general *prise de conscience* concerning the consequences of wet-nursing in the last third of the century.[44] Similar evidence of parental concern with the physical well-being of their children put out to nurse can be assembled for Paris, for example, in the letters that anxious parents wrote in the early nineteenth century to the mayors of communes where their babies were placed with nurses.[45] It is impossible, however, in the absence of any continuous series of documents on this subject to say exactly how or when popular attitudes about the care provided by wet nurses changed.

Surveillance in the Villages: Parish Priests and Mayors

Official concern about the quality of infant care provided by the rural wet nurses certainly developed significantly in the last three decades before the Revolution as a result of the general infant welfare movement. One manifestation of this concern was the effort to provide some kind of surveillance in the country over the wet nurses and the care they dispensed to the nurslings. Thus, as already noted, the Parisian police officials in the 1770s tried to introduce traveling inspectors and resident surgeon-inspectors. Both institutions proved too expensive and quickly disappeared. The *meneurs* and *meneuses*, whom the police also tried to use for the purpose of surveillance, were too closely identified with the wet nurses by their interests and general culture to exercise an independent control over them. When Parisian police officials wanted to discover whether a child with a rural wet nurse was living or dead, well cared for or neglected, whether a nurse was pregnant, or whether she was keeping more than one nursling, or when the magistrates in Paris wanted someone in a village to supervise a change of nurses for a baby or to force an unpaid nurse to return a baby, inevitably they turned to the parish priest. The priest controlled the indispensable record of births and deaths in the parish. He was literate, and for this reason he was also often called upon by wet nurses who needed to communicate with the parents of their nurslings. And the priest was independent insofar as he had no personal financial interest in wet-nursing, as the *meneur* did.

In 1728 the lieutenant-general of police of Paris appealed to the *curés* of the wet-nursing regions, through their bishops, for their cooperation in issuing certificates of character according to a specified format to potential nurses and in informing the lieutenant-general of abuses.[46] Soon after the royal declaration of 1769 Lieutenant-General Sartine surveyed the *curés* to discover their reactions to the operation of the new Bureau of Wet Nurses. Their responses evince a widespread familiarity with the details of the wet-nursing business but varying degrees of zeal on the priests' part for the task of surveillance. Some, at least, were reluctant to lodge complaints against their own parishioners. Others felt that the inspection of a baby's condition was incompatible with the dignity or decency of their office. Still others complained that the large number of hamlets composing their parishes and the great distances between them, in addition to the number of tasks assigned them by the wet-nursing regulations, made it impossible for the priests to accomplish all that was expected of them.[47]

With the Revolution, the new statute of local government, and the secularization of vital registration, the principal responsibility for surveillance over rural wet nurses passed from the parish priests to the mayors of rural communes. The change probably contributed to the efficiency of surveillance and communications. The archives of wet-nursing communes between the late 1790s and the early Restoration (when the Bureau of Wet Nurses appointed local salaried employees in the country) contain many printed inquiries from the bureau requesting information on the condition of specific babies, whose names were inserted in the blanks, as well as manuscript letters from anxious parents.[48] Sometimes the mayors have scribbled notes on their inspection or a draft of their reply in the margins or on the back of these letters. Some mayors left lists of the nurslings in their commune and notes on the condition in which they found the babies ("*femme* Rollet—fairly well kept, cradle and firescreen; *femme* Duchamps—fairly well but lacks a cradle"). The wet nurses' accounts with the bureau were the subject of many letters between the head of the bureau and the mayors, who wrote on behalf of the women of their communes. The mayors, of course, kept the *certificats de renvoi* that the nurses brought back from Paris with the information on the nurslings with whom they returned. They also supervised changes of nurses and the surrender of babies to specific people designated by the parents upon notification of these changes by the bureau, but many times parents, nurses, and *meneurs* made these changes without notifying the bureau, the mayor, and sometimes even the parents. For after the Revolution, when Parisian authorities finally could count upon relatively efficient officials in the rural communes to supervise the wet nurses, the Parisian authorities themselves had begun to lose their once comprehensive control of the business in the capital (see chapter 5).

The Parents

The parents who placed their babies with wet nurses came overwhelmingly from the large population of artisans and shopkeepers of Paris. This population, because of its political role in the Revolution, has been well studied by historians.[49] Research shows that a majority of the working people of eighteenth-century Paris was engaged in a perpetual struggle to avoid insolvency and indigence, a struggle that became more difficult as the cost of living and particularly of bread rose faster than wages.

The cost of wet-nursing, about 7 or 8 *livres* a month for one child, was a major item of expenditure in the very tight budget of Parisian working families. "In fact," the philanthropist Piarron de Chamousset asked in 1756,

> how would it be possible for a lackey who earns 40 *écus* [120 *livres*] a year, or 1 *pistole* [10 *livres*] a month, to pay 14 *livres* a month for two children whom he might have out to nurse at the same time? His wife could not find in her earnings the wherewithal to survive; and small as that resource is, it is also interrupted around the period of childbirth, when expenses increase. The fate of a poor worker is, so to speak, more pitiable. Out of earnings of 30 *sols* a day, which stop on holidays & Sundays without his expenses diminish-

ing, he has to pay for his food, that of his family, and the rent, which is always expensive in Paris. How could he possibly with every imaginable economy, take from such a small income the means to pay the wet nurse's monthly wage, if his wife does not have enough milk to nurse her children, or if the multitude of her household occupations prevents her from doing it?[50]

A recent historian, Dominique Risler, came to a similar conclusion using Labrousse's series of wages and prices. A journeyman artisan in late eighteenth-century Paris, Risler said, earned 20 to 25 *livres* a month, and his wife earned half as much, bringing the family's income up to 40 *livres* a month. Of this amount, 50 percent went for food (in normal years), 15 percent for clothing, 6 percent for light and heat, and 13 percent for the rent, which was often paid late. The cost of wet-nursing for one baby represented an additional 20 percent of income in this hypothetical budget, which was strained nearly to the limit without this expense.[51]

It is hardly surprising, then, that many parents fell behind in their payments to the wet nurses and often stopped paying altogether. When this happened the wet nurse returned the baby to Paris and obtained a police judgment against the parents for the remainder of the money due (after 1769 the Bureau of Wet Nurses, which had already advanced the money to the nurse, obtained the judgment). The annual number of judgments against Parisian parents for nonpayment of wet nurses' wages rose substantially between the decade of the 1720s, the date of the first surviving records, and the 1750s, then fell by about 25 percent in the next decade, the last for which these records survive. The mean number of judgments per year was thirty-four in the 1720s (records survive for only six years), 205 in the 1730s, 536 in the 1740s, 1,116 in the 1750s, and 816 in the 1760s.[52] The explanation for this trend in the number of nonpayers is undoubtedly as much or more related to patterns of enforcement as it is to the reality of economic hardship and nonpayment. The numbers do show that in the worst decade, the 1750s, at least 1,100 parents each year, perhaps 10 percent of those who placed babies with wet nurses, had fallen so far behind in their payments that the nurses had returned their babies and obtained a judgment against the parents that put them in jeopardy of arrest. The amount the parents owed was usually the value of several months of wet-nursing. Of 277 judgments obtained in 1737, the mean value of each debt was 33 *livres*, for between four and five months of wet-nursing.

The occupational pattern of the nonpayers does not appear to differ significantly from that of all parents who placed their babies with rural wet nurses. Among the 277 nonpayers of 1737 only twenty-two were domestic servants, and sixteen were widows or single women. The list includes masters as well as apprentices and journeymen, in addition to a large number of guild artisans for whom no status is specified, a few "bourgeois," and a few unskilled laborers. The judgments for later years, for example those of 1758–60, often specify the wife's occupation as well as the husband's when the two differ (when the wife's occupation is not specified, she probably worked alongside her husband at the same occupation). Most of the wives were street-dealers selling such products as fruit, tobacco, or clothing. Several were laundresses, dressmakers, or midwives. A small number of the people sentenced for nonpayment of wet nurses was not the parents of the baby being nursed but had nevertheless assumed responsibility for all or part of its nursing. These people were usually either the baby's grandparents or a midwife who had placed the baby on someone else's behalf.

Under police legislation governing the wet-nursing business in Paris the nurses' wages were privileged obligations for which debtors could be imprisoned after a summary hearing until their debts were repaid. Many fathers were imprisoned for debts to nurses, but their incarceration was probably brief and largely ceremonial. Charitable companies, mostly organized in the seventeenth century to assist prisoners as an act of piety, bought the release of the impecunious fathers. The most important of these organizations was the Compagnie des Messieurs, founded in 1654 and headed in the eighteenth century by successive members of the *parlementaire* family, the Joly de Fleury. While their mother society, the Compagnie des Dames, visited and assisted prisoners directly, the Messieurs worked to deliver debtors by negotiating settlements with the prisoners' creditors and paying the debts. The objects of their charity included "merchants, artisans and masters with shops in Paris . . . when they are in prison because of their trade and profession" and "collectors of the *taille*," who were often detained for others' debts, but the category of *"prisonniers pour mois de nourrice"* grew most rapidly in the eighteenth century and came to absorb the biggest portion of the company's income. Nursing debts were treated differently from the other debts handled by the company, in that they were always paid in full and without the customary three-month delay (to chastise the debtor?) but still after information was obtained on the prisoners' "morals, rank and residence, wealth, the number of their children." In 1774 the Messieurs decided to assist prisoners for nurses' debts no matter how small the debt, reversing a position taken in 1754 that they would only help those who owed more than 35 *livres*. The prisoners' release was often accompanied by processions, masses, and other religious manifestations.[53] The Compagnie des Messieurs had at its disposal not only its own funds but also annual gifts from the king and special grants made by the Grand Aumônier de France on such occasions as a coronation, the birth of a dauphin, and royal anniversaries.[54] In this indirect way the state may be said to have subsidized the nursing expenses of urban working families in the Ancien Régime.

The whole carefully contrived system of nursing assistance to poor artisans and tradesmen, patched up in 1769 with the bureau's guarantee to the wet nurses, broke down again twenty years later at the beginning of the Revolution. The economic crisis that precipitated the Revolution and the unemployment crisis for many servants and artisans in the luxury trades that resulted from the political unrest and emigration directly affected parents' ability to pay wet nurses' wages. In the political circumstances of 1789 the municipality of Paris, which took over the Bureau of Wet Nurses from the defunct police administration, could not consider imprisoning the soaring number of debtors; in 1792 imprisonment for debt was legally abolished. If the debtors had been imprisoned, it is doubtful that the traditional sources of charity could have come to their assistance. Without the power to compel payment by the parents, the Bureau of Wet Nurses could not continue to guarantee the wet nurses' wages. As a result, fewer nurses must have come to Paris, and many of those who did may have bypassed the official placement bureau. When the bureau emerged from the administrative chaos of the revolutionary decade, it was placing each year about half the number of babies that it had placed at the end of the Ancien Régime.[55]

On September 15, 1791, after repeated pleas from the city of Paris and others, the National Constituent Assembly decided to mark the completion of the Constitution with a traditional gift from the sovereign to free the fathers imprisoned in Paris for nursing debts. When it was discovered that there were only three such prisoners in Paris, the act was extended to all Parisians who had judgments standing against them for nursing debts. The total number of debtors benefiting from the decree was 5,597. Some of the judgments went back to 1776, but 75 percent of them dated from the three years of the Revolution, 1789 to 1791. The amount of their debt was 225,788 *livres*. The average debtor thus owed about 40 *livres*, the cost of five months of nursing. Two-thirds of the debt was owing directly to the wet nurses, whom the bureau had been unable to pay because of the difficulty it had collecting from parents. Proponents of the decree in the Assembly observed that about one-half of the debtors were enrolled in the National Guard and that 6,000 letters had been received from rural priests and municipalities soliciting payment of the nurses. Thus the measure, it was argued, was not only an act of humanitarian charity but also a patriotic obligation with more than local impact.[56]

Beyond the approximately 10 percent of parents who failed to pay the wet nurses, a much smaller number of parents abandoned all responsibility for the babies they had placed in the country. In this event, when the nurse was not being paid and both the nurse and the police were unable to locate the parents or any relatives or guardians who would take the baby back, then the baby was turned over to the foundling hospital. The records of these belated abandonments are scattered through the papers of the police commissioners assigned responsibility for supervising the wet-nursing business in the capital. Random sampling of years reveals that there were twelve cases in 1742, one in 1745, six in 1755, four in 1765, fourteen in 1755, and thirty-five in 1784.[57]

The parents who abandoned babies with a wet nurse whom they had contracted to pay were not typical patrons of the wet-nursing bureau. In contrast to the simple nonpayers, who were usually married workmen from the lower ranks of guild artisans and unskilled laborers but still within the normal socioeconomic range, the parents who abandoned babies with wet nurses were often unmarried, many were domestic servants, a few were soldiers, a few others were criminals in prison, and most were destitute. An eight-month-old girl returned to Paris by her wet nurse and turned over to the foundling hospital in 1784 was the illegitimate offspring of a coachman, whose whereabouts were unknown, and a woman who was not living in Paris and was described as "absolutely incapable of providing for the baby's feeding and maintenance." The father of another baby girl abandoned the same year was a Swiss Guard, who had deserted three months before the baby was returned. The whereabouts of the mother, who was not married to the father, were unknown. In the case of a third illegitimate baby abandoned in 1784, the midwife originally took responsibility for the nurse's wages, then asked to be discharged from this responsibility when the baby was about seven months old. Many of the parents had disappeared with the deliberate intention of shaking off their creditors: they left "furtively," moving out in the middle of the night, without paying the rent, "after having contracted many debts."

Often the death of one or both parents precipitated the baby's abandonment. A wine merchant and his wife died within three months of one another in October 1741 and January 1742, leaving no property but some furniture and personal effects that did not bring enough to pay their debts. In February 1742 a wet nurse, unpaid, brought their one-year-old daughter to the mother's brother, who turned the baby over to the foundling hospital because he had four children of his own and claimed to be "completely incapable of providing for his niece." Another one-year-old girl, abandoned in 1784, was the daughter of a servant and his wife who both died in the hospital. Their property was sold to pay their debts. Both grandfathers were indigent and unable to take the baby.

In most cases when the nurse returned a baby and it was turned over to the foundling hospital, the reason was that the parents had disappeared, without manifesting the least concern for the fate of their children who were out to nurse, or that the parents had died. In some cases, however, the parents themselves, without attempting to conceal their whereabouts, asked that their baby, returned

by the wet nurse, be placed in the foundling hospital. In a pattern
that Claude Delasselle has shown was characteristic of many eighteenth-century parents who abandoned their babies at birth, these
parents, facing difficult family or financial circumstances, acted
on the belief that the hospital could care for their child better than
they until they had overcome their difficulties and could reclaim
the child.[58] Thus Jean Chevrelier, a master tailor in Paris, and his
wife declared in March 1742

> that because of the hardness of the recent past and the lack of work
> they were reduced to the most extreme necessity. That in this
> condition and having been unable to pay the nurse's wages for Jean
> Michel Chevrelier, their 5-month-old child, . . . his nurse brought
> the said child back to them last Saturday. And since they do not
> know how they can provide for his food and maintenance being
> burdened with another child sixteen months of age whom they have
> great difficulty supporting, [they were advised to place the baby
> at the foundling hospital] to be nursed and raised there until God
> grants them the grace to be in a position to take him back.

In the same difficult year a cook in the service of an officer in
the Army of the Meuse, unable to pay for his daughter's nursing,
instructed the nurse to turn the two-and-one-half-year-old infant
over to the hospital and send him a certificate with the day, hour,
and date of the transaction, evidently so that he could reclaim her
later. In a poorly spelled and ungrammatical letter the cook asked
the wet nurse to let him know "if my daughter is in good health
[*en bon point*] and if she walks alone and kiss my daughter for me
and give my compliments to your *curé*." In 1775 a fruit-dealer's
wife wrote to the *meneur* to announce that she had left Paris for
Saint Malo, where she planned to spend two years. She asked that
her six-month-old baby be placed in the hospital, where she would
reclaim it on her return.

Delasselle has pointed out that the foundling administration
made it very difficult and expensive for parents to reclaim babies
once they had abandoned them, precisely to discourage such temporary arrangements. It is also true that babies left with the foundling hospital were much less likely to survive than those placed
by their parents with a wet nurse, although those abandoned after
six months or a year with a wet nurse must have had a better
survival rate than those abandoned at birth.

The Nurslings

Of course, the group that was most affected by the wet-nursing business, although it necessarily played only a passive role in it, was the babies. Perhaps the best figures we have on the fate of those children are those recorded by Jacques Tenon from the registers of the Bureau of Wet Nurses of Paris for the years 1770 to 1776. During those seven years 66,259 nurslings were placed by the bureau, 45,412 nurslings placed by the bureau were returned to their parents, and 21,002 nurslings placed by the bureau died while in the country with their wet nurses. These figures suggest a mortality rate of 31 to 32 percent. Tenon calculated that the mean period of time spent in the country by the survivors was nineteen or twenty months. The mean age of those who died at the time of their death was five or six months.[59]

From the same source, Tenon selected samples of 250 babies placed in 1786 with nurses from each of four provinces—Burgundy, Champagne, Normandy, and Picardy—and followed these babies for two years. Of the 1,000 babies placed in all four provinces, ninety-one died in the first month.[60] At the end of one year, 257 of the 1,000 had died, and 128 had been returned to their parents. At the end of the two-year period through which Tenon followed his sample, 312 had died, and 499 had been returned, leaving 189 who were still with their wet nurses at two years of age. Comparing the first-year mortality of nurslings placed in the four different provinces, Tenon observed that the mortality of vine-growing provinces was above the overall mean (32.8 percent for Champagne and 29.2 percent for Burgundy, compared to 25.7 percent for the entire sample), while the forage- and grain-growing provinces had below average mortality (23.6 percent for Picardy and 17.2 percent for Normandy). Tenon attributed these differences to the lesser availability of milk in the vine-growing provinces and the fact that viniculture required more work by women, who consequently neglected their nurslings.[61]

If Tenon's figure of 25.7 percent or 257 per 1,000 is taken as a rough equivalent of infant mortality for the Parisian babies placed with rural wet nurses in the 1780s, one may compare the mortality of that group with the mortality of other infants raised in different circumstances at about the same time. Paul Galliano found a lower infant mortality, 177 per 1,000, among 11,293 babies born in nineteen parishes of the southern *banlieue* of Paris in the years from 1774 to 1794 and nursed at home by their own mothers.[62] Working with the earliest available national data on births and deaths by age, Dominique Dinet determined infant mortality for France as a whole to have been 186 per 1,000 in the Year X (1801–2), 200 in the Year XI (1802–3), and 186 in 1806.[63]

Much less precise are the figures from Lyon, perhaps the only other major city in France where the wet-nursing business reached proportions comparable to those of the capital, but with the difference that this activity was completely unregulated and unsupervised in Lyon. Writing in 1770 the physician Jean-Emmanuel Gilibert, a violent critic of Lyon's unsupervised wet-nursing business, estimated on the basis of information he collected from the *curé* of one nursing parish outside the city and from Lyonnais parents that two-thirds of the babies born in the city, "bourgeois as well as artisan," died with their wet nurses, compared to the one-quarter mortality that he thought was to be expected of babies raised by their mothers or by "wise, prudent and enlightened nurses."[64] Prost de Royer, the lieutenant-general of police of Lyon, made the same estimate in 1778: two-thirds of the 6,000 babies born each year in Lyon died with their wet nurses. Moreover, Prost said that only one-half of the 2,000 who returned to the city were in good health.[65] Lyonnais babies placed with unsupervised wet nurses almost certainly were subject to a higher mortality than Parisian nurslings. But the estimates of eighteenth-century reformers like Gilibert and Prost de Royer were probably exaggerations. Garden thinks only 1,500 to 2,200 Lyonnais babies, including 500 to 700 foundlings, died each year in the country with their wet nurses in the late eighteenth century. That figure represents 25 to 37 percent of the city's annual births and a higher proportion of the number of babies placed with rural wet nurses, a number not known for Lyon.[66]

Everywhere in eighteenth-century France the mortality of foundlings was much higher than that of children placed with rural wet nurses by their parents, principally because of the difficulty of procuring nurses to breast-feed the foundlings. The foundlings' mortality, in fact, was catastrophic: 68.5 percent of babies under one year of age admitted to the foundling hospital of Paris in 1751 died before reaching their first birthday, and 1751 was a good year for the hospital. In 1781, 85.7 percent of newborns admitted in the last six months of the year died before their first birthday; 92.1 percent died before their eighth birthday.[67]

There were, then, three different levels of infant mortality for children born in the cities of late eighteenth-century France. The lowest, perhaps 180 to 200 per 1,000 (or a little higher), was the normal for a baby nursed by its mother, a pattern that was rare in the largest cities. In the middle, perhaps 250 to 400 per 1,000, was the infant mortality of babies placed at birth with rural wet nurses. The highest level of infant mortality, perhaps 650 to 900 per 1,000, prevailed among newborns abandoned at the foundling hospitals and generally placed in the country, several to each nurse, to be raised artificially.

Jean-Pierre Bardet identified these three levels of infant mortality in Rouen from surviving records on abandoned children and on children of large, poor families whom the city assisted financially for one year while the baby was nursed either by a wet nurse or by the mother. Bardet found that 90.8 percent of children abandoned as newborns died before reaching their first birthday as compared to 38.1 percent of assisted children placed with wet nurses (fifty-two cases) and 18.7 percent of assisted children nursed by their mothers (150 cases).[68] In explaining the remarkable differences between the three levels of infant mortality, Bardet points out that the assisted children benefited not only from the advantage of breast-feeding but also from greater attention and supervision, either from a wet nurse who looked after only one nursling and was located close enough to the city to be visited by the parents or, even better, from the baby's own mother.

For the two of three Parisian babies placed with rural nurses by their parents who survived to return to the city at the age of eighteen months to two years, what difference did the experience make in their lives? Our present-day psychological theories concerning the impact of maternal deprivation on infantile development may not be applicable to these circumstances, where wet-nursing was so normal a part of the life cycle that it required an independent mind, a strong will, and even courage on the part of a mother to keep her newborn baby and nurse it herself. Something of the banality of wet-nursing in the artisan world of eighteenth-century Paris is suggested by a passage from the memoirs of Madame Roland on her return to the city from the wet nurse: "At two years of age I was brought back to the paternal house. I was often told of the surprise I expressed on seeing in the streets at night the illuminated lamps which I called pretty bottles, of my reluctance to use what is properly called a chamber pot, because all I knew for such purposes was a corner of the garden, and of the mocking look with which I asked whether the salad bowls and soup bowls which I pointed to were also made for that."[69]

But the light and trivial tone of this recollection does not reflect the full impact of wet-nursing on Madame Roland and at least some other individuals in the eighteenth century. Madame Roland in particular, escaping from the parochial artisanal milieu by dint of her intelligence and her reading, joined the enlightened critics of wet-nursing and broke from her own upbringing in nursing her only child. Perhaps the major psychological impact of wet-nursing was on people of Madame Roland's generation and awareness (Talleyrand is another example),[70] who were the first to assert that the way their parents had chosen to raise them was a form of abandonment that betrayed parental indifference toward the children's welfare.

The psychological impact of wet-nursing on the surviving children is a subject best studied in individual cases. Sources are scarce. Most wet nurses were probably illiterate. What written record they left, with the assistance of scribes, is primarily concerned with business (their wages, clothing, and schedules of the *meneur*) and scattered in personal papers, if it was preserved at all. Parents, perhaps a little more likely to write, did not see the babies until they returned home, and then the letters stopped. Memoirists occasionally referred in their memoirs to their own wet-nursing experience but generally devoted less attention to the subject than a post-Freudian historian would want. Chapter 4 examines three unusually well-documented nursing experiences from the early 1780s; only one of the three involves a wet nurse directly.

Notes

1. For Lyon, where the intermediaries were called *messageres*, see the book by that city's lieutenant-general of police, Prost de Royer, *Mémoire sur la conservation des enfants*, ch. 2; for nineteenth-century

Bordeaux, where the intermediaries were called *courtières*, see Dr. André-Théodore Brochard, *De l'industrie des nourrices dans la ville de Bordeaux, conseils aux jeunes mères* (Bordeaux: Féret, 1867), 9–61.

2. Ordinance of January 30, 1350, Title XXXIX, regulating the wages of wet nurses and of *recommandaresses*, in Decrusy, Isambert, and Jourdan, *Recueil général des anciennes lois françaises*, 4:610.

3. LeNoir, *Détail sur quelques établissemens*, 63–64.

4. BN, MF, 21,800, fols. 65–66 (Reglement pour les nourrices, Aug. 17, 1685), 88, 89, 94-97, and Paul Galliano, "Le fonctionnement du bureau parisien des nourrices à la fin du XVIIIᵉ siècle," in *Actes du 93ᵉ Congrès national des sociétés savantes. Tours, 1968.* Section d'histoire moderne et contemporaine, 2 (Paris: Bibliothèque nationale, 1971), 68–69.

5. *Code des nourrices*, 1–6.

6. Galliano, "Le fonctionnement du bureau parisien des nourrices," 71–72. Throughout the eighteenth century Frenchmen were about twice as likely to sign their names in marriage registers as their brides. See Michel Fleury and Pierre Valmary, "Les progrès de l'instruction élémentaire de Louis XIV à Napoléon III d'après l'enquête de Louis Maggiolo (1877–1879)," *Population*, 12 (1957), 71–92.

7. *Code des nourrices*, 7–13; see also BN, MF, 21,800, fols. 79–86, "nourrices et recommandaresses," an annotated early draft of the royal declaration of Mar. 1, 1727.

8. *Code des nourrices*, 21–23.

9. *Ibid.*, 27–31.

10. *Ibid.*, 32–34.

11. *Ibid.*, 35–38.

12. Flandrin, "L'attitude à l'égard du petit enfant," 164–67. See also the collection of diocesan statutes in the Bibliothèque Nationale, under the call number B 2298, especially those of Meaux (1691, p. 7), Troyes (1680 and 1688, p. 5), and Beauvais (1700, p. 20).

13. Morel, "Théories et pratiques de l'allaitement," 399–400, 402, 411.

14. *Code des nourrices*, 42–49.

15. *Ibid.*, 50–57.

16. BN, MF, 14,300, fols. 7–9, 40–45.

17. *Ibid.*, fols. 20–22.

18. AD Eure, II F 4097, "Feuille d'ordre délivrée à Toussaint Clairet, Meneur de la Paroisse de Muzy, Diocèse d'Evreux, Election & Poste de Dreux, lors de son arrivée à Paris, le 4 juillet 1769," a printed model of the table prescribed in the declaration of July 24, 1769.

19. BN, MF, 14,300, fols. 36–37.

20. BN, NAF, 22,746, Papiers de Tenon, fols. 176–77, 257; J. J. Gardane, *Détail de la nouvelle direction du Bureau des nourrices de Paris* (Paris,

1775), xxviii–xxxv; Framboisier de Beaunay, *Instructions utiles à MM. les curés, vicaires, ou desservans des villes, bourgs & paroisses où il y a des nourrissons de Paris, ainsi qu'à MM. les médecins ou chirurgiens inspecteurs, & aux meneurs & meneuses* (Paris, 1776), 27–34, 53–151 (table of surgeon-inspectors and *meneurs*). Gardane was the physician attached to the Bureau of Wet Nurses in Paris; Framboisier was its director.

21. *Code des nourrices*, 60–64.

22. Risler, "Nourrices et meneurs," 37. The *meneurs* and *meneuses* were not permitted to deal directly with parents but had to work through either the *bureaux des recommandaresses* or the Foundling Hospital.

23. Framboisier de Beaunay, *Instructions*, 53–151.

24. AAP, 283.

25. BN, MF, 14,300, fol. 20.

26. Chamoux, ed., "Mise en nourrice et mortalité des enfants légitimes," 418–22.

27. Prost de Royer, *Mémoire*, 15–17.

28. BN, MF, 14,300, fols. 20–22, 29–33, 78–79, 85.

29. BA, AB, 11,070; BN, MF, 21,800, fols. 109–10.

30. BA, AB, 11,064.

31. BN, MF, 21,800, fol. 111.

32. BA, AB, 11,064, 11,070, 11,149.

33. Risler, "Nourrices et meneurs," 21, 35–37. Enough wet nurses did take the riverboats in the eighteenth century to put their imprint on these conveyances. Thus the Napoleonic physician Desgenettes wrote in his memoirs, recalling a canal boat ride between Padua and Venice in 1785: "The boats which make this trip reminded me of the one from Auxerre debarking at the Port Saint-Paul in Paris, except that, instead of wet nurses, we had actors and monks with us." Baron René Nicolas Dufriche Desgenettes, *Souvenirs de la fin du XVIIIe siècle et du commencement du XIXe, ou mémoires de R.D.G.*, 1 (Paris: Firmin Didot Frères, 1835–36), 229.

34. BN, MF, 14,300, fol. 11.

35. Ganiage, "Nourrissons parisiens en Beauvaisis," 271–73, 287.

36. BN, MF, 14,300, fols. 12–14, and Framboisier de Beaunay, *Instructions*, 36.

37. AAP, 283.

38. Jean Ganiage, *Trois villages d'Ile-de-France au XVIIIe siècle. Étude démographique*, Institut National d'Études Démographiques, Travaux et Documents, Cahier no. 40 (Paris: Presses universitaires de France, 1963), 78–79.

39. BN, MF, 14,300, fols. 78, 38–39, 89–90, 86, 87–88.

40. *Ibid.*, fols. 56–57, 55–56, 91.

41. On the conflict between Enlightenment medical theory and the wet nurses over practices of infant care, see Morel, "Ville et campagne"; Morel and Loux, "Prime éducation"; Françoise Loux and Marie-France Morel, "L'enfance et les savoirs sur le corps: pratiques médicales et pratiques populaires dans la France traditionnelle," *Ethnologie française*, 6 (1976), 309–24. For two good examples of medical criticism of wet nurses, see Gilibert, "Dissertation sur la dépopulation," 273–327, and Montmignon, "Observations sur le régime et le gouvernement des nourrissons," in Framboisier de Beaunay, *Instructions*, 41–51. Montmignon was surgeon-inspector of the nurslings of Paris at Château-Thierry.

42. BN, MF, 21,800, fol. 82.

43. BA, AB, 11,322.

44. Garden, *Lyon et les lyonnais*, 120–24.

45. See, for example, AD Eure, AC Beaubray, 5 Q 4.

46. "Une circulaire sur les nourrices (XVIIIᵉ siècle)," *Bulletin de la Société française d'histoire de la médecine*, 18 (1924), 405–6, and *Ordonnances synodales du diocèse de Soissons* (Soissons, 1769), 259.

47. BN, MF, 14,300, fols. 25–26, 46–47, 52–53.

48. See, for example, AD Eure, AC Beaubray, 5 Q 4; AC Houlbec-Cocherel, 1 Q 1; AC Verneuil, 5 Q 7; AD Oise, AC Milly-sur-Thérain, 13 Q 1.

49. Jeffrey Kaplow, *The Names of Kings: Parisian Laboring Poor in the Eighteenth Century* (New York: Basic Books, 1972); George Rudé, *The Crowd in the French Revolution* (New York: Oxford University Press, 1959), and Albert Soboul, *Les sans-culottes parisiens en l'an II. Mouvement populaire et gouvernement révolutionnaire, 2 juin 1793–9 thermidor an II* (Paris: Librairie Clavreuil, 1958).

50. [Claude-Humbert] Piarron de Chamousset, *Deux Mémoires: le premier, sur la conservation des enfans, et une destination avantageuse des enfans trouvés . . .* (Paris, 1756), 12–13.

51. Risler, "Nourrices et meneurs," 41–42.

52. AN, Y 9510–9511, Minutes de sentences de police contre les parents qui ne payaient pas les mois de nourrice de leurs enfants, 1723–1775.

53. Marcel Fosseyeux, "L'assistance aux prisonniers à Paris sous l'ancien régime," *Mémoires de la Société de l'histoire de Paris et de l'Ile-de-France*, 48 (1925), 110–29, and *Réglemens de la compagnie de messieurs qui travaillent à la délivrance des pauvres prisonniers pour dettes dans toutes les prisons* (Paris: de Butard, 1774).

54. BN, CJdF, 1304, fols. 16, 81–82.

55. BN, NAF, 22,746, Papiers de Tenon, fols. 255–57, "Observations sur le décret relatif aux prisonniers pour mois de nourrices"; AD

Paris, 3 AZ 140, letter from Bailly, mayor of Paris, to Pastoret, Paris, June 1, 1791; AN, AD XIV 9.

56. In addition to the sources cited in the previous note, see Camille Bloch and Alexandre Tuetey, eds., *Procès-verbaux et rapports du Comité de Mendicité de la Constituante, 1790–1791* (Paris: Imprimerie Nationale, 1911), 44, 91, 93, 132, 298, and AN, F⁴* 32, "État général des débiteurs de mois de nourrices, dont les enfants leur ont été rendus ou sont décédés chez leurs nourrices, avant l'époque du 15 septembre 1791, et contre lesquels il y a des contraintes par corps décernées."

57. AN, Y 13,381, 13,391, 14,067, 14,070, 14,824, 14,834.

58. Delasselle, "Les enfants abandonnés," especially 212.

59. BN, NAF, 22,746, fol. 254.

60. Tenon probably meant the first month following the registration of their placement at the bureau rather than the first month of life, although he did record the dates of birth as well as of placement. The difference was usually only a matter of one or two days.

61. BN, NAF, 22,746, fols. 3, 81–145, 258–59.

62. Galliano, "La mortalité infantile," 149–50.

63. Dominique Dinet, "Statistiques de mortalité infantile sous le Consulat et l'Empire," in *Hommage à Marcel Reinhard. Sur la population française au VIIIe et au XIXe siècles* (Paris: Société de démographie historique, 1973), 215–30, especially 217.

64. Gilibert, "Dissertation sur la dépopulation," 325–27.

65. Prost de Royer, *Mémoire*, 19.

66. Garden, *Lyon et les lyonnais*, 140.

67. Dupoux, *Sur les pas de Monsieur Vincent*, 116–17.

68. Bardet, "Enfants abandonnés et enfants assistés," 27–34.

69. Jeanne-Marie Phlipon de Roland, *Mémoires de Madame Roland*, ed. by Berville and Barrière, 2d ed., 1 (Paris, 1821), 8.

70. See the grousing passage that Talleyrand devoted to his infancy in *Mémoires du Prince de Talleyrand*, ed. by the duc de Broglie (Paris, 1891), 1:6–8.

4

Three Histories of Infant-Feeding

THREE UNUSUALLY WELL-DOCUMENTED experiences of infant nursing from the Île-de-France and Picardy in the early 1780s are examined in this chapter. The three cases illustrate three distinct social conditions. At the lower end of the social scale is the case of an infant boy born early in 1783 (his first tooth appeared in mid-July) to a watchmaker named Nicod (or Nicot), who lived at the time in the Faubourg Saint-Germain in Paris. Nicod's son spent the first two years of his life in a village near Noyon, perhaps sixty miles north of Paris, with a poor wet nurse named Marie-Reine Féré, the wife of André Billart (or Billard). Our documentation for this case consists of thirteen letters from the wet nurse and her husband (dictated to scribes whose spelling was phonetic) responding to the meticulous communications of the watchmaker and his wife.[1]

The example of middle-class infant care is better known: it is a baby girl named Marie-Thérèse-Eudora, born October 4, 1781, to Jean-Marie Roland de la Platière, who later served as minister of the interior in the Girondin governments of the Revolution, and to Jeanne-Marie Phlipon, his more famous and talented wife. At the time of their daughter's birth Roland, then forty-nine, held the office of inspector of manufactures in the Generality of Picardy, stationed in Amiens, while Madame Roland, at twenty-nine, was an enthusiastic disciple of Jean Jacques Rousseau and promoter of her husband's career. The major sources on Eudora's nursing are the letters (later published) that Madame Roland wrote to her husband during his prolonged absences in Paris and a memoir that she wrote about her nursing experience in 1782 entitled "Advice to my daughter [then six months old], for the time and in the event of her becoming a mother."[2]

73

The third example of infant care in France at the end of the Ancien Régime comes from the summit of society, the court of Versailles. The baby, a boy known to us only as Bombon, was born July 1, 1780, in the imperial city of Regensburg, where his father, the marquis de Bombelles, served as the minister of France to the Diet of the Holy Roman Empire. Some months after the birth the marquise, Angélique-Charlotte de Mackau, returned with Bombon to Versailles to take up her service in court as a lady-in-waiting on Madame Elizabeth, Louis XVI's sister. The mother's letters to her husband in Germany, seized as émigré property during the Revolution, are the basis of our knowledge of this aristocratic infancy.[3]

The three cases presented here are, of course, atypical. The selection is skewed toward the upper end of the social scale. At a time when at least nine of ten urban children were placed with rural wet nurses, two of these three were nursed by their own mothers. The letters clearly indicate the two mothers' feelings that what they were doing was unusual. At least two of the three children were their parents' first or only child, and all three survived their infancy.

Nevertheless, the three cases of infant-feeding examined here are instructive. They provide, in two instances, a basis for judging the impact of Enlightenment critique of wet-nursing on the educated classes and the attitudes and circumstances associated with the upper-class withdrawal from the system of rural wet-nursing in the late eighteenth and early nineteenth century.[4] These cases also show the limits imposed on the movement away from wet-nursing by the long shadow of infant mortality, medical ignorance, and the understandable tendency in these circumstances to view infant-rearing as primarily a physical problem with little bearing on the mental and emotional development of the child.

The Watchmaker's Son

The Parisian watchmaker Nicod and his wife placed their infant son in the country with the wet nurse Marie-Reine Féré. The nurse and her husband, André Billart, were poor. He wrote as a social inferior to the watchmaker: "Though our condition is mediocre, you never fail to respect it" (September 16, 1783). Like many of the rural poor on the eve of the Revolution, Billart often traveled away from home for prolonged periods to find work, while his wife contributed her wet-nursing wages to their "economy of makeshifts."[5] On September 16, 1783, Billart wrote Nicod that he had been away from home for three months. Six months later he announced that the family had decided to move from their home in Le Frétoy "to Rollot in Picardy near the city of Mondidier. Since that place is more prosperous and commercial than Le Frétoy, because of the stocking frames, we have decided to live there and put our small property up for rent" (March 4, 1784). But it is not clear that they did move, for a month later Billart was working in Paris while his wife remained at home. The wet nurse gently rebuked Nicod for giving her husband money that the watchmaker should have sent her (April 12, 1784). In a letter of June 20 the nurse asked Nicod if he would go to Madame Matreque's place in the Faubourg Saint Antoine "to find out if my husband is still working there. Give him my compliments, that I kiss him, and please say, sir, that when he writes me letters that he kindly pay the postage." On December 30 Billart was still in Paris. His wife sent him New Year's greetings for herself and their daughter via Nicod and asked the watchmaker to tell her husband "to try to help me a little for I am having difficulties and am overcome on all sides." But Billart had his own financial problems, for he evidently borrowed money from Nicod. On March 28, 1785, when the wet nurse was about to return the baby, she explained to the watchmaker that her husband had been delayed in satisfying him by an indisposition but would do so soon.

Marie-Reine Féré was a stranger to the watchmaker Nicod and his wife before they hired her to nurse their son. Parents and wet nurse were brought together under the auspices of the municipal Bureau of Wet Nurses. The bureau appears twice in Marie-Reine Féré's letters to Nicod, once when it asked her to bring the baby back to Paris, apparently in error, and another time when Nicod left a package there to be transported to the nurse (April 12, 1784, and July 25, 1783).

The normal intermediary between parents and wet nurse, the *meneur* or *meneuse*, also played only a minor role in this instance. Marie-Reine Féré and the Nicod family relied upon their *meneur* principally to transport packages of clothing from Paris. The wet nurse invariably accompanied her requests with a schedule of the *meneur*'s next journey to Paris: "The *meneur* departs on the 4th of this month; he will arrive the 7th. I beg you to bring him the clothing on the first day of his arrival" (November 3, 1783). He was not very reliable. On September 16, 1783, André Billart wrote that he was "extremely angry with him" for his failure to deliver a package. The next year the nurse wrote that she had not seen the *meneur* for three or four months and did not know whether he was in Paris or not (December 30, 1784).

In this particular instance the primary channel of communication between wet nurse and parents was their direct correspondence, for which the nurse asked the parents to pay the postage (June 16, 1783). The nurse's letters, the only ones that survive, follow a fairly uniform format: a formal salutation, a scarcely informative phrase about their son's good health (on July 17, 1783, "He is very well and as plump as ever"), and a detailed inventory of the clothes that the growing child was forever in need of. The conscientious father also had one more channel of communication with and means of surveillance over the wet nurse: like the lieutenant-general of police and the Bureau of Wet Nurses, he wrote directly to the wet nurse's parish priest to solicit information on his son's condition and the treatment he received (September 16, 1783).[6] There were other miscellaneous intermediaries between the parents and the wet nurse. When the time came to return Nicod's two-year-old son to Paris, the nurse was not feeling up to making the journey. For 9 *livres* a friend agreed to accompany the child and his clothing on the trip in the *meneur*'s wagon. On her return journey the friend carried Nicod's gifts for the successful wet nurse (March 28 and April 7, 1785).

Marie-Reine Féré raised Nicod's son and her own daughter (the *soeur de lait*) with little fanfare and little outside assistance. Her letters to Nicod are most informative about the baby's dress, since he provided clothing. For the first few months of his life Nicod's son was routinely wrapped in swaddling bands, although advanced medical opinion had attacked this practice since about 1740 for forcing the baby into an unnatural position and making it difficult to keep the baby clean.[7] In the same letter in which she announced the first tooth (July 17, 1783), the nurse wrote that she was dressing the baby in clothes that she owned because those sent by Nicod were too small and "he will no longer let himself be tied up in swaddling-cloth, because of his agility and strength." Two months later her husband, complaining about the *meneur*'s failure to deliver clothing from Nicod, wrote that "your child was dressed at the age of five months because of his plumpness" (September 16, 1783).

Once out of his swaddling bands, the baby appears to have worn a shirt with a halter or heavy dress over it, high socks and shoes, and a cap and bonnet on the head. Nicod sent red leather shoes, which the wet nurse set aside for Sundays (March 4, 1784). She bought him wooden clogs for weekdays (? [month covered by seal] 13, 1784). The attention paid to protecting the baby's head is especially striking. On March 4, 1784, the nurse asked Nicod to send cotton bonnets and baby's caps (*béguins*) to put inside. "I asked you for cotton bonnets," she explained, "because he has humors in the head, and the cardboard bonnets are too hard." In the same letter she asked for a head pad (*bourrelet*) "because I hope your child will be walking before long." Another time she complains that his bonnets are not warm enough and asks for money to buy another "for he has cradle cap [*une crasse tête*]" ([?] 13, 1784).

The only mention of the baby's feeding was in the postscript of a letter written by Billart two months after the first tooth: "I forgot to tell you that your child weaned himself, voluntarily on his part, and without any alteration in his health" (September 16, 1783). Billart's evident embarrassment in announcing what was regarded as one of the most difficult events of infancy derives from the fact that wet nurses were expected to breast-feed for a longer period, at least a year.

The nurse's letters suggest that she worked hard to keep the baby clean. His shirts were in bad condition, "as I put one on every day. I had to scrub them very often. That wore them out quickly" ([?] 13, 1784). Toward the end of the baby's second year the wet nurse tried unsuccessfully to toilet-train him:

He is very lazy. He does everything under him. If he is playing in the house he comes to sit down in his chair to make under him. He gives me laundry enough for two. For the entire month I put him on the pot and I could not get him to make on the pot and I put him there at least four or five times a day. He doesn't do anything on the pot. I leave him there a long enough time. As soon as he is seated on his chair he does everything under him. This makes me very unhappy (December 30, 1784).

From the wet nurse's letters it would appear that Nicod's son enjoyed good health throughout his first two years. Marie-Reine Féré only expressed her anxiety once and then only in a contingency that might affect the baby's appearance: "We are afraid of the smallpox which is raging through the country; it would be unfortunate for the child if it spoiled his face since he has a pretty face" (July 25, 1783). Otherwise she reassured the parents, carefully noting in each letter the number of his teeth, which mostly appeared without mishap. Once she noted simply, "Your little boy is indisposed because of his tooth" (November 24, 1783). From her letters it would appear that his most serious problem was a rash he had during his second year. The surviving letters do not actually inform the parents of this rash but only offer reassurances, which suggest that the parents discovered the rash for themselves on a visit in one direction or the other (which is not discussed in the letters). In a letter that could have been written soon after this hypothetical visit, the nurse was unusually prolix in her comments upon the baby's health: "Don't ask about your child. He is very well. I wish you both as perfect health as his. With regard to his rash [*dartres*], there is no danger at all. I am certain that it is teeth [that are causing the rash]. He has one which is breaking through. He still needs one more for his last. He continues to have a big appetite" ([?] 13, 1784). The tendency to explain all infant ills by teething was characteristic of the time.[8] But here this explanation is used to emphasize the transitory character of the rash. A surgeon confirmed the wet nurse's diagnosis: "With regard to that rash, do not worry. The surgeon told me it was normal and would clear up by itself" (December 30, 1784). This is the only professional consultation that appears in the nurse's letters. Was the surgeon called at the parents' insistence?

Marie-Reine Féré's last latter to the Nicods (April 7, 1785) reminds the present-day reader of an element that was missing from her earlier letters and that must have been muted in actuality: an emotional relationship between the baby boy and his surrogate mother. After thanking the parents for their gifts, the nurse wrote, "I am very happy that your little boy arrived home safely. It seems very strange to me not to see him anymore." After a remark about her own health, she continues, "My little girl asks me every day for him, the little brother." In thirteen letters the wet nurse never once identified Nicod's son by name, nor did she do so for her own daughter, whom she only mentioned twice.

Madame Roland's Daughter

Jeanne-Marie Phlipon, the future Madame Roland, had a background very similar to that of Nicod's son, only thirty years earlier. Her father also was an artisan in the luxury trades of Paris: he was an engraver. She was the second of seven children, "but all the others died while out to nurse or in coming into the world, as the result of various accidents."[9] She spent the first two years of her life in the country near Arpajon with a wet nurse selected by a great aunt who spent her summers there. In her memoirs Madame Roland presents the relationship with her wet nurse as a successful one, which was sustained in later years through visits by the nurse to Paris and by the girl to the nurse's cottage in the country. But one specific memory suggests that as an adolescent, at least, she found it difficult to reconcile her feelings for her nurse with the obligations she felt toward her mother. The wet nurse "rushed to my side when she learned that a cruel death had taken my mother from me." (Madame Phlipon died suddenly of apoplexy in 1775, when her daughter was twenty-one.)[10] "I still remember her appearance: I was on the bed of sorrow; her presence recalling to me too vividly a recent loss, the first affliction of my life, I fell into convulsions which frightened her. She withdrew; I never saw her again; she died soon afterwards."[11] Was it a feeling of guilt for her mother, the grave and distant woman, the incomplete mother, which caused the daughter to drive away the wet nurse at this moment? Or guilt at her own preference for the hired nurse over the mother? The father was little consolation: he was insensitive, a gambler, and no more capable of appreciating his precocious daughter than his pious wife was.[12]

Manon (as the girl was called) sought relief from the unsatisfactory relationships of her family of origin in her books, in an adolescent flirtation with convent life, in the relationships she formed in her twenties with a succession of older men, in her infatuation with Rousseau, and in a new ideal of family life, which she never realized so fully as in the months she spent nursing her only child. She perceived the society she had been born into as artificial, corrupt. To the nursing mother of 1781, only six weeks after her own delivery, this corruption could hardly have been better represented than by the spectacle of another new mother, a neighbor in Amiens, putting her baby out to nurse. Madame Roland described the scene to her husband, who was in Paris:

> Mme d'Eu gave birth yesterday at noon to a girl. Her husband is completely ashamed of it; she is in a foul mood over it. I have never seen anything so grotesque. I went out this morning to go see them. . . . Good God! how bizarre it strikes me to find a newly delivered mother alone, without a child! The poor baby was sucking its fingers and drinking cow's milk in a room far removed from its mother, waiting for the hired woman who was to nurse it. The father was in a great rush to have the ceremony of the baptism over, so the little creature could be sent to the village.
>
> Really, my friend, it is not my fault, but I respect them both still a little less since I have been witness to their indifference.[13]

Madame Roland would follow nature: she would nurse her own baby. But, as Rousseau had demonstrated, to follow nature in the midst of a corrupt society was not the easy path; it could require, in fact, something akin to heroism. Madame Roland appreciated heroic roles, as she was later to show in another context. Of the doctors and neighbors who urged her to hire a wet nurse, especially after she fell ill, she wrote to her husband, "Let them talk, all those people who don't count for anything on nature, which they have never had the courage to follow with consistency: I shall be a nurse in spite of them."[14] Another time she wrote to Roland of how carefully she had to watch her diet and avoid indulging herself lest she communicate her fancies to her daughter. "In truth," she concluded, "looking at the matter closely, nursing a baby is a course in morals, and I think some women do well not to try it."[15]

In deciding not to send her baby off to a rural wet nurse Madame Roland took on more than a physical task for herself. She also assumed the ultimate moral responsibility for the infant's welfare, which rested under the wet-nursing system with the father. For it was fathers like the watchmaker Nicod and M. d'Eu who procured the nurses in the hours following the wife's delivery, fathers who generally corresponded with the Bureau of Wet Nurses, the *meneurs*, the wet nurses themselves, and their parish priests, and fathers who had to pay the nurses monthly or face imprisonment as debtors. Madame Roland assumed the ultimate responsibility for the baby's welfare herself. This responsibility entailed round-the-clock supervision. "Since your departure I live only in my bedroom," she wrote to Roland; "that way I have my eye continually on the baby."[16] And in the memoir to her daughter she warned, "Nothing is indifferent for such delicate creatures; the mother's eye should watch everything around them."[17] The father's responsibility in the task of infant-rearing was to serve as a support and reserve force for the mother, "the only person who could replace me."[18] When illness struck Madame Roland and threatened the future of her nursing, she called upon Roland, who was then in Paris, for guidance and advice, and he returned to assist his wife during her illness.[19]

In Eudora's infancy the Roland household was a small collective, isolated for the most part from kin or neighbors, in which the wife had primary responsibility for child care and the husband for his career, and each partner backed up the other in the other's primary area. The role of nursing mother gave Madame Roland a familial and a social status that her own mother, for one, never enjoyed. In 1782, at least, she expressed her satisfaction with this status: "I can imagine nothing a woman could do preferable to caring for her children: it is the most sacred and at the same time the sweetest of duties."[20]

Aside from her husband, Madame Roland's principal auxiliaries in the task of raising her baby were two formal social groups—the medical profession and domestic servants—whose services she purchased in the market. The enlightened mother's quest for professional understanding and assistance, in books on infant care and through visits by doctors and surgeons, contrasts strikingly with the nearly complete absence of the medical profession from the wet nurse's correspondence with Nicod. But Madame Roland's attitude toward medicine was far from the attitude of passive obedience to the doctor's orders. None of the three authorities whose books she cited in her writings of this period—Madame Le Rebours, Rousseau, and the *Encyclopédie*—was strictly speaking a licensed medical doctor. Madame Le Rebours was a midwife, whose popular "Advice to mothers who wish to nurse their babies" was first published in 1767. In a preface to the second edition the author explicitly disclaimed any scientific basis for her work, which she said was based on "practical experience," by which she referred to her own motherhood as well as her professional practice.[21] Madame Roland cited the midwife as an authority on two specific points of infant feeding and recommended her work to her daughter in glowing terms: "I had read attentively the *Avis aux mères* of Me. Le Reboul [*sic*], whose wisdom and exactitude I cannot praise enough."[22]

Rousseau's *Émile* and the *Encyclopédie* certainly had a much more profound effect on Madame Roland's life than the midwife's manual, but the nursing mother found fault with what both works had to say about specific details of infant care. Her reference to the *Encyclopédie* illustrates the ambivalence of her relationship to the medical knowledge of her day. "I will tell you," she wrote to Roland, "that my little girl worries me with her vomiting and her acidity. In the moments of freedom she allows me, I go leafing through the *Encyclopédie* and other works under the words *children, nurse, diseases of infants*, etc. I assure you that the learned dissertations and beautiful precepts appear very stupid or very inadequate when it's a question of applying them. All those people will certainly cure me of reasoning, for I see that the ablest do not have common sense when you relate them to the facts."[23] Clearly, Madame Roland wanted and expected human knowledge to illuminate the task of raising a baby and to help her accomplish this task successfully. Yet she was skeptical of whether the medicine of her day was yet capable of doing either.

The same combination of longing for a medical understanding of and medical solutions to her baby's physical problems and skepticism about contemporary medical knowledge characterized Madame Roland's relations with the physicians and surgeons whom she invariably consulted in each crisis, however minor. Did the baby pass wind often? Madame Roland was not very worried about it, but she nevertheless discussed the subject for an hour with the surgeon Ancelin when he came to visit a servant in the house. Ancelin felt the baby's hands, found them cold, and attributed the problem to a hardening of the fibers caused by this cold in the extremities, which made the humors flow back to the center of the body where they caused the disorders. But he could not suggest any way of keeping the baby's hands warm without inhibiting their freedom of movement or enveloping them in cloth that, the mother pointed out, the baby would inevitably suck. "The reasoner ran on with long words to avoid the problem of prescribing simple rules I asked him for, and I decided I would just carry on as I was doing, letting the baby play with its hands uncovered in my room, where I am careful to keep the air rather warm."[24] When the baby had diarrhea, the doctor sent instructions to continue feeding it the ordinary diet. Madame Roland disagreed. She wanted to cut back and serve it lighter foods, and she would have done so except that the servants agreed with the doctor and gave the baby more to eat after Madame Roland went to bed.[25]

Still, Madame Roland continued to consult the medical profession in her restless search for understanding and solutions. At one time the physician d'Hervillez found that Eudora was suffering from worms, confirming her mother's diagnosis, and prescribed a remedy that Madame Roland administered. She then questioned the doctor on how to get the baby on a schedule, but he had no suggestions.[26] In an almost desperate tone she once wrote Roland, then in Paris, "If you find some doctor who has observed babies, studied what they need, try to get from him some suggestions for me. I feel like an ignoramus, and I think it requires much more attention and care of a certain kind to raise them correctly than we are accustomed to believe."[27] Characteristic of Madame Roland's search for understanding was her careful effort to measure the baby and relate its size to norms at that age and to earlier measurements of the baby as an indication of its health and of the success or failure of its regimen.[28]

Madame Roland's longing for the advice of well-informed medical professionals was matched by her impatience with the assistance of the inevitable domestic servants.[29] She blamed the servants for all sorts of mishaps with the baby and especially for giving in to the baby's will and contravening her instructions. To get Eudora to sleep, for instance, the maids first got into the bad habit of rocking the baby, until the mother forcefully intervened; then, when Madame Roland had to give up nursing temporarily, they fed the baby in its cradle. Madame Roland was adamant about not allowing the baby to become spoiled. Each time Eudora contracted a bad habit because of the servants' indulgence, she insisted on breaking the habit as soon as she discovered it. The whole household then had to endure Eudora's prolonged cries without

responding under the mother's stern eye.[30] Still, Madame Roland
could not reduce the baby's diet when it had diarrhea, as she
wanted to, because of "the feeling of Marie-Jeanne and the *bonnes
femmes* who are always afraid that the little creatures are not eating
enough" and who would feed the baby after its mother was in
bed "thinking they were doing a service for both of us."[31]

The servants' crimes were not all well-meaning or indulgent.
Madame Roland accused her former cook, "the horrible Josephine,
whom I absolutely hate," of causing the baby's diarrhea by feeding
it spoiled milk that the cook swore she had seen being drawn from
the cow.[32] The mother's anger with the servants did not rest on
individuals; it extended to the whole class. After the discovery
that a nursemaid had been surreptitiously rocking the baby to
sleep, Madame Roland wrote to her husband, "You cannot trust
these hired people [*cette gent mercenaire*] for anything. The attachment which they show for you is only mechanical, if it is not a
game. This part of the species which I liked to look on with a
good eye, because it is in a state of suffering, is no more worthy
than the other."[33] Indeed, her low opinion of the moral, as well
as physical, qualities of the poor was a major reason for Madame
Roland's antipathy to wet nurses.[34]

Ideally Madame Roland might have liked to raise her baby
without the intervention of the servant class at all, but this would
have been difficult in the absence of her husband or any other
close relatives and in the underdeveloped state of professional
knowledge. The difficulties of successful infant care in eighteenth-
century conditions were dramatically illustrated in the case of
Madame Roland's daughter because of the mother's decision to
feed the baby artificially when her breast milk failed. Artificial
feeding of infants was the subject of much speculation among
eighteenth-century physicians, philanthropists, and administrators, who were concerned with preserving the lives of the growing
numbers of abandoned children, especially those infected with
venereal disease, whom it was impossible to place with wet nurses.
But the experiments undertaken in this period in different foundling hospitals were uniformly discouraging.[35]

When Madame Roland's milk failed after eight weeks of nursing,
the doctors urged her to hire a wet nurse, and the neighbors
offered their condolences on the collapse of her hopes of nursing

the baby through its teething. But Madame Roland was determined not to give Eudora to a wet nurse. She first tried to feed the baby through a piece of bread wrapped in a knotted cloth, which was dipped in sweetened rice-water, "an expedient imagined with the speed required in the circumstances." She soon changed the formula to heated cow's milk diluted with barley water and sweetened with honey. The feeding apparatus presented more problems. The knotted cloth was abandoned because of the difficulty of removing it from the baby's mouth to moisten it again every time the baby had sucked the bread dry. Eudora would not drink from a spoon or a bottle made with an end to fit her mouth, and a sponge released the milk too easily causing her to choke. Finally, Madame Roland settled on a piece of cloth with holes in the end from which the baby sucked the milk, which was poured slowly and continuously over the cloth. When the baby showed signs that it was not getting enough nourishment, she increased the proportion of milk in the formula and began to supplement it with light soups with a base of bread, bouillon, or butter.[36] But Madame Roland was worried. The baby did not grow for a month, and the mother was afraid it would not survive the teething crisis unless it could be restored to the breast.[37] So Madame Roland, having recovered from her illness, resorted to various expedients to restore her milk flow, even paying a poor woman to allow her to nurse that woman's baby a few times a day in the hope that its sucking would provoke the resumption of lactation.[38] Despite her husband's expressions of concern for her health and to the astonishment of her surgeon, Madame Roland triumphantly succeeded in completely restoring her milk flow and resuming the nursing of her baby after an interruption of about seven weeks.[39]

The subsequent relationship between mother and daughter in the ten years that remained of Madame Roland's life after she completed nursing Eudora suggest that the mother either lost interest in the maternal role that was once so important to her or that she always interpreted this role to be essentially a physical relationship that ended with weaning, leaving behind an indissoluble emotional bond. A major argument for maternal nursing in the eighteenth century was the belief that a baby imbibed physical and especially moral qualities with the milk on which it was nursed in addition to those which it inherited from its parents.[40] Perhaps it was in part because eighteenth-century medical theory neglected the impact of environment and the psychological development of children after weaning that Madame Roland tended to neglect her daughter after she had met the child's physical needs but felt cheated when Eudora grew up as distant emotionally from her mother as Madame Roland had been from hers. After an absence of three months in Paris during Eudora's third year, Madame Roland returned home to find her daughter did not recognize her. "There I am, like the women who did not nurse their children," she complained to a friend; "yet I deserved better than they, and I am no further along! . . . I wish [the child] still needed milk, and I had it to give her."[41] Eudora was left behind again, in a convent near the family's new home in Villefranche-sur-Saône, when her parents went to Paris during the Revolution. Many years later, in the midst of a long and quiet life, Eudora protested that Lamartine's popular *History of the Girondists* had glorified her mother at the expense of her father.[42]

A Baby at Versailles

When the marquis de Bombelles became a father, he wrote home from Regensburg to family and friends in France to announce the good news. His letters, which do not survive in the archives, evidently also announced the intention of the marquise to nurse the baby herself, for the congratulatory letters that the marquis received in reply and which are preserved in the archives almost all comment upon this unusual course of action. In the main the correspondents express approval and admiration. Only the marguise d'Harvelay feared that the mother's health might suffer from nursing: "It is a big enterprise," she cautioned, "especially when one is not very strong" (July 20, 1780). Several of the letters express their delight with the idea of maternal nursing by painting a verbal genre scene in the manner of Jean-Baptiste Greuze. In the most elaborate of these the writer imagines "my Angélique holding her son in her arms, giving him existence from her own substance, following with a maternal eye the milk which the baby sucks in and gulps down. I see my Marquis in the ecstasy of feeling contemplating the mother and the child and giving the mother the kisses which his heart dictates to him and even those which he does not dare give the baby for fear of interrupting him" (July 11, 1780). The parents evidently shared their friends' aesthetic of family life. When the marquise was about to wean her baby a year later, she wrote to her husband, "One of my great regrets in weaning him is caused by Hain, who was supposed to paint him with me, sucking me. But perhaps he will be able to do it even though he no longer sucks" (July 23, 1781).

In early 1781 the marquise de Bombelles had returned to Versailles, without her husband but still nursing her son, to take up her service with Madame Elizabeth at the royal court. The highest personages there took an interest in her enterprise. When the king's minister the comte de Maurepas heard that the marquise was nursing, he asked her about her son's age and health (May 26, 1781). The queen, who had once expressed an interest in nursing her children,[43] asked after Bombon several times and stopped to look at and compliment the baby once when she met the marquise walking with him (May 12 and June 13, 1781).

Although the court took a sympathetic interest in the nursing mother, it did not provide the ideal setting for bringing up a baby. On the eve of Bombon's first birthday, for example, the marquise complained to her husband, "I would certainly like to celebrate it, but there is no way. You know what a Sunday is like when one is on duty for the week [*lorsqu'on est de semaine*]. I scarcely have the time to suckle him" (June 30, 1781). The common accusation by eighteenth-century moralists that upper-class French women put their social lives ahead of their maternal obligations certainly did not apply to the marquise de Bombelles. She left the theater near the beginning of the second play one evening to feed Bombon before he went to sleep. The play promised to be "charming," she wrote, "but I was well compensated by seeing my little child, who was very pleased with my return" (July 2, 1781). When the baby was recovering from a cough on the eve of the mother's week of service, she wrote the marquis, "So long as Bombon is well I will do what I can to show my zeal for Madame Elizabeth. But if he has the least thing wrong, nothing in the world could make me leave him" (May 20, 1781). At the end of a week of service the marquise expressed her longing for another style of life, one built around the home and nuclear family, a life that she, anticipating later sociologists, associated with the bourgeoisie: "The court is

a dog of a place. I shall long regret the sweet and tranquil life I
led at Ratisbon [Regensburg] and I feel perfectly that my lot should
have been to be a goodwife [*une bonne femme*] occupied solely with
her husband, her children, and her household. For the pleasures
of the court, of what is called good taste [*le bon ton*], have no
attraction for me, and I have too bourgeois a way of thinking for
that place" (May 31, 1781). But the question raised by the interest
of her friends and of the court in the marquise's nursing is whether
her own longing for a bourgeois style of family life was not general
to aristocratic society on the eve of the Revolution.

The marquis, even though absent, was his wife's confidant and
partner in her idyll of family life centered on the baby. It appears
that his personal involvement and contribution to his son's welfare
began with the boy's birth. Eighteenth-century medical theory
still held that a woman should abstain from sexual relations while
she was nursing because intercourse was supposed to spoil or
diminish the flow of milk and could lead to a new conception that
would stop the flow entirely.[44] The friends and relatives who
responded to the marquis's announcement of his wife's delivery
and nursing assumed that the father was sacrificing his conjugal
right. "I am charmed," wrote one correspondent to the marquis,
"that Madame de Bombelles has decided to nurse, and that the
abstinence of the nursing state has not frightened you" (July 13,
1780). Another declared, "How deserving she [the marquise] is,
how generous you are!" (July 17, 1780).

After the marquise returned to France, she wrote her husband
almost daily with abundant descriptions of Bombon's latest *gestes*.
One day the baby took a soup spoon from his mother's hands and
began feeding himself. The marquise was sad that the father could
not share her pleasure at seeing the baby's progress. "Why does
he have to be deprived of the only real pleasures, pleasures which
so few people feel as he does?" (May 10, 1781). The marquis was
also interested in the nursing mother's health. This was the reason
he urged her to wean the baby when it had reached one year of
age (July 7, 1781). But the mother put off weaning the baby
another few weeks until its first teeth finally appeared. Nursing,
after all, was her responsibility. The father took over the son's
education after the mother had nursed him through the perils of
infancy and assured his physical survival. After Bombon was suc-

ccssfully weaned, the marquise wrote with pride to her husband: "I believe that this child will be well made for raising. He has a sweetness and sensitivity which will give you plenty of means to work with, and along with that his vivacity. In truth, he is charming, and you will have a good field to cultivate" (August 4, 1781).

The marquis's role as an absent but intimate partner of his nursing wife resembles Roland's role. By contrast, the auxiliary role of kin outside the nuclear family in bringing up the baby is much more prominent in the aristocratic family. The marquise brought the baby along with her for a visit to her husband's sisters in Paris and Villiers. They fussed over Bombon and gave him toys. When Bombon's first tooth finally appeared, the husband's sisters were among the first people the mother informed, confident that they "will surely be very pleased" (January 9 and 19, July 14, 1781). With her own mother, who lived in Montreuil, the marquise was on even closer terms. There is no evidence that the marquise's decision to nurse her child derived from or implied any alienation from her parents as Madame Roland's might have. Bombon's grandmother saw her grandson often and shared all his mother's anxieties and joys about the boy's coughs, teeth, and such (March 24 and July 14, 1781). Out of concern for her daughter's health the grandmother was an early member of the party advocating that Bombon be weaned at eleven months (May 15, 1781). When he finally was weaned at thirteen months, the grandmother took sole charge of the baby at her house for several days to ease the separation from the mother. The marquise, who was quite anxious about the weaning, expressed herself as reassured that Bombon would be at Montreuil, "where he will be well cared for by *maman* who absolutely insists on having him with her, although I told her that he would prevent her from sleeping the first few nights. It is a mark of love which she gives you as well as me, for which I am grateful. And she is busy getting everything together which could amuse the baby, such as a rug to play on and toys" (July 21, 1781).

For advice on caring for her baby the marquise de Bombelles did consult the medical profession, but with neither the exclusive faith in science nor the critical attitude toward traditional medicine that characterized Madame Roland's relations with professionals. Like Madame Roland, the marquise had read Madame Le Re-

bours's book and cited it as an authority on specific questions of
nursing (July 7, 1781). She also knew enough of Tissot, the enlightened Swiss author of the very popular "Advice to the People
on its Health" (first edition, 1762), to tease her husband about
visiting Lausanne without consulting the famous physician about
raising children (June 13, 1781). The physician or surgeon whom
the marquise consulted personally about nursing and infant care
(his precise qualifications were never specified) was a man named
Constannau. But his position was more like that of a family friend
or perhaps a subordinate member of an aristocratic household than
an independent professional, for the marquise wrote, "he visits me
every morning with more exactitude than if he were a man I paid"
(May 17, 1781). The marquise quoted Constannau's advice in
several letters to her husband and seems to have respected it, but
no more than the advice of a non-professional *bonne femme*. In
resisting her mother's advice to wean the baby in May, the marquise wrote, "Constannau is of my opinion. In addition, Madame
de Lan [?], a lady's-maid of Madame Elizabeth who had five children, told me that nothing was so dangerous as weaning a baby
at the moment that its teeth are coming out" (May 15, 1781).

The marquise de Bombelles also measured Bombon, as Madame
Roland measured Eudora, but the purpose of this gesture differed
in the two cases. Madame Roland measured Eudora to give precision to her observation of the baby's physical development and
to relate that development to the feeding methods the mother had
adopted. She measured the baby's health and the efficacy of her
own intervention. For the marquise de Bombelles measurement
of Bombon was a matter of ceremony. Bombon's measurement
was the only event that marked his first birthday. He was twenty-
six inches tall, the marquise reported to her husband; "when you
are back in Ratisbon, measure the ribbon on the piece of wood
where we measured him every three months since his birth and
tell me how much he has grown since the month of April" (July
2, 1781). Bombon's height was a fact for the baby album, part of
the family cult, not a medical record.

The servant whom the marquise de Bombelles depended upon
to look after her baby during her frequent absences at court was
not a lieutenant bound to execute the mother's minutely defined
tactics of infant care, but a governess whose sole task was to care

for Bombon and to whom the marquise appears to have allowed considerable autonomy. Madame Giles had been hired in Regensburg to be the baby's governess until he was weaned. The marquise was so pleased with the care she gave Bombon that she asked her husband in May to buy an inexpensive watch in Geneva as a gift for the governess (May 22, 1781). A few weeks later, before the watch arrived, Madame Giles aroused her mistress's anger and confusion by announcing that she wanted to go home to her husband and children. "It is a very natural feeling," the marquise wrote her husband, "but you will agree that after the assurances which she had given us to wean the baby and not to leave it until it would no longer need her, I was not expecting to see her leave at the moment when the baby's teeth are going to appear and when it needs her most." The marquise thought she would have to hire the court wet nurse for awhile to wean the baby, as another servant in her household was too young and inexperienced to help with the weaning (June 14, 1781). But Madame Giles was persuaded to stay another two months, through the baby's weaning, especially by the promise that a watch—the news of which the marquise conveyed to the governess indirectly—was to be the reward for the successful completion of her task. "So true it is that you cannot count on the attachment of those people except insofar as it is guided by interest" (July 2, 1781).

To replace Madame Giles immediately after the weaning the marquise sought to accustom the baby over a few days to Agatha, another servant of her household, and set her maid, "who understands children perfectly," to watch Agatha and report back to the marquise on the care she gave Bombon. Had Agatha not succeeded, she planned to hire "a governess whom I will keep until the child is a little bigger" (August 10, 1781). To her great relief, Agatha and Bombon got along well together so it was not necessary to introduce "a new face" (August 12, 1781). In all of this the primary criteria for judging the servants were the efforts they made on the baby's behalf and their compatibility with Bombon, not their obedience to the mother's orders, which seemed to be the primary consideration for Madame Roland.

On the whole Bombon appears to have enjoyed a healthy and uneventful infancy. He was "beginning to walk very well" at the end of his tenth month after refusing two months before to be placed in a walker which his mother had had made "to teach him to walk" (March 24 and May 26, 1781). During the daytime hours when his mother was often away at court, he gradually and cheerily became accustomed to eating soups and moistened bread (May 15, 1781). But at night the mother nursed him indulgently: "He drinks and eats perfectly and could very easily do without sucking all day long. But at night he cannot do without me. He is accustomed to falling asleep in the evening at my breast, to sucking every time he wakes up. This regimen succeeds so well with him, and bothers me so little that I am in no hurry to wean him" (June 13, 1781). In contrast to Madame Roland, the marquise felt no urgency about putting the baby on a schedule or preventing him from being spoiled.

The major drama of Bombon's first year was the long wait for the appearance of his first tooth, an event that was fearfully awaited as it was regarded by the marquise as "one of the most dangerous epochs of infancy" (July 18, 1781). On March 24, at the end of Bombon's ninth month, his mother was "enraged" that his teeth had not yet appeared. She refused to wean the baby until the teething crisis was past. Finally, on July 13, in the baby's thirteenth month, the first tooth broke through "as white as milk" and "without the least little pain." After confirming the fact by tapping a glass against it, the marquise broke down in tears and trembling for two hours. The good news was quickly spread around the court, to the extended family, and with the first post to Zurich, where the marquis was then traveling (July 14, 1781). A second tooth broke through four days later (July 18, 1781).

When Bombon had overcome the teething crisis without incident, his weaning could no longer be postponed. The doctors were consulted and found the baby strong enough to withstand the next trial and the mother so weakened as to make the weaning urgent. The process itself, for which plans were laid over a week in advance, involved a physical separation of mother and child lasting several days (July 21, 1781). Sunday, July 29, was the day of separation, anxiously anticipated by the mother, when Bombon was sent with his governess to his grandmother's house at Montreuil. The marquise received news of each night's events but did not see Bombon again until August 4, and then Bombon was still not allowed to see his mother, who watched her baby playing in the garden for three hours from behind the blinds inside the *salon* (August 6, 1781). On August 10 the baby spent the morning with its mother, although it remained at Montreuil for another few days while the marquise completed her week on duty at court and recovered from the pains which accompanied the cessation of nursing (August 10, 1781). The weaning was a success. Bombon slept through the night for the first time, he had not gotten any thinner, and the marquise felt "he loves me just as much as when I was nursing him" (August 12, 1781). With teething and weaning behind her, the marquise breathed easier: "That puts two very worrisome epochs behind us without incident. Everything allows us to hope that we shall preserve this dear treasure. Once he has all his teeth and has been inoculated [against smallpox] we can feel very much at ease" (August 4, 1781). The shadow of infant mortality, which hung menacingly over all classes at the end of the Ancien Régime, had nearly been lifted from Bombon.

Conclusions

The three histories of infant-feeding related in this chapter help to clarify the interplay of cultural, socioeconomic, and technological considerations in eighteenth-century wet-nursing.

The case of Nicod's son (or those of the upper-class infants cited in note 4 of this chapter) shows that wet-nursing was not invariably associated with parental indifference or hostility toward small children, as the Enlightenment critics of wet-nursing (including Madame Roland) and some recent historians of the family have argued. On the other hand, the cases of the Rolands' daughter Eudora and of the eldest son of the marquis and the marquise de Bombelles illustrate the diversity of motives and family styles that lay behind the adoption of maternal feeding by a prominent minority in the 1780s. For Madame Roland the decision to nurse was associated with a radical break from her family of origin, from the traditions of infant care and of medicine, and from the social peers who lived around her. For the marquise de Bombelles, who took the same step in full awareness of its originality within her society, maternal nursing implied no such radical break from or rejection of other elements in that society, no cutting adrift of the nuclear family from kin, and no new science of baby care.

Lacking any letters from Nicod or his wife, one cannot know why they placed their baby with a wet nurse. Probably it was because of the high cost that the mother's nursing the baby would have entailed for the family shop and household. Hiring a peasant woman was cheaper and more convenient. Monsieur Nicod wrote the nurse and her parish priest regularly to see that the baby was well clothed and that all was well. The responsibility was his. Although Madame Nicod's contribution to household and business was too important to sacrifice for nursing and infant care, her status in the workshop-household was subordinate.

With the Rolands and the Bombelles, the milieux of family and work were differentiated; indeed, they were often separated by long journeys. The nursing mothers had a status in the family milieu parallel to their husbands' status on the outside. The tensions between mother and servants and the tendency to seek professional medical advice rather than rely on folk wisdom in the task of child-rearing are additional manifestations of the growing isolation of home and family from the wider world and the differentiation of social functions. Placing a baby out of the house and allowing a stranger into the house, except in a carefully prescribed social role, were both beginning to be viewed as intolerable by the upper strata. The marquise de Bombelles conceded that it was "a very natural feeling" on the part of Madame Giles to wish to return to her own family, even as she fumed over the governess's breaking her agreement to stay until Bombon was weaned. The faults with which Madame Roland taxed her servants—overfeeding the baby, rocking her to sleep—were the very faults with which Enlightenment medicine taxed the rural wet nurses and the reasons why Madame Roland did not place Eudora with a wet nurse.

The decision by the educated classes at the end of the eighteenth century to nurse their babies at home was also associated with a new science and a new material culture of infant-rearing. With home nursing the swaddling bands were abandoned, baths probably became more frequent, and feedings were put on a regular schedule. But social and cultural change ran ahead of scientific and technological change in one respect. Until a safe substitute for breast-feeding could be discovered, even the well-to-do could not dispense entirely with wet nurses, urban working women would continue to send their babies away to the country, and a very high proportion of abandoned children would die year after year.

Notes

1. AD Seine-et-Oise, E 2644.
2. Jeanne-Marie Phlipon de Roland, *Lettres de Madame Roland, 1780–1787,* ed. by Claude Perroud, 1 (Paris: Imprimerie nationale, 1900), and Jeanne-Marie Phlipon de Roland, "Avis à ma fille, en âge et dans le cas de devenir mère," in *Oeuvres de J.M.Ph. Roland, femme de l'ex-ministre de l'intérieur,* ed. by L. A. Champagneux, 1 (Paris: Bidault, an VIII), 301–44.
3. AD Seine-et-Oise, E 432 and 434.
4. Caution is called for in interpreting this evidence. Instances abound of educated families in the late eighteenth century who resembled the Roland and Bombelle families in their child-centered intimacy but who nonetheless continued to place their babies with rural wet nurses. One striking instance is the family of General de Martange, cited by Philippe Ariès as exemplary of "a concept of the family which had become identical with that of the nineteenth and early twentieth centuries." See Ariès, *L'enfant et la vie familiale,* 453, and, for the reference to his son's wet nurse in Martange's correspondence, *Correspondance inédite du Général-Major de Martange, aide de camp du Prince Xavier de Saxe, Lieutenant Général des Armées (1756–1782)* [ed. by Charles Bréard] (Paris: A. Picard et Fils, 1898), 385. For another example, see Le conseiller et la comtesse d'Albis de Belbèze, *Une famille de parlementaires toulousains à la fin de l'Ancien Régime, correspondance du Conseiller et de la Comtesse d'Albis de Belbèze (1783–1785),* ed. by Auguste Puis (Paris: Édouard Champion, 1913).
5. Olwen H. Hufton, *The Poor of Eighteenth-Century France, 1750–1789* (Oxford: Clarendon Press, 1974).
6. See also AD Seine-et-Oise, E 2644, three letters of Feb. 10 and 23, and Mar. 20, 1786, from Debras, *curé* of Babeuf, to Nicod, concerning another child, a daughter, whom he put out to nurse with a woman in that parish.
7. Morel, "Ville et campagne," 1011–12.
8. For a Freudian analysis of this preoccupation with teething see David Hunt, *Parents and Children in History: The Psychology of Family Life in Early Modern France* (New York: Harper & Row, 1972), 117–24.
9. Roland, *Mémoires,* 6.
10. Gita May, *Madame Roland and the Age of Revolution* (New York: Columbia University Press, 1970), 46.

11. Roland, *Mémoires*, 7.
12. May, *Madame Roland*.
13. Roland, *Lettres*, 53.
14. *Ibid.*, 132–33.
15. *Ibid.*, 169.
16. *Ibid.*, 71–72.
17. Roland, "Avis à ma fille," 320.
18. *Ibid.*, 321.
19. Roland, *Lettres*, 79.
20. Roland, "Avis à ma fille," 342.
21. Madame L. R. [Marie-Angélique (Anel) Le Rebours], *Avis aux mères qui veulent nourrir leurs enfans*, 2d ed. (Paris: P. F. Didot, le jeune, 1770), xii–xiii.
22. Roland, "Avis à ma fille," 305–6. See also Roland, *Lettres*, 100.
23. Roland, *Lettres*, 168–69. On Rousseau see Roland, "Avis à ma fille," 340–42.
24. Roland, *Lettres*, 66–67.
25. *Ibid.*, 100.
26. *Ibid.*, 171–74.
27. *Ibid.*, 169.
28. *Ibid.*, 92, 176.
29. For a very suggestive discussion of the triangle of bourgeois mothers, doctors, and servants in this period, see Jacques Donzelot, *La police des familles* (Paris: Éditions de Minuit, 1977), ch. 2.
30. Roland, *Lettres*, 72, 154.
31. *Ibid.*, 100.
32. *Ibid.*, 115.
33. *Ibid.*, 72.
34. Roland, "Avis à ma fille," 312, 320.
35. Morel, "Théories et pratiques de l'allaitement."
36. Roland, "Avis à ma fille," 318–22.
37. Roland, *Lettres*, 92, 100.
38. "I should observe, to the honor of the indigent class, that it is much more difficult to find among them mothers who will take money to give their babies to be nursed, than it is common in the other class to see women pay to have theirs nursed." Roland, "Avis à ma fille," 312.
39. Roland, *Lettres*, 142–43, 150.
40. Étienne van de Walle and Francine van de Walle, "Allaitement, stérilité et contraception: les opinions jusqu'au XIXe siècle," *Population*, 27 (July-Oct. 1972), 698.
41. Letter of June 7, 1784, reprinted in Roland, *Mémoires*, 294–95.

42. May, *Madame Roland*, 146, 176–77, 291.

43. Balandra, *Les nourrices des rois*, 59.

44. Jean-Louis Flandrin, *Familles. Parenté, maison, sexualité dans l'ancienne société* (Paris: Librairie Hachette, 1976), 198–200; Flandrin, "L'attitude à l'égard du petit enfant," 182–87; van de Walle and van de Walle, "Allaitement, stérilité et contraception." Flandrin suggests that wet-nursing was a solution, sanctified by the Roman Catholic Church, to the woman's dilemma of meeting her obligations to both husband and baby. But wet-nursing, of course, only shifted the dilemma from the mother to the wet nurse. Parents who placed their baby with a rural wet nurse had no means of insuring that the wet nurse would abstain from sexual relations with her husband. The best the parents could hope for (and the regulations of the wet-nursing bureau reflect this hope) is that the nurse would inform them as soon as she discovered she had become pregnant. Sexual abstinence might, however, be enforced on live-in nurses. There was mention in chapter 1 of the nurse of the future Louis XIV who was dismissed because she was seen talking with her husband in the palace garden. In 1823 the poet Victor Hugo's mother hired a woman to nurse her grandson at the grandparents' house in Blois with the understanding that "for one year [the wet nurse] would not cohabit with her husband." When the nurse's husband and children moved into the garden house where she was living, in spite of the agreement, the grandparents dismissed the wet nurse. Unable to find another without a family, they began to feed the baby goat's milk. Two weeks later the baby died. Victor Hugo, *Oeuvres complètes*, ed. by Jean Massin (Paris: Le Club français du livre, 1970), Tome II, vol. 2, 1403–27.

Étienne Aubry (1745–81), *Les adieux à la nourrice*.
Sterling and Francine Clark Art Institute, Williamstown, Mass.

Jean-Baptiste Greuze (1725–1805), *La privation sensible*.
Cabinet des estampes, Bibliothèque Nationale, Paris.

Jean-Baptiste Greuze (1725–1805), *Retour de nourrice*.
Cabinet des estampes, Bibliothèque Nationale, Paris.

Bureau de la Direction Générale des Nourrices.
From a collection of lithographs by Marlet entitled *Nouvaux tableaux de Paris* (1821?).

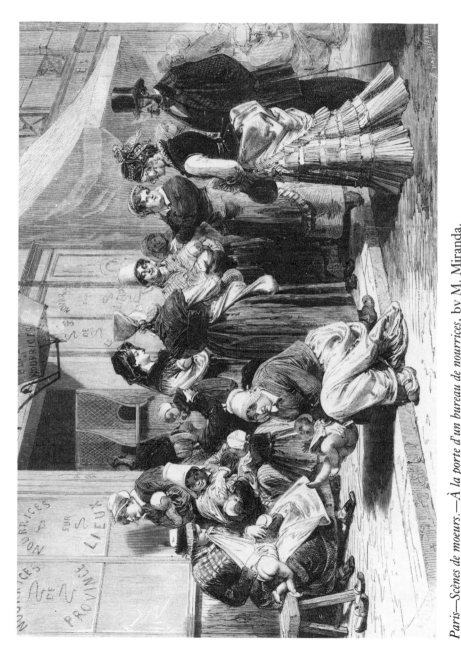

Paris—Scènes de moeurs.—À la porte d'un bureau de nourrices, by M. Miranda.
From *Le Monde illustré, Journal hebdomadaire*, Nov. 7, 1874, p. 300.

A lithograph from the collection *Les nourrices*, by Gédéon (Paris, 1866?). The interior of a third-class railway coach carrying wet nurses and nurslings. One nurse in the midst of cleaning her charge says to her companion, "We should have warned the gentleman that we would use musk."

A lithograph from the collection *Les nourrices*, by Gédéon (Paris, 1866?).
The illiterate wet nurse in the country dictates to the schoolmaster a
letter to the nursling's parents. " 'Monsieur, Madame,' " she says, " 'The
baby whom you confined to our solicitude is in the most perfect state
of health.' Say there, too, teacher that they should send some linen,
sugar, soap and especially the money they owe us."

"Protection du premier âge, Loi du 23 décembre 1874."
Medal signed by J. C. Chaplain.
Archives of the Prefecture of Police of Paris.

PART II
The Nineteenth Century

5

The Wet-Nursing Business
from the Revolution to
the Roussel Law

I N NINETEENTH-CENTURY FRANCE wet-nursing continued to be a fact of everyday life and a significant commercial enterprise. The great writers of the century were generally hostile to wet-nursing.[1] Popular literature and illustration were more often neutral or sympathetic. A favorite subject for illustration was the scene outside the nurses' placement bureau, where buxom peasant women in a variety of provincial coifs nursed, changed, and fondled babies, chatted with guards and with one another, and suffered the scrutiny of new fathers and grandmothers. After mid-century another favorite scene was that of wet nurses and babies sharing benches with other travelers in crowded railway cars.[2]

The demand for wet nurses continued strong in the nineteenth century and may even have expanded because wet-nursing served the cities and the cities were expanding rapidly. The demand probably did not increase in direct proportion to urban growth. Educated and comfortable families had been decreasing their use of rural wet-nurses since the late eighteenth century. Many in the nineteenth century hired live-in nurses, a rapidly expanding sector of the wet-nursing business. In comparison with the eighteenth century many more mothers at this social level must have nursed their own babies. In many factory towns and industrial quarters of older cities wet-nursing was not widely adopted. But a good deal of the urban growth in nineteenth-century France was not related to industrialization. The ranks of shopkeepers, craftsmen, and single mothers were also increasing in the cities, and these groups continued to rely on rural wet nurses. No safe or simple substitute for breast-feeding existed until the very end of the century, when sterilized milk, sterilizing equipment, and feeding bottles with rubber nipples became available on the market.

While the demand for wet nurses was expanding, the supply of impoverished rural women recently delivered and willing to nurse another woman's child—never a very elastic supply—was certainly declining. The effects of this decline could be postponed for awhile by the expansion of the area of recruitment as a result of new roads and railroads. But by the 1860s there were severe shortages of capable wet nurses. As in the eighteenth century, the dearth of nurses coincided with middle-class criticism and resulted in reform and reorganization of the wet-nursing business. The passage of the Roussel Law "for the protection of infants and especially of nurslings" in 1874 and the demise in 1876 of the Bureau of Wet Nurses of the City of Paris (founded in 1769 in the previous major reform) marked the end of an era in the wet-nursing business, but not the end of the business itself.

General Survey

Before the Roussel Law wet-nursing in France was subject exclusively to municipal regulation, when it was subject to any regulation at all. As a consequence, the sources of knowledge for French wet-nursing as a whole are scattered or nonexistent until the late 1890s, when the registration requirements of the Roussel Law finally began to bear significant fruit (see chapter 7). Before the Roussel Law local officials had no record of the total number of infants being nursed commercially in their jurisdictions. Of course, the children who died while with rural wet nurses left the traces of their short lives in the burial registers of the communes in which they died. Historical demographers have collected data on these isolated infants and used the information to construct a social description of the wet-nursing business. In addition, records were at least kept, if not always preserved, for infants put out to nurse by municipal or departmental agencies, such as the departmental administrations for foundlings or municipal welfare agencies that contributed toward and sometimes found placements for infants of poor families. Such records, when they are available, allow the historian—as, for that matter, they allowed nineteenth-century administrators—to calculate mortality rates, the average duration of placements, and other descriptive statistics, but only for the indigent population they concern. For infants born above the level of poverty the documentation on wet-nursing is the skimpiest. Public placement bureaus were established in a few cities in addition to Paris in the eighteenth century, but in the nineteenth century these had all disappeared or were declining in favor with urban parents, who generally preferred to place their infants either through private placement bureaus or through personal contacts.[3] In some cities the wet nurses who came to the private bureaus themselves were subject to police regulation. But during the first three-quarters of the nineteenth century, even in these cities the police never effectively kept track of the infants placed by the private bureaus—where they were placed and whether they died or were returned. And the best policed cities had no way of estimating with any assurance the number of newborns who were put out to nurse in the country through direct personal arrangements.[4]

Thus, any survey of wet-nursing practices in France during the first three-quarters of the nineteenth century is impressionistic. The best informed sources within the cities, among those who were likely to record their impressions, were the doctors. Dr. Charles Devilliers conducted an informal survey of colleagues in various French cities during an extended debate on wet-nursing and infant mortality in the Academy of Medicine in the late 1860s.[5] The responses to Devilliers's survey and other scattered medical reports, which are brought together here indicate a pattern of increasing reliance on maternal nursing by the middle and upper classes and a widespread, almost underground network of rural wet-nursing serving the shopkeepers and workers of many provincial cities.

The second city of French wet-nursing was Lyon, a major industrial center in the early nineteenth century whose principal product was silk woven on hand looms in thousands of small independent workshops.[6] Louis-René Villermé described the nursing practices of the Lyonnais silk workers in his survey of the conditions of French textile workers in 1840: "Almost all the newborns of weavers living in the city and its suburbs are placed with wet nurses in the neighboring departments of the Ain or the Isère, or even in Savoy, because the mothers can make a lot more money working in the silk shops than raising their children themselves. They take the babies back from the nurse sometime after they are weaned, and usually when they are walking alone." Villermé estimated that in the Croix-Rousse, a suburb of silk workshops, about three-quarters of the newborns were put out to nurse.[7] Dr. F. Imbert, who taught at the secondary school of medicine in Lyon, emphasized the favorable conditions for the supply of nurses: "We are neighbors of certain areas where living is cheap. The worker can place his child in the country for a low price, sending him only eight or ten leagues away" (as compared with thirty leagues for placements from Paris). Writing in 1847, Imbert noted that only the well-to-do in Lyon did not resort to wet-nursing. "Here maternal nursing implies a certain degree of comfort. It implies that the husband's work suffices for the family and requires, on the wife's part, only household duties." [8] Devilliers's Lyonnais correspondents in the 1860s confirmed the earlier reports. Women living in Lyon, they contended, did not nurse their babies.

> If a few women belonging to rich families do nurse their own children, they did it as much as possible in the countryside surrounding Lyon. Since shopkeepers' wives have, in general, as much importance in their businesses as their husbands, they cannot nurse for themselves; and besides, they usually live far from their shops, so they have to resort to the wet-nursing bureaus. It is the same with female silk-workers and wives of silk-workers, who earn almost as much as their husbands and have an interest in putting their children out to nurse in the country. Perhaps the largest number of nursing mothers is to be found among the wives of railway clerks and workers.[9]

Wet-nursing was so widespread in nineteenth-century Lyon because of the extent of its pre-industrial population of independent shopkeepers and artisans, who worked *en famille*. The wives of workers employed in newer, larger enterprises, where men worked alone, did not resort to wet-nursing. Nor did the well-to-do.

The wet-nursing business of nineteenth-century Lyon was no longer exclusively in the hands of the ignorant and unsupervised *messageres* graphically described by Lieutenant-General of Police Prost de Royer in 1778. A former employee of the Parisian Bureau of Wet Nurses established a bureau in Lyon in 1779 and received letters patent in 1780. The bureau had trouble succeeding against the unauthorized competition. In 1803 it was reestablished as a private enterprise under administrative supervision. A second bureau was opened with official sanction in 1832, and there were three by the 1860s.[10] In 1853 departmental authorities in the Rhône issued a decree governing the wet-nursing business in Lyon and the surrounding communes. The decree was modeled on Parisian regulations but went beyond the existing regulation of private wet-nursing bureaus in Paris in several respects. All bureaus were required to register with the prefect, to keep careful records, to provide for quarterly inspections of nurslings in the country, and to pay nurses quarterly (whether or not the parents had paid the bureau).[11]

Wet-nursing in other manufacturing centers of eastern France was unorganized. In Reims Villermé found that workers' children were generally raised on bottles, "especially when the care of raising them is entrusted to women who make a profession of nursing." The textile workers of Sedan were more fortunate. "For a modest sum, and by saving, many of the workers in the city put their newborn children out to nurse in Luxemburg, where they are breast-fed, and not bottle-fed like the children of the workers of Reims. They owe this advantage to the proximity of a poor region where manpower is very cheap, and where the peasants, who have difficulty finding any means of earning money, need only very little." [12] Similar circumstances probably account for the prevalence of rural wet-nursing reported by Devilliers's correspondent in the watch-making center of Besançon. Although Besançon had no wet-nursing bureau, nearly all of the city's infants were placed in the surrounding country to be nursed. "The woman in the watch factory, earning 2 fr. 50 c. or 3 fr. a day, finds it more economical to shift the cares of maternity to a hireling." The public administration in the Doubs placed abandoned babies with wet nurses for 15 francs a month and with dry nurses for 12. Most children placed by their own parents were breast-fed.[13] In Mulhouse paternalistic manufacturers intervened when the death rate of their workers' infants, placed with rural wet nurses, reached 38 to 40 percent. The manufacturers organized a society that paid new mothers their full wages for six weeks of maternity leave and provided rooms in the factories, where returning mothers could leave their babies and stop in to nurse them periodically. The mortality of babies kept under these arrangements, according to the manufacturers, was 24 to 28 percent.[14]

In the port city of Marseille a significant demand for wet nurses was served by no fewer than fourteen placement bureaus. Dr. Gibert estimated in 1875 that 50 percent of new mothers in the city hired wet nurses, in the following proportions: "Twenty percent take live-in nurses, 10 percent entrust their children to nurses living in the commune of Marseille or in the vicinity, and 20 percent send their children far away, with that neglect and that kind of abandonment which characterizes this sector of infant nursing." The bureaus placed some 2,000 babies a year through the intermediary of *meneuses*, who generally carried the babies into the country and found nurses for them there. The babies were placed in the departments of the Basses-Alpes, the Hautes-Alpes, and the Ardèche, and a growing proportion (already one-half) in Piedmont. Local regulation of the business began in 1873 under pressure from the local branch of the Société protectrice de l'enfance.[15]

Wet-nursing in Bordeaux was described in 1867 by Dr. André-Théodore Brochard, a recent arrival who had already written about wet-nursing in the Paris region. Conditions were much worse in the southwestern port. "Most of the women in Bordeaux do not nurse themselves," Brochard wrote. The wet nurses serving the city and the *meneuses* or *courtières* who procured them were subject to no medical or administrative supervision. "Each year the customs administration and the *octroi* [municipal excise tax] can say how many bottles of wine, how many sacks of coffee entered Bordeaux or how many were exported to the rest of France and abroad. But no one can say how many newborns from this city were sent out to nurse, how many are living, how many are dead." According to the mayor, Bethmann, the *courtières* carried babies out of Bordeaux in baskets, without bothering to feed them, and placed them, after bargaining over the price, "with poor peasant women who agreed to raise these poor little creatures as they raise their cattle and their poultry, for a minimal quarterly wage. The difference between the price agreed upon with the mother and the price paid the wet nurse is the *courtière*'s profit." Nineteenth-century Bordeaux had an unusually high illegitimate birth rate. Many of the babies sent out to nurse in these circumstances may have been the offspring of unmarried servant girls.[16]

The evidence from Strasbourg suggests that there was no significant wet-nursing activity there. In the early 1820s a group of physicians proposed to the mayor that he establish a municipal bureau of wet nurses modeled on the Parisian institution. Their principal concern was that unmarried mothers who offered their services as wet nurses might be infected with venereal disease. No action was taken on the doctors' proposal.[17]

Dr. Couillard, from the agricultural canton of Issoire (department of the Puy-de-Dôme), reported in 1875 that "in general children are nursed by the mother and sometimes, in the bourgeoisie, by a live-in nurse. . . . Some modest shopkeepers, too busy to raise the child, place it with a wet nurse." Moreover, in recent years as lace-making had spread rapidly through the rural districts many young mothers had turned their babies over to older women or children, who bottle-fed them, so that they could spend their time more profitably making lace.[18]

In the Hérault Dr. Bringuier observed in 1875 that the practice of maternal feeding was spreading in the towns. Still, the principal towns of the department had placement bureaus "which, by means of intermediaries [*entremetteuses*], procure live-in nurses or facilitate the placement of babies in neighboring departments." The department of the Hérault itself, because of the general level of prosperity, provided only a few wet nurses who charged 35 to 50 francs a month. For this reason workers' children and abandoned children were placed in the departments of the Tarn and the Aveyron.[19] Devilliers's correspondent at the port of Cette in the Hérault emphasized that maternal nursing was predominant in all classes and dry-nursing almost unknown. The wives of customs officers, who lived together in large barracks, often took babies to nurse under close parental supervision. Customs officers' wives also served as wet nurses in Le Havre. There, Devilliers's correspondent reported, "In the upper class of society the current practice is for women to nurse their children. In the class of shopkeepers and honest workmen, nursing mothers are less numerous, and the children are raised, some in town and some in the country, either on the breast or on the bottle." Le Havre had no placement bureau.[20]

This impressionistic survey of nursing practices in the provincial cities and towns of nineteenth-century France leads one to conclude that everywhere the well-to-do were tending toward maternal feeding or, at least, closely supervised live-in nurses. The principal demand for rural wet-nursing care came from the class of shopkeepers and independent artisans, in addition to single working mothers (usually subsidized by public authorities) and the public authorities responsible for abandoned children. The nursing practices of families of unskilled workers varied with the conditions of supply and access. If the industrial town were located near a poor and populous rural district with no competing occupation for women, then the female factory workers might place their babies with wet nurses in the rural district. Otherwise the babies were bottle-fed close to home, before the era of safe bottle-feeding. Placement bureaus for wet nurses were common in the larger cities. They were, for the most part, completely unsupervised and seem in some places to have offered the consumer only live-in nurses or the services of a *meneuse* who promised to place the baby with rural wet nurses.

Until the end of the nineteenth century, after the Roussel Law was passed, it is not possible to present a statistical survey of the geographic distribution of wet-nursing in France. But an interesting substitute is provided through Louis-Adolphe Bertillon's maps representing infant mortality by department in the years 1857 to 1866. Regions in which wet-nursing was common registered relatively high infant mortality ratios, not, for the most part, because of poor infant care provided by the wet nurses, but rather because of a faulty (but necessary) calculation, which related all infant deaths occurring in a department to the infant population determined from births during the previous year in the department. Thus, the nurslings counted in the numerator but not in the denominator of this ratio in the rural departments where they were sent; likewise, they diminished the infant mortality of the urban departments (the Seine, the Rhône) where they were born.

In presenting his findings in 1874 to a legislative committee concerned with a bill to protect nurslings, Bertillon observed that the highest infant mortality in France occurred in fourteen departments around Paris and ten departments of the Rhône and Alpine region, "two centers of high mortality owing solely to the emigration of children and the wet-nursing industry." The two Alsatian departments also showed relatively high infant mortality, ranking sixty-seventh and seventy-first among eighty-seven departments. Otherwise, the northern border from Lorraine to the Channel had relatively low levels (the department of the Nord, ranking forty-seventh, had the highest infant mortality in this region), and the west and southwest, including the Breton and Cotentin peninsulas, the lower Loire, Poitou and the western part of the Massif central, Gascony, the Pyrenees, and western Languedoc, had the lowest levels of infant mortality in France. Thus, there is the paradoxical pattern that the lowest infant mortality in mid-nineteenth-century France was to be found in the remote, economically underdeveloped departments, while the highest occurred in Eure-et-Loir, the Yonne, the Ardèche—poor departments located in reasonable proximity to the growing cities, for which they provided wet-nursing services. The industrialized departments of the Eure and Seine-inférieure registered the very highest levels of infant mortality because of a combination of rural wet-nursing and widespread bottle-feeding.[21]

Trends in Paris

The extent and pattern of wet-nursing in nineteenth-century Paris are much better documented than they are for other parts of France because so much more of the business in the capital fell under administrative supervision or regulation. However, even in Paris, before about 1880 (when the Roussel Law began to be effectively implemented) public authorities had only incomplete information about babies placed in the country by the private bureaus and none at all about babies placed individually through private contacts.

Despite these lacunae in the evidence, it is possible to trace significant trends in the wet-nursing business in Paris between the end of the Ancien Régime and the Roussel Law through a series of statistical soundings. The first sounding consists of a rearrangement in tabular form (Table 1) of the statistical description of infant-feeding patterns in the capital in 1780 by Jean LeNoir, lieutenant-general of police.[22] The remainder of the babies who were placed with wet nurses in the provinces comprised a majority,

Table 1
Nursing patterns for Parisian babies, 1780

Total number of births	21,000
Nursed by mothers	fewer than 1,000[a]
Nursed commercially	more than 20,000[b]
In parental home	fewer than 1,000
In Paris	"difficult to estimate"
In *banlieue/environs*	2–3,000 "from wealthy families"
In provinces	remainder [at least 15,600]

[a] Less than 5 percent.
[b] More than 95 percent.

since it must have included the 10,000 infants placed by the municipal Bureau of Wet Nurses and the 5,600 placed by the foundling hospital. In the last decade of the Ancien Régime all social classes in Paris put their children out to nurse, generally through public agencies (for all except the wealthy) and at a distance that was inversely proportional to the family's wealth.

A report to the General Council of Hospitals for the Year X (1801–2) presents a different sort of breakdown for the 21,018 babies born that year in Paris (Table 2).[23]

In comparing the figures for the Year X with LeNoir's estimates for twenty years earlier, note first of all the much larger proportion of newborns thought to have been nursed by their own mothers:

Table 2
Nursing patterns for Parisian babies, Year X (1801–2)

Total number of births	21,018
Nursed by mothers	10,667[a]
Receiving assistance	5,004
Nonindigent (estimated)	5,663
Nursed commercially	10,351[b]
Abandoned	3,820
Nursed or died in *hospice*	1,510
Placed in country	2,310
Others placed in country	6,531
By municipal bureau	4,531
By "wealthy people" (estimated)	2,000

[a] 51 percent.
[b] 49 percent.

51 percent compared to 5 percent in 1780. This figure is obviously speculative in both reports; the digital precision of the figure for nonindigent infants raised by their own mothers should not fool anyone: it is the result of subtraction and not registration. But the large difference begs for an explanation nonetheless. Had the Enlightenment critique of wet-nursing, spread by the Revolution,[24] had an effect in encouraging maternal feeding? Had the devalued currency of the 1790s discouraged the wet-nursing business like so many others? Or does this report grossly underestimate the number of wet nurses obtained without the intermediary of public agencies? The hospital report of the Year X also shows a decline in the number of abandoned babies compared with the 1780s, which is attributable to various municipal and national reforms in the administration of public assistance and of assistance to foundlings.[25] The report ignores the category of rural nurses brought into the parental home, the live-in nurses, probably because no public agency placed live-in nurses. It is also conceivable that this form of domestic service went into temporary eclipse during the Revolution.

The final sounding, for 1869, consists of figures brought together from various sources (Table 3).[26]

The figure in Table 3 for infants "nursed by mothers"—32,408— is simply the difference between the total number of births and the number of newborns reportedly nursed commercially. The

Table 3
Nursing patterns for Parisian babies, 1869

Total number of births (enlarged Paris)	54,937
Nursed by mothers	32,408[a]
Nursed commercially	22,529[b]
Abandoned children placed in country	2,756
Others placed by municipal bureau	2,129
At parents' expense	1,624
Assisted	505
Placed by private bureaus (circa ⅔ in country, ⅓ at home)	11,644
Placed by parents (estimated)	6,000

[a] 59 percent.
[b] 41 percent.

principal uncertainty in the figures for 1869 is the estimate of the number of infants "placed by parents." The estimate cited in this table—6,000—was made by Armand Husson, director of the General Administration of Public Assistance of Paris. Others put the figure higher, at 9,500.[27] If the latter figure is correct, the proportion of Parisian infants commercially nursed in 1869 was 47 percent. By still another calculation, Gustave Lagneau estimated on the basis of census counts and birth and death registrations that 27,005 of the 54,520 infants born in the department of the Seine in 1856, and 29,136 of the 60,889 born in 1861, were nursed outside the department.[28] In other words, 50 percent in 1856 and 48 percent in 1861 were placed with rural wet nurses. The total percentage of babies commercially nursed, including those by live-in nurses, would be still higher. In sum, the number of Parisian infants reported in Table 3 to have been commercially nursed in 1869—22,529, or 41 percent of births—should be regarded as a conservative estimate.

Comparing now the three soundings for 1780, 1801–2, and 1869, the proportion of Parisian infants commercially nursed declined substantially over the last decade of the Ancien Régime and the subsequent decade of Revolution and may have declined somewhat more in the first seventy years of the nineteenth century. Much of this decline may be attributable to the spread of maternal nursing in the middle and upper classes. At the same time the number of infants nursed commercially and, consequently, the demand for wet nurses were higher in 1869 than they had been in 1780. The capital and its female working population had, after all, grown tremendously in this ninety-year period. One other change stands out in the figures from 1869: the wet-nursing business in Paris was falling more and more into private hands, leaving primarily charitable placements to the official agencies.

The wet-nursing business in Paris in the early nineteenth century was heading for a crisis. The problem was in one respect economic in character: as the demand for wet nurses was expanding, the supply of able nurses was contracting. In another respect it was a problem of social attitudes: a growing section of the population came to reject the practice of commercial nursing as inhumane, deadly (as it was, increasingly), and even unpatriotic (for its effects on the national population). The decline of the municipal Bureau of Wet Nurses and the successs of the new private bureaus were symptomatic of the deteriorating situation, for the private bureaus generally provided a poorer quality of service at a higher price to the parents, while their operations were less closely supervised by the public authorities.

The pre-Revolutionary Bureau of Wet Nurses of the City of Paris was a privileged institution. It enjoyed a legal monopoly on the lodging and placement of rural wet nurses who came to Paris, usually accompanied by *meneurs* or *meneuses*, seeking a baby to nurse (except for those who took foundlings). In these conditions the bureau placed about 10,000 babies a year from the time of its founding in 1769 until the Revolution. The bureau survived the Revolution, one of the very few privileged institutions of the Ancien Régime that did. although it emerged from the decade of the 1790s seriously weakened. Its business, like so many other businesses, was nearly suspended amid the economic and monetary distress around the Year IV.[29] Of more lasting effect were two changes of law and custom associated with the Revolution: the abolition of imprisonment for debt and the drying up of private charity. These two changes significantly reduced the means available to the Direction des Nourrices to obtain the revenues it required to cover its payments to the nurses. In order to maintain the guarantee to the nurses it was compelled henceforth to incur large annual deficits, which were made up by regular subsidies from the local government or occasional munificent gestures by old-fashioned sovereigns, who proclaimed that they were liberating the poor fathers of Paris from their obligations when, in fact, they were only reducing the municipal government's subsidies to the Direction.[30]

With the restoration of monetary order in the Consulate, the Direction des Nourrices found itself with a more or less stable business of 4,000 to 5,000 placements a year, about half of the pre-Revolutionary level. It appears that the explanation for this permanent decline in the business of the bureau was free enterprise. During the troubled years of the Revolution some of the *meneurs*, and perhaps some midwives, had begun to place babies on their own, bypassing the official bureau for larger profits, although their business remained clandestine so long as the Direction held onto its legal monopoly.[31] A fateful step was taken under the

Consulate when the Bureau of Wet Nurses was placed under the supervision of the new Conseil général des Hospices rather than the prefect of police, the successor to the pre-Revolutionary lieutenant-general of police. In the long run the effect of this decision, as the Prefect of Police Dubois correctly foresaw in his protest against the transfer, was to emphasize the charitable character of the bureau, encouraging the poor payers to be remiss in their obligations while driving away the good payers, who were reluctant to place their babies with "some sort of hospital." [32] All that prevented the immediate evolution of the Bureau of Wet Nurses into another institution of public assistance, largely supported by municipal subsidies, was the yet undeveloped state of private placement bureaus.

A basic reform of the bureau, implemented in October 1821, transformed definitively the balance of public and private agencies in the wet-nursing business of Paris. The principal reasons for the reform were frequently reiterated complaints about the utter disorder of the books kept by the Bureau of Wet Nurses and concern over the absence of any effective supervision of the wet nurses in the country. [33] The remedy for these abuses was to replace the peripatetic *meneurs*, characterized as "generally illiterate," by a new bureaucracy of stationary employees who would communicate with one another through regular written reports. In each rural *arrondissement* where the bureau placed its babies, a local employee, assisted by a physician or a surgeon, would recruit nurses, dispatch them to Paris under the supervision of a *surveillante* as they were needed, inspect them upon their return with the babies, and, at regular intervals thereafter, convey wages and packages to the wet nurses and make regular reports on each baby to Paris. In the capital other employees would collect the nurses' wages from the parents and forward written communications from the country concerning their children. The reorganization of 1821 resembled the unsuccessful efforts of pre-Revolutionary police authorities to replace the *meneurs* in the functions of rural surveillance of the wet nurses and collections from the parents. The difference was that the nineteenth-century reformers persisted in the effort.

The new system had an immediate and catastrophic effect on the number of children put out to nurse through the agency of the municipal bureau (see Table 4). [34] Placements dropped from

5,096 in 1821 to 3,497 in 1822, 2,882 in 1823, and as low as 848 in 1832. The short-term explanation for this precipitous fall is simple: the fifty-two *meneurs* released by the bureau went into business for themselves, and they took with them their clientele— parents, wet nurses, and also midwives who directed business their way for a bounty. Thus the reform of the municipal bureau in 1821 had the ironic effect of decisively encouraging the hitherto clandestine private placement bureaus.

For the last half century of its existence the Bureau of Wet Nurses of the City of Paris was engaged in a long struggle to recover its traditional place in the wet-nursing business—an alternative to the ruthless free enterprise of the private placement bureaus and to the abjectness and costliness of a public charity. In this struggle the hospital administration tried two successive strategies, both of which failed. From the 1820s through the 1840s it called for the revival of the bureau's pre-Revolutionary privilege, which had never been formally revoked. Successive prefects of police, supported by ministers of the July Monarchy and the economic liberalism of the times, blocked all these efforts to abolish the private bureaus by writ of authority and insisted that if the municipal bureau were to survive in the nineteenth century, it would have to compete in a free market only slightly tempered by police regulation and supervision of the private placement bureaus.[35]

In 1850 the hospital administration abandoned its endeavors to revive the bureau's privilege in favor of a new competitive effort to attract parents and wet nurses from private bureaus back to the municipal bureau. To make the municipal bureau more attractive to the parents, the city undertook to pay all administrative costs associated with its placement bureau, including the cost of health care for the babies in the country. For the nurses the municipal bureau accelerated its schedule of payments and began to provide free meals in Paris in addition to the free lodging already provided. But in 1850 the municipal bureau still shied away from full participation in the competitive wet-nursing business of the capital: the bureau would not pay bounties to midwives and obstetricians to direct the parents of newborns its way, a practice it considered unworthy of a public administration.[36] Finally, in 1867, the hospital administration overcame this last scruple, to little avail.[37]

Selling Mothers' Milk

The Bureau of Wet Nurses survived until 1876, and its annual total of placements even recovered for certain periods—moderately in the mid-1840s, significantly in the early 1850s and again in the early 1870s (see Table 4). But these signs of life were almost entirely the effect of injections of public charity, either in the form of grants of assistance to poor mothers who placed their babies through the municipal bureau (to prevent them from abandoning the babies) or in the form of subsidies to the deficit-ridden institution to make up for the losses sustained because of parents who

Table 4

Placements by Parisian wet-nursing bureaus, Year VII (1799–1800) to 1874

	Municipal Bureau				Municipal Bureau		
Year	Placements	Deaths	Mortality (Percent)	Year	Placements	Deaths	Mortality (Percent)
VII	4,769	1,182	24.8	1823	2,882	—	—
VIII	3,863	1,152	29.8	1824	2,887	—	—
IX	4,080	1,075	26.3	1825	2,590	—	—
X	4,531	—	—	1826	2,277	—	—
XI	4,944	—	—	1827	1,977	—	—
XII	4,834	—	—	1828	1,876	482	25.7
XIII	4,914	—	—	1829	1,472	364	24.7
XIV–1806	5,864	—	—	1830	1,276	374	29.3
1807	4,500	—	—	1831	919	246	26.3
1808	4,751	—	—	1832	848	198	23.3
1809	4,851	—	—	1833	1,110	232	20.9
1810	4,943	—	—	1834	1,213	374	30.8
1811	—	—	—	1835	1,246	833	66.9
1812	—	—	—	1836	1,286	327	25.4
1813	4,387	1,107	25.2	1837	1,199	306	25.5
1814	4,427	1,466	33.1	1838	1,203	341	28.3
1815	4,971	1,557	31.3	1839	953	252	26.4
1816	5,081	1,444	28.4	1840	843	243	28.8
1817	4,530	1,409	31.3	1841	810	181	22.2
1818	4,915	1,484	30.2	1842	1,814	693	38.2
1819	5,531	1,832	33.1	1843	1,699	526	31.0
1820	5,716	1,567	27.4	1844	1,725	556	32.2
1821	5,096	1,281	25.1	1845	1,783	469	26.3
1822	3,497	1,217	34.8	1846	1,914	720	37.6

Table 4 (cont'd.)

| Year | Municipal Bureau | | | | | Private Bureaus |
| | Placements | | | Deaths | Mortality (Percent) | Placements |
	Voluntary	Assisted	Total			
1847	505	1,025	1,530	534	34.9	—
1848	445	830	1,275	415	32.5	—
1849	529	922	1,451	530	36.5	—
1850	725	990	1,715	474	27.6	—
1851	1,074	1,346	2,420	—	—	6,426
1852	1,278	1,967	3,245	958	29.4	7,157
1853	1,447	2,523	3,970	1,034	26.0	7,642
1854	1,326	2,702	4,028	1,458	36.2	8,114
1855	1,544	1,809	3,353	1,056	31.5	8,064
1856	2,201	605	2,806	—	—	9,148
1857	1,899	176	2,075	—	—	9,988
1858	1,637	205	1,842	—	—	10,381
1859	1,789	245	2,034	—	—	11,370
1860	1,512	637	2,149	574	26.7	11,315
1861	1,517	752	2,269	851	37.5	11,683
1862	1,452	743	2,195	607	27.7	11,202
1863	1,364	1,012	2,376	812	34.2	11,354
1864	1,612	568	2,180	751	34.4	11,491
1865	1,470	504	1,974	767	38.9	11,906
1866	1,574	399	1,973	529	26.8	11,646
1867	1,557	408	1,965	611	31.1	11,477
1868	1,713	465	2,178	789	36.2	11,055
1869	1,624	505	2,129	621	29.2	11,644
1870	1,246	409	1,655	726	43.9	8,455
1871	487	135	622	208	33.4	5,386
1872	994	2,474	3,468	1,282	37.0	9,857
1873	1,067	3,662	4,729	2,120	44.8	10,081
1874	657	3,544	4,201	1,811	43.1	—

Source. George D. Sussman, "The Wet-Nursing Business in Nineteenth-Century France," *French Historical Studies*, 9 (Fall 1975), 326–27.
Note. Dash = not available.

freeloaded on the bureau's promise to pay the nurses.[38] Recognizing
that the Bureau of Wet Nurses was no longer serving the purpose
of providing moderately priced and reliable wet-nursing services
for working families of Paris, the hospital administration finally
began to advocate its abolition in the mid-1860s, though this step
was not actually taken until 1876.[39]

In 1828, seven years after the municipal bureau had been re-
organized and its *meneurs* released, the prefect of police of Paris
issued the first ordinance regulating the private wet-nursing business, which also served to give the private bureaus a legal status
that they had lacked up until then and that the hospital authorities
continued to contest. The police ordinance of August 9, 1828, and
its successor of June 20, 1842, drawing upon eighteenth-century
police regulations, set certain minimal requirements for wet nurses:
each had to bring to Paris a certificate from her mayor testifying
to her age, her good morals, the age of her youngest child, her
possession of a cradle and a fire screen; none was permitted to
nurse more than one infant at a time, nor to have someone else
pick up an infant for her; each was required to carry back to her
village the birth certificate of the infant she took. Furthermore,
the police ordinances required wet nurses, *meneurs*, and the directors of private placement bureaus to register with the prefecture,
which began to conduct sanitary inspections of the hiring and
lodging centers.[40]

In practice police supervision of the private bureaus developed
slowly and was apparently never very rigorous.[41] The most sympathetic observers remarked upon the salubrious appearance of
some of the private wet-nursing bureaus that they had visited in
Paris. But all would have agreed with the Deputy Théophile Roussel's observation in 1874, nearly fifty years after police regulation
had begun, that "the majority of the bureaus seemed to us to be
in a very defective condition." Of approximately a dozen private
bureaus in the capital, only the three or four that specialized in
providing live-in nurses for the wealthy (about one-third of the
placements by the private bureaus) did a lucrative trade and could
afford to maintain healthy and attractive establishments.[42]

Whatever their qualities, the private bureaus were certainly successful with Parisian parents and rural wet nurses. By the 1860s
they were providing over 11,000 nurses a year, about one-fifth of

Parisian births, one-half of all wet nurses serving Paris, and five or six times as many as the municipal bureau was providing. For years the hospital authorities tried to understand the reasons for their rivals' success in spite of the obvious advantages offered by the municipal bureau: for the nurses, a guaranteed wage, and for the parents, the system of medical and administrative supervision in the country.

Many of the wet nurses must have simply followed their *meneurs* when the latter were released by the Direction des Nourrices in 1821. They stayed with the private bureaus no doubt in part because of the prospect of higher wages and gratuities, which were less and less likely at the municipal bureau as its placements became increasingly charitable.[43] At the municipal bureau, where many parents failed to pay, the wet nurses were frequently reduced to the guaranteed minimal wage of 10 francs a month (12 francs after 1850). But with infants obtained through the private bureaus, if the parents ceased to pay the nurse, she returned the baby at once and took a new one. In the private bureaus the nurse was not submitted to a humiliating medical inspection with the risk of being rejected, and she was generally hired promptly in contrast to the long waits and cumbersome administrative formalities characteristic of the municipal bureau.[44] Finally, at home in the country the wet nurse was free of any serious medical or administrative surveillance, free to take a second nursling from another source, to wean the baby prematurely, or to substitute a foundling for a wealthy infant who died—if the worst tales that were told are true.

As for the parents, most hospital administrators believed that they simply followed the advice of their midwives and obstetricians in transferring their patronage from the public to the private bureaus.[45] And the midwives and the obstetricians, they insisted, were corrupted by the bounties that the private bureaus paid them. "The nurse is always good enough if the bounty is high," a bitter public official observed in 1848.[46] When the competition among the private bureaus became acute, they made an agreement among themselves to pay the midwives 6 francs for each baby placed with a rural wet nurse and 10 francs for each live-in nurse hired. In 1867 the bounty for an ordinary placement rose to 10 francs. Virtually everyone condemned the bounty as an unprofessional fee that also worked to discourage maternal nursing. But the competitive wet-nursing business was unable to extricate itself from the system, into which even the municipal bureau was eventually drawn.[47] Another reason for the parents' preference for the private bureaus was the personal relationships formed and maintained among the working class of Paris by the *meneurs*, who brought the parents firsthand reports (of whatever accuracy) of their infants in the country, in contrast to the professionally prepared, written reports provided at regular intervals by the municipal bureau.[48]

In retrospect the issues in dispute between the municipal and the private bureaus were peripheral to the central problem of the wet-nursing business. In 1863 Vée, the first hospital official to advocate the abolition of the municipal bureau, asked a very pertinent question: what would happen if the Direction des Nourrices won the contest, drove the private bureaus out of existence, and inherited their 10,000 annual placements?[49] It could only have hoped to attract a sufficient number of wet nurses if it had, in this event, abandoned the guaranteed wage to the wet nurses, which pulled its general wage level down. And if the municipal bureau had abandoned the guarantee, the municipal government would have had to dole out more public assistance for nurses' wages. For wet nurses in the numbers that the growing capital city demanded were simply not available at prices that working people could afford, and good nurses were scarcely available at all. This is the internal crisis that overtook the wet-nursing business in Paris in the 1860s, that is probably behind the high mortalities registered by all nursing bureaus, public and private, and that provoked a public clamor against the business in all its manifestations.

The evidence of an internal crisis was dreadfully visible in the last decade of the municipal bureau's existence. In 1866 the Direction raised the level of the monthly wage it guaranteed to its wet nurses from 12 to 20 francs. Still unable to recruit enough wet nurses, in 1871 the bureau began to place some of its babies with "dry nurses," "more or less impoverished women" who raised the newborns on animal milk dispensed through the clumsy "English bottles" provided by the Direction. By 1874, 35 percent of the newborns placed by the bureau were placed with dry nurses. The effect of this policy was a sharp increase in the overall mortality of the bureau's babies, for while 20 to 25 percent of the babies who were breast-fed died, the figure for those raised on the bottle was 40 to 50 percent. The overall mortality for infants placed by the bureau was 41.6 percent in the years 1871 to 1874. It had been 33.8 percent in the decade 1861 to 1870, 30.3 percent in the five years of the decade 1851 to 1860 for which figures are available, 32.4 percent in the decade 1841 to 1850, and 26.3 percent in the decade 1831 to 1840, not counting the exceptionally high mortality of 1835 (66.9 percent), which looks like an error or perhaps the effect of the cholera epidemic (see Table 4). The nurslings' mortality rose gradually over the century and sharply in the early 1870s because good wet nurses became more difficult to find. This scarcity occurred at the same time that public tolerance for such high levels of infant mortality was declining. The quality of the parents served by the municipal bureau in its last decade deteriorated with the quality of the nurses: charitable placements, delinquent payers, infants abandoned by their parents, and infants who communicated syphilis to their nurses all multiplied.[50]

A similar crisis seems to have afflicted the wet-nursing services of the foundling administration of Paris. Despite frequent increases in its wet nurses' monthly wages (to 12 francs in 1855, 15 francs in 1862, and 18 francs in 1876), the director of public assistance observed in 1866 that "the conditions for the selection of nurses are poorer than formerly." [51] No accurate data exist on the quality of wet-nursing services provided by the private bureaus, but Roussel concluded from his investigations in 1874—in a judgment that fairly sums up many critics' observations—that most commercial nursing practiced at a distance from the families had become nothing but "a disguised form of artificial nursing."[52]

Criticism and Reform

The internal crisis of the wet-nursing business in the 1860s— or the visible effects of that crisis—roused the latent hostility of the middle class and medical professionals against the idea of hired women replacing mothers and of the neglect and abuse of infants that were inseparable from that practice. The revolt of conscience against wet-nursing began with a few individuals, nearly all medical practitioners in city and country, who formed associations and wrote books to promote their ideas. From there the movement spread to the Academy of Medicine and eventually to the National Assembly. The Direction des Nourrices of the City of Paris was as much a victim of this movement of opinion as it was of its own internal difficulties.

The person who claimed and generally received credit for initiating this movement in the 1860s was Dr. Alexandre Mayer. The tone of his effort is expressed in a pamphlet he published in 1865 outlining his proposal to create a Société protectrice de l'enfance:

> We are going to conduct a crusade against an inconceivable, absurd, and barbaric custom, the custom which has prevailed of abandoning, a few hours after its birth, a cherished being, whose coming was ardently desired, to a coarse peasant woman whom one has never seen, whose character and morality one does not know, and who goes off, bearing our treasure, to an unknown corner of the provinces whose name is sometimes not even marked on the map of France.
>
> The whole thing is so revolting to good sense and morality that in twenty years people will refuse to believe it ever happened.[53]

Mayer was successful at interesting a number of prominent citizens and many medical colleagues in his crusade. The inaugural meeting of the Société protectrice de l'enfance, authorized by the government, was held in Paris in January 1866, with 228 members. Three years later membership reached 804, and separate societies had been founded in Brussels, Lyon, Metz, Bordeaux, Beauvais, and Le Havre.[54]

The initial efforts of the society, in addition to organization and propaganda, were primarily directed toward protecting children put out to nurse. In 1868 the society sought to reorganize the private wet-nursing business of the capital as a philanthropic enterprise to be known as the Agence générale des nourrices. The proposed agency would abolish the *meneurs* and replace them with a network of rural doctors paid to recruit wet nurses, inspect nurslings, and report to Paris monthly on the babies' condition. Public authorities had already attempted the identical reform unsuccessfully on two occasions, in 1769 and 1821. The idea was not tested a third time, because the society was only able to raise one-quarter of the 100,000 francs it felt were needed to establish the new agency.[55] In its stead the Société protectrice de l'enfance organized an unpaid network of "patronage committees" and medical inspectors in the rural nursing regions serving Paris to supervise and assist the wet nurses. By 1872 this network comprised 153 patronage committees, 426 "physician-inspectors," and 56 "delegated inspectors" in places where there were no physicians, the whole network extending over thirty-five departments that received nurslings from Paris.[56]

But the success of the society was limited to rallying middle-class and medical opinion. It never received the cooperation it sought from wet nurses, private placement bureaus, or the working parents who placed their babies in the country. In frustration Mayer once accused the shopkeepers and artisans of Paris of sending their infants away "with the desire of not seeing them again." [57] Frustration may also explain a number of bizarre proposals with which the society became associated, including the establishment of large, closely regulated, nursing or maternal colonies on the edge of cities, a law to require maternal breast-feeding, and regional fairs where wet nurses would present their infants to be judged for prizes like cattle. Still, the Société protectrice de l'enfance did raise the issues and did press for legislative solutions.[58]

About the same time that the society was founded, two rural doctors published books exposing the most obscure and least attractive aspects of the wet-nursing business. One of the authors, André-Théodore Brochard, had served for eighteen years as medical inspector for the Direction des Nourrices in his native *arrondissement* of Nogent-le-Rotrou (Eure-et-Loir). Wet-nursing was the sole occupation for the peasant women of the area. Each year the municipal bureau placed over 300 babies in the *arrondissement*, while the private bureaus and individual Parisians placed nearly three times as many. Brochard's brief was against the private bureaus, whose nurses, he claimed, were entirely unsupervised by the bureaus, the *meneurs*, the Prefecture of Police (despite the ordinance of June 20, 1842), doctors, or the village mayors. Women whom Brochard, in his capacity as medical inspector for the municipal bureau, rejected as unfit to be wet nurses always managed to return from Paris with babies from the private bureaus. Some nurses were so unfit that their nurslings always died, yet they had no trouble procuring new babies and they were regularly paid; indeed, "certain houses of the capital" evidently preferred these nurses. The *meneurs* Brochard characterized as crude and uneducated men, "who, when the occasion presents itself, recruit at the same time girls or women for other establishments of the capital." Their wagons were called "Purgatories," because the babies they carried were about to enter heaven. Deaths were so common that when the village church bells tolled in the Perche, people said, " 'It's nothing, a little Parisian died!' "

Brochard did not confine his case to anecdotes. He collected from the mayors of each of the fifty-four communes in the *arrondissement* a list of the babies placed with wet nurses in 1858 and 1859 either by the private bureaus or by the parents directly, searched the civil register for the names of those who died there, and compared the mortality of babies placed by the private bureaus with that of babies placed by the municipal bureau. The difference he found was dramatic: 42 percent mortality for the private bureaus compared to 17 percent for the municipal bureau. Patronage committees in the nursing villages, as advocated by the Société protectrice de l'enfance, could never control the abuse in Brochard's opinion. The only solution was to abolish the private bureaus and bring all wet-nursing anywhere in France under the control of the Direction des Nourrices.[59]

Brochard's proposal drew little support. Even his medical colleagues, who shared his general feelings about wet-nursing, had to question the mortality statistics he presented; those for the municipal bureau were too low and those for the private bureaus were too high.[60] Brochard's book, nevertheless, had a great impact, especially as it dramatized the prevailing ignorance about the effects of wet-nursing on mortality. It also provoked several efforts to get a more accurate picture of mortality among nurslings, including one sponsored by the minister of the interior, but all such efforts were stymied by the absence of any registration of placements before the passage and implementation of the Roussel Law.[61]

In the same year that Brochard's book appeared—1866—the Academy of Medicine received a report on wet-nursing from another rural district that opened with the stark sentence "A profound disorder is ravaging the Morvan." The author, Dr. Charles Monot, had practiced medicine for ten years in the canton of Montsauche (department of the Yonne) in an area of Burgundy called the Morvan and had served as mayor of his commune, cantonal physician, and cantonal representative of the administration of *Enfants assistés* (abandoned children) of the department of the Seine. The disorder that he perceived to be spreading through and destroying the Morvan was the emigration of its women immediately after childbirth to serve as live-in nurses in Paris. The traffic had expanded over the last forty years with the swelling demand of middle-class families. It had become "the most important business of the Morvan." In the seven-year period from 1858 through 1864 Monot counted 2,884 births in the ten communes of the canton of Montsauche and 1,897 departures for Paris. Two-thirds of the women who gave birth left to become live-in nurses in Paris.

The first victim of the nurse's departure was her own child, for whom it was "often the death sentence." The prospective nurse left as soon as possible after her delivery because the "younger" her milk, the better her chances of procuring a good placement. She took her baby with her to Paris, so that she could show evidence of her capacity as a nurse (if the baby had died or if there was anything wrong with it, a healthy one could be borrowed or rented). Once the nurse was hired, the *meneuse* carried her baby back to the Morvan and left it with another nurse or a neighbor. Monot counted 449 children of live-in nurses who died in the canton during the years 1858 to 1864, "victims of the live-in nurse business." And there were more costs. The nurses' husbands stopped working and soon followed their wives to Paris; nurses were corrupted in Paris; families were broken up; and the Morvan was sapped of its productive forces.

With almost all of the women able to nurse going to Paris to nurse in the homes of the well-to-do, Monot observed, there should not be many wet nurses left in the Morvan. Yet the country was full of "Petits-Paris." They came from the private bureaus, or with returning wet nurses, or with unregistered *meneuses* who would pick up two to four babies directly from the midwives in Paris and carry them back to the country, where they would then look for nurses with whom they could be placed. Every commune had three or four *meneuses*. Nobody knew how many babies were being nursed in the communes, neither the Prefecture of Police of Paris nor the local mayors. Monot's book showed more imagination in describing the disorder than in prescribing a treatment. The well-to-do mothers in Paris, he felt, should nurse their own children, reducing the demand for live-in nurses. In addition, he would have the police administration extend its regulations to wet nurses who were hired by individual contact rather than through a placement bureau; he would make several small adjustments to the police ordinance of 1842; and he would have the police enforce the ordinance for a change.[62]

In 1866 Victor Duruy, the minister of public instruction, sent Monot's book to the Academy of Medicine for its judgment. The report on the book by the Academician Hippolyte Blot opened a discussion of the wet-nursing business at the summit of the French medical profession that continued for thirty-four meetings over nearly four years. The critical condition of the wet-nursing business in Paris, although not generally recognized nor clearly understood, nevertheless was partially responsible for the length and intensity of the medical discussion of wet-nursing in the late 1860s, after a century-long hiatus of professional interest in the subject. The developing unification of Germany was another, less professional reason for the doctors' renewed interest in wet-nursing. As early as October 1866 Félix Boudet, a leading participant in the discussion, underlined the connection between commercial wet-nursing, which seemed unique to France, the heavy infant mortality associated with wet-nursing, and depopulation and the importance of reducing mortality and increasing the population at a time when France was surrounded by states nearly as populous as she.[63]

Long and intensive as the discussion of wet-nursing in the Academy of Medicine was, it was not as illuminating or as productive as the eighteenth-century dialogue of physicians and laymen on infant care. The reason may be that the doctors of the Second Empire had no new understanding of infant hygiene to propagate and no new notion of the role of the state in public welfare. The strongest message of their discussion was the century-old exhortation: mother, be your own wet nurse. "We should . . . maintain and proclaim everywhere and at the top of our voices the necessity of maternal nursing," said Armand Husson, director of the Administration of Public Assistance in Paris. Dr. Boudet declared, "The monstrous mortality which strikes infants sent out to nurse . . . is . . . a national calamity. . . . It is the result of the unnatural practice, which is spreading more every day among French mothers, of renouncing maternal feeding." With the same moralistic tone Boudet lashed out at the new threat of bottle-feeding, reported to be well-established in Normandy and spreading throughout France.[64]

Lacking any new insight into the causes of infant mortality, the doctors could only declaim their opposition to social trends that they could not even measure accurately. A maverick in the discussion, Dr. Antoine-Sulpice Fauvel, eschewed his colleagues' moralistic approach. Fauvel saw the resort to wet nurses as an economic necessity rather than a choice for many urban mothers. "The problem," he argued, "comes from the fact that the number of good nurses is not proportionate to the number of infants to be nursed." This "penury of good nurses" naturally weighed most heavily on the poor, who were compelled to take poor nurses ("poverty feeds poverty") with all the terrible consequences for infant mortality.[65]

The majority view within the Academy of Medicine, expressed at the conclusion of the discussion in March 1870, was that the problems of the wet-nursing business in France could be controlled within the existing framework of social custom and economic institutions by means of a more severe and extensive system of medical and administrative supervision and regulation. Dr. Fauvel disagreed. He thought that what was needed was money, not more regulations. Only money, most likely in the form of state subsidies to indigent parents, would reduce infant mortality by eliciting the supply of milk and good care that were lacking.[66]

Probably the most important effect of the wet-nursing discussion in the Academy of Medicine was the impetus it gave to the statistical study of infant mortality. In February 1867, the Academy appointed a Committee on the Mortality of Nurslings. The committee, chaired by Husson, asked the minister of the interior to conduct an official investigation of infant mortality in the ten departments that received the most nurslings from Paris. The official investigation, completed two years later, resulted in a finding of 52 percent infant mortality for Parisian nurslings placed in the ten departments, compared to 20 percent mortality for infants born and raised in those departments. In releasing this report on March 16, 1869, the minister of the interior, Forcade de la Roquette, appointed a committee of legislators, officials, magistrates, and doctors (including Husson, Boudet, Blot, and Paul Broca from the Academy of Medicine) to study the causes of infant mortality and the means of reducing it. Within the Academy a permanent Committee on Infant Hygiene was established on April 12, 1870. Under the leadership of Boudet, it set about designing a program of research by which doctors all over France would contribute to a statistical study of the practices of infant hygiene and the causes of infant mortality.[67]

The government committee drafted a bill to extend governmental supervision of nurslings, but the Franco-Prussian War, the overthrow of the Second Empire, and the revolt of the Paris Commune interrupted the progress of the bill. After these events, Boudet, a member of the committee, passed its bill on to Roussel, a physician who had specialized in the study of pellagra before becoming a deputy to the National Assembly in the Third Republic. Roussel introduced the bill "relative to the protection of infants and, in particular, of nurslings" on March 24, 1873. The Roussel Law was adopted by the National Assembly December 23, 1874.[68]

In presenting this bill Roussel claimed that fundamentally it was "only the re-establishment and adaptation to the present conditions of our society of legislation which, under the Ancien Régime, seems to have protected with a certain efficacity the children of the bourgeois of Paris against the abuses of the wet-nursing business."[69] And, indeed, many provisions of the Roussel Law were nothing but the eighteenth-century regulations of the lieutenant-general of police of Paris applied to all of France. But the significance of the Roussel Law, and of the decade of agitation and discussion that preceded and prepared the way for it, lay in the requirement of registration of all children under the age of two placed with a nurse or a guardian outside the parents' home for pay. This registration, which was incumbent both on parents and wet nurses, made it possible for the first time to determine exactly how many babies in France were placed with wet nurses and how many of them died. The system of registration took many years to organize. It was largely in place, however, by the 1890s, when the Pasteurian revolution led to the first critical breakthrough in infant hygiene since the Enlightenment doctors had called for frequent baths, loose clothing, and maternal nursing. When the time came to test and propagate sterilized feeding methods, French doctors had both clinical and statistical access to the babies, thanks to the provisions of the Roussel Law for medical surveillance and registration of nurslings.

Notes

1. I have already referred in Chapter 1 to Émile Zola's extremely hostile portrait of all aspects of the wet-nursing business in the novel *Fécondité* (1899), one of the *Quatre Évangiles*. Equally hostile is the story "Nounou" by Pierre Hamp (1917). Like Zola, Hamp suggests a connection between the wet-nursing business and the procurement of prostitutes. The story is in *Gens* (Paris: Éditions de la Nouvelle Revue Française, 1917), 100–8. I am grateful to Ned Newman for bringing this to my attention. Gustave Flaubert depicted Emma Bovary visiting her baby girl, who was placed with a wet nurse in wretched circumstances, during an idle walk with her lover, and beating a hasty retreat when the baby threw up on the mother's shoulder. *Madame Bovary*, trans. by Max Aveling (New York: Universal Library, n.d.), 99–102. Honoré de Balzac made a small plea for maternal nursing by working women in the portrait of Madame Sauviat, the wife of a tight-fisted scrap-metal dealer in the Auvergne: "She nursed her child herself in her chair, in the midst of her shop, continuing to sell scrap-iron while the baby sucked. Since her milk cost nothing, she let her daughter suck for two years, and the baby was none the worse for it. Véronique became the most beautiful child in the old part of town; passers-by stopped to stare at her." *Le curé de village*, in *La comédie humaine*, Bibliothèque de la Pléiade, vol. 8 (Paris: Éditions Gallimard, 1949), 541.

2. Marlet, *Nouvaux tableaux de Paris* (Paris [1821?]), illustration of the Bureau central des nourrices (I am again grateful to Ned Newman for this photograph); Gédéon, *Les Nourrices* (Paris: A. de Vresse [1866?]), a collection of seventeen amusing lithographs; illustration by M. Miranda entitled *Paris—Scènes de moeurs.—À la porte d'un bureau de nourrices*, in *Le Monde illustré, journal hebdomadaire* (Nov. 7, 1874), 300; P.-J. Stahl, *Mon petit frère, ou une visite la nourrice* (Paris: J. Hetzel et Cie. [1876?]), a children's book with illustrations by E. Valton. I think that the group in the foreground of Honoré Daumier's painting of *The Third-Class Carriage* at the Metropolitan Museum of Art in New York City may represent a wet nurse and nursling, with the *meneuse* sitting beside her and the *frère de lait* (although he looks a little old for that role) falling asleep on the opposite shoulder of the *meneuse*.

3. On the eighteenth-century placement bureaus outside Paris see Bloch, *L'assistance et l'état*, 108–9.

4. See the remarks on this subject by Armand Husson, director of public assistance in the city of Paris, in *Bulletin de l'Académie impériale de médecine*, 34 (1869), 921–26.

5. *Bulletin de l'Académie impériale de médecine*, 32 (1866–67), 165–94.

6. Robert J. Bezucha, *The Lyon Uprising of 1834: Social and Political Conflict in the Early July Monarchy* (Cambridge, Mass.: Harvard University Press, 1974).

7. Louis-René Villermé, *Tableau de l'état physique et moral des ouvriers employés dans les manufactures de coton, de laine et de soie*, 1 (Paris: J. Renouard, 1840), 394–95, 398.

8. Dr. F. Imbert, *Des crèches et de l'allaitement maternel, lettre au docteur Barrier* (Paris and Lyon, 1847).

9. *Bulletin de l'Académie impériale de médecine*, 32 (1866–67), 176.

10. Garden, *Lyon et les lyonnais*, 124; J.-M. de Gérando, *De la bienfaisance publique*, 2 (Paris: Renouard, 1839), 15, and *Bulletin de l'Académie impériale de médecine*, 32 (1866–67), 189–92.

11. *Arrêté* of Nov. 27, 1853, in Département du Rhône, *Recueil des actes administratifs du Département du Rhône, année 1853* (Lyon, 1853), 409–20. In brief visits to the Archives départementales du Rhône and the Archives municipales de Lyon I was unable to discover any records related to the enforcement of this or other wet-nursing regulations in Lyon. The archivists in both places were not aware of the existence of any such records.

12. Villermé, *Tableau*, 242, 271–72.

13. *Bulletin de l'Académie impériale de médecine*, 32 (1866–67), 173–75.

14. *Ibid.*, 34 (1869), 934–37, and Brochard, *De l'industrie des nourrices*, 63.

15. Gibert, "Étude de statistique sur la mortalité des jeunes enfants à Marseille et questions relatives à la conservation des nouveau-nés," in Académie de Médecine, *Recueil de mémoires publiées par la Commission permanente de l'hygiène de l'enfance*, 1, 1st fascicule (1875), 69, 73, and Jean-Baptiste-Victor Théophile Roussel, *Assemblée nationale. Année 1874. Annexe du procès-verbal de la séance du 9 juin 1874. Rapport fait, au nom de la commission chargée d'examiner la proposition de loi de M. Théophile Roussel, relative à la protection des enfants du premier âge et en particulier des nourrissons* (Versailles: Imprimerie de Cerf et fils, 1874), 120–22.

16. Brochard, *De l'industrie des nourrices*, especially 27, 29, 60–61; see also Pr. Pierre Guillaume, *La population de Bordeaux au XIXe siècle, essai d'histoire sociale* (Paris: Librairie Armand Colin, 1972).

17. AC Strasbourg, Fonds de Police, 85–478.
18. Couillard, "Résumé d'une étude statistique et géologique sur le canton d'Issoire (Puy-de-Dôme)," in Académie de Médecine, *Recueil de mémoires publiées par la Commission permanente de l'hygiène de l'enfance*, 1, 1st fascicule (1875), 81–83.
19. Bringuier, "Étude sur l'hygiène de l'enfance dans le département de l'Hérault suivie d'une statistique médicale des mort-nés," in Académie de Médecine, *Recueil de mémoires publiées par la Commission permanente de l'hygiène de l'enfance*, 1, 1st fascicule (1875), 18–19.
20. *Bulletin de l'Académie impériale de médecine*, 32 (1866–67), 181–82, 167.
21. Bertillon, *La démographie figurée*, and Roussel, *Rapport fait*, 107–10.
22. LeNoir, *Détail sur quelques établissemens*, 63.
23. "Rapport sur le Bureau de la Location et de la Direction des Nourrices," in *Rapports au Conseil général des Hospices, sur les hôpitaux et hospices, les secours à domicile, la Direction des Nourrices* (Paris, fructidor an XI), 10, n. 1 (hereafter cited as *Report of the Year XI*).
24. "At Lyons, in the Year III, a procession in honor of the transferring of Rousseau's ashes to the Pantheon was composed, among others, 'of young men worthy of Emile, of young girls worthy of Sophie, of mothers from among those who had not neglected their duty by giving their children to wet nurses.' " Crane Brinton, *The Jacobins: An Essay in the New History* (New York: Macmillan Co., 1930), 210.
25. Dupoux, *Sur les pas de Monsieur Vincent*, ch. 8, esp. 153.
26. For the placements by the municipal bureau, see AAP, 592[6], De Nervaux, Report of Mar. 31, 1875, p. 4, n. 1. For the other figures, Roussel, *Rapport fait*, 160, 170.
27. *Bulletin de l'Académie impériale de médecine*, 34 (1869), 906, 921–23.
28. Gustave Lagneau, *Mortalité des enfants nés dans le département de la Seine* (Paris: G. Masson, 1873), 7–8.
29. *Report of the Year XI*, 7.
30. AAP, 592[6], Vée, Report of Jan. 7, 1863, p. 11. Napoleon made one such gift to celebrate his accession to the Imperial title and another on the birth of the king of Rome; the Bourbons made one for the birth of the duc de Bordeaux; and Napoleon III made several.
31. See *ibid.*, 13–14, for Vée's suggestion.
32. AN, F[15] 1937, letter from Dubois, prefect of police, to the Minister of the Interior, 29 floréal Year IX.
33. For complaints about the bookkeeping of the Bureau des Nourrices, see AN, F[15] 1937, letters to the Minister of the Interior from Pasquier, prefect of police, Paris, May 16, 1811, and from Bellart, procureur général du Roi, Paris, July 21, 1817. For the reforms themselves see AAP, 709[1], Administration générale des Hôpitaux,

Hospices civils et Secours de Paris, *Instruction sur le service des préposés à la surveillance des enfans placés dans les départemens par l'intermédiaire de la Direction des Nourrices* (Paris, 1823); AAP, 709², *Instruction sur le service des médecins et chirurgiens chargés de la surveillance des enfans placés dans les départemens par l'intermédiaire de la Direction des Nourrices* (Paris, 1823); AAP, 592⁶, Davenne, Report of May 30, 1850, pp. 9–11, and Vée, Report of Jan. 7, 1863, pp. 15–17; AD Oise, AC Milly-sur-Thérain, 13 Q 1, printed letter from Peligot to mayor, n.d. The reform of the Bureau des Nourrices was modeled upon a similar reorganization of the wet-nursing services of the Hospice des Enfants-Trouvés in 1819. Dupoux, *Sur les pas de Monsieur Vincent*, 234–41.

34. The most complete source for the annual number of placements by the municipal bureau and the annual number of deaths occurring among its charges is a manuscript table marked "Direction municipale des nourrices—statistique," in AAP, 592⁶. This table covers the period from the Year XI to 1850 with some gaps. I was able to confirm the accuracy of these figures and to supplement them for other years from the following sources: *Report of the Year XI*, 10–11; AN, F¹⁵ 1937, "États de situation du Bureau des nourrices de la Ville de Paris," 1813–19; AAP, 709⁷, S. Pierret, Report of July 25, 1829; AAP, 592³, *Rapport de la Commission chargée de l'examen du budget de la Direction des nourrices pour 1854, séance du 9 juin 1853* (Paris, 1853), 4; AAP, 592³, Davenne, "Projet de Budget de la Direction des nourrices pour 1857," Paris, May 22, 1856, p. 2; AAP, 592⁶, Vée, Report of Jan. 7, 1863, p. 29; AAP, 592⁶, A. Husson, Reports of Jan. 8 and Feb. 28, 1866, pp. 5, 23; AAP, 592⁶, De Nervaux, Report of Mar. 31, 1875, p. 4, n. 1. The figures for the wet nurses registered each year by the private bureaus, reported in the same table but discussed later in this chapter, were found in André-Théodore Brochard, *De la mortalité des nourrissons en France, spécialement dans l'arrondissement de Nogent-le-Retrou (Eure-et-Loir)* (Paris: J.-B. Baillière et fils, 1866), 97, and Roussel, *Rapport fait*, 152. Both Brochard and Roussel obtained their figures from the Prefecture of Police, where they apparently no longer exist. The breakdown of placements by the municipal bureau into the categories "voluntary" and "assisted" only appears in the records from 1847. The first figures I could find for placements by the private bureaus were from 1851.

35. AAP, 592⁶, Davenne, Report of May 30, 1850, pp. 12–15, and Vée, Report of Jan. 7, 1863, pp. 17–23. A statement of the police position can be found in Dr. Boys de Loury, "Mémoire sur les modifications à apporter dans le service de l'administration des nourrices," *Annales d'hygiène publique et de médecine légale*, vol. 27 (1842), 5–35.

36. AAP, 592[6], Davenne, Report of May 30, 1850.

37. AAP, 592[6], De Nervaux, Report of Mar. 31, 1875, p. 5, and Roussel, *Rapport fait*, 157–58, 203–4.

38. On the initial decision of 1842 to place babies supported by public assistance see AAP, 592[3], *Rapport de la Commission*, 4. On nonpayment and underpayment by "unassisted" parents see AAP, 592[6], Husson, Reports of 1866, pp. 11, 14–15. In 1864 Husson noted, the Direction des Nourrices collected only about 50 percent of the amount due from parents; of 1,416 parents who owed money to the Direction for that year, 501 paid nothing, 235 paid part of what they owed, and 681 paid all.

39. The first hospital official to advocate abolition was Vée, head of the Division des Secours et des Enfants-assistés (AAP, 592[6], Report of Jan. 7, 1863). Husson, director of the Administration générale de l'Assistance publique, took this position in 1866 (AAP, 592[6], Reports of Jan. 8 and Feb. 28, 1866), and his successor De Nervaux again advocated abolition in 1875 (AAP, 592[6], Report of Mar. 31, 1875). A decree of Nov. 22, 1876, finally abolished the Direction (AAP, 592[2]).

40. The ordinance of Aug. 9, 1828, may be found in APP, D B/61, and that of June 20, 1842, is appended to Husson, Reports of 1866, pp. 25–28 (AAP, 592[6]).

41. The police administration did renew its correspondence with mayors in the nursing communes to keep track of the wet nurses hired through the private bureaus and their nurslings. See AD Eure, AC Beaubray, 5 Q 4, correspondence from 1830–59.

42. Boys de Loury, "Mémoire," 20–27; AAP, 592[6], Husson, Reports of 1866, pp. 12–13, 24–25; Roussel, *Rapport fait*, 143–59 (the quotation is from p. 146); Alfred Donné, *Conseils aux mères sur la manière d'élever les enfans nouveau-nés, ou de l'éducation physique des enfans du premier âge* (Paris: J.-B. Baillière, 1842), 98–99.

43. AAP, 592[6], Vée, Report of Jan. 7, 1863, p. 35.

44. AAP, 592[6], Davenne, Report of May 30, 1850, pp. 10–11, and Boys de Loury, "Mémoire," 19.

45. The parents may not even have known the difference, since some private bureaus represented themselves as branches of the municipal bureau. Boys de Loury, "Mémoire," 18.

46. AAP, 592[6], "Note sur le service du louage des Nourrices," Nov. 2, 1848.

47. Roussel, *Rapport fait*, 157–59.

48. AAP, 592[6], L. Faulcon, "Notice sur la direction des nourrices adressée au Conseil général des hospices civils de Paris," n.d. (written sometime between 1832 and 1843), 4–5.

49. AAP, 592⁶, Vée, Report of Jan. 7, 1863, pp. 32–33.

50. AAP, 592⁶, De Nervaux, Report of Mar. 31, 1875, pp. 3–8, and Roussel, *Rapport fait*, 209–12.

51. *Bulletin de l'Académie impériale de médecine*, 32 (1866–67), 95, and Dupoux, *Sur les pas de Monsieur Vincent*, 238.

52. Roussel, *Rapport fait*, 15.

53. Alexandre Mayer, *De la création d'une société protectrice de l'enfance pour l'amélioration de l'espèce humaine par l'éducation du premier âge* (Paris: Librairie des sciences sociales, 1865), 4–5.

54. Félix-Henri Boudet, *Coup d'oeil sur l'origine et les oeuvres de la Société protectrice de l'enfance* (Paris: Imprimerie de F. Malteste, 1869).

55. Alexandre Mayer, *Des moyens pratiques de ramener à ses limites naturelles la mortalité du premier âge en France, mémoire* (Paris: Imprimerie de F. Malteste, 1869), 4.

56. Alexandre Mayer, *De la mortalité excessive du premier âge en France considérée comme cause de dépopulation et des moyens d'y remédier* (Paris: J.-B. Baillière, 1873), 22.

57. Testimony to the Roussel committee, Jan. 16, 1874, in Roussel, *Rapport fait*, 97.

58. Mayer, *De la création d'une société protectrice de l'enfance*, 11–15; Mayer, *De la mortalité excessive du premier âge*, 23–30; Alexandre Mayer, *Projet de loi et de règlement concernant la protection des enfants placés en nourrice* (Paris: Imprimerie de F. Malteste, 1870); Roussel, *Rapport fait*, 25–26, 68–69, 97; *Bulletin de l'Académie impériale de médecine*, 32 (1866–67), 84, 258–60, 283–84, 369–70; and 34 (1869), 1147–48.

59. Brochard, *De la mortalité des nourrissons en France*, v, xi, 32, 40, 44–45, 50, 55, 61–62, 72–73, 99–104, 151–55.

60. *Bulletin de l'Académie impériale de médecine*, 32 (1866–67), 358–62.

61. APP, D B/63, Théophile Roussel, "Proposition de loi ayant pour objet la Protection des enfants du premier âge et en particulier des nourrissons, Assemblée Nationale, Année 1873, Annexe au procès-verbal de la séance du 24 mars 1873," pp. 15–17.

62. Charles Monot, *De l'industrie des nourrices et de la mortalité des petits enfants* (Paris: A. Faure, 1867), 23–24, 29, 32–33, 35–36, 38–40, 42–48, 51–63, 69, 76–79, 92–94, 134–55.

63. *Bulletin de l'Académie impériale de médecine*, 32 (1866–67), 80–81.

64. *Ibid.*, 34 (1869), 934, 909–10.

65. *Ibid.*, 946–58, 972–75.

66. *Ibid.*, 978–88; 35 (1870), 251–60, 264–71.

67. Charles Devilliers, *Rapport de la commission de l'hygiène de l'enfance* (Paris: Imprimerie de E. Martinet, 1872); *Bulletin de l'Académie impériale de médecine*, 34 (1869), 254–65; AAP, D B/63, Roussel, "Proposition de loi," pp. 16–17.

68. Jean-Baptiste-Victor-Théophile Roussel, *Candidature à l'Académie de médecine. Titres et travaux scientifiques du Dr. Théophile Roussel* (Paris: Imprimerie de E. Martinet, 1868); J. B. Duvergier and J. Duvergier, *Collection complète des lois, décrets, ordonnances, règlements et avis du Conseil d'État*, 74 (Paris, 1874), 461–66.

69. APP, D B/63, Roussel, "Proposition de loi," p. 19.

6

Two Nursing Regions

Dᴜʀɪɴɢ ᴛʜᴇ ᴇɪɢʜᴛᴇᴇɴᴛʜ ᴄᴇɴᴛᴜʀʏ and well into the nineteenth, the principal regions supplying wet nurses to Paris were to the north and west of the capital, especially Picardy and Normandy. Only a small trickle of nurses came to Paris from the south or east, generally on the riverboats along the Yonne or Marne. Of 104 wet nurses counted in the register of the *recommandaresse* Anne Delaunay in July 1732, eighty-seven came from dioceses to the north or west of Paris (Chartres, Soisson, Beauvais, Rouen, Meaux, Évreux, Amiens, and Senlis), sixteen came from Paris or unidentified dioceses, and only one came from the south or east (Sens).[1] Norman coifs predominated in the street in front of the Bureau of Wet Nurses through the Bourbon Restoration.

What inhibited access to the wet-nursing market of Paris for the poor regions to the south and east during the eighteenth and early nineteenth centuries were the difficult conditions of overland transport in that direction. The road-building activity of the July Monarchy and Second Empire and the simultaneous development of the railway network changed the situation abruptly. From mid-century the wet nurses from central France, Champagne, and Burgundy began to take over the Parisian market. Of 7,642 wet nurses registered at the twelve private bureaus in Paris in 1872, 4,509 or 59 percent came from departments to the south or east of the city (including 2,145 or 28 percent from the four departments of Burgundy), 2,261 or 30 percent came from departments to the north or west, and 873 or 11 percent came from the department of the Seine or (a very small number) from unidentified departments and other countries.[2] Nineteenth-century opinion viewed Burgundian women as especially qualified to make good wet nurses. The king of Rome, Louis-Philippe's grandchildren, and the Prince Imperial are all said to have been nursed by women from the Morvan region of Burgundy.[3]

The same shift of the locus of wet-nursing from north and west to south and east occurred with the foundling population of Paris in the nineteenth century. In 1690 all the foundlings of Paris were placed with wet nurses in Normandy and Picardy. Late in the eighteenth century the foundling hospital began to place some of its babies through *meneurs* based in Troyes (Champagne), Autun, Auxerre, and Sens (all in Burgundy). By the year XIII (1804–5), some 20 percent of Parisian foundlings were being placed in departments to the south and east of Paris. In 1820, 26 percent of the foundlings were in the southeastern departments, including 24 percent in the four Burgundian departments (the Côte-d'Or, Nièvre, Saône-et-Loire, and Yonne). The proportion in the southeastern departments reached 38 percent in 1830 and exceeded one-half (55 percent) in 1856, by which time the major roads and railroads were nearly completed. During the first three-quarters of the nineteenth century the foundling administration closed all its offices in such departments of the north and west as the Eure, Seine-inférieure, Oise, and Seine-et-Oise, while opening new offices in poorer and more distant departments of the south and east. In 1876, 69 percent of Parisian foundlings were placed in the southeastern departments.[4] The Norman countryside around Évreux (department of the Eure) and the Morvan region of Burgundy (between the departments of the Yonne, Nièvre, Saône-et-Loire, and Côte-d'Or) typify the regions that provided wet-nursing services to Paris in the first and last quarters of the nineteenth century, respectively.

The Department of the Eure in the Early Nineteenth Century

An unusual source of information about wet-nursing in the department of the Eure survives in the form of a register of the Direction des Nourrices of the City of Paris, the only source on individual placements by the municipal Bureau of Wet Nurses in the nineteenth century to have survived the fires of 1871 or routine bureaucratic disposal of old papers.[5] The register was evidently prepared around 1822 as a part of the general reorganization of the Direction and straightening out of its books, and it was kept up until 1825. It contains information on individual placements from 1814 through 1825 in four of the rural *arrondissements* where the Direction recruited its nurses: Évreux and Louviers in the department of the Eure, Épernay in the department of the Marne, and Fontainebleau in the department of Seine-et-Marne. For each infant placed the register contains spaces for the following information: an identification number, the child's name, the nurse's name, her commune and canton, the date when the child was put out to nurse, what happened to the child—whether he or she died, was returned, was expunged from the books (probably because the nurse and parents came to a private arrangement), or was still with the nurse in 1825—the date of the child's return or death, and the amount of the monthly wage the parents agreed to pay the nurse. There are also spaces to record the payments made, and these are only filled in from 1822. There is no information on the occupations of the child's parents or the nurse's husband, or the birthdate or age of the nurse, the child, or the nurse's own child (the *frère de lait*), or on the parents' address in Paris.

The register contains information on 1,648 placements during the years 1814–25, about 3 percent of the total number of placements by the Direction des Nourrices during these years. Out of 1,653 infants placed in the four *arrondissements* (including five stray placements before 1814), 438 or 26.5 percent of the total died while they were out to nurse in the country (Table 5). Mortality

Table 5

Placements and deaths in four *arrondissements* in which the Bureau of Wet Nurses placed its Parisian babies, 1814–25

Arrondissement (years)	Placements	Deaths	Mortality (%)
Épernay (1814–25)	451	133	29.5
Évreux (1806, 1812–24)	826	204	24.7
Fontainebleau (1813–25)	269	78	29.0
Louviers (1814–23)	107	23	21.5
Total[a]	1,653	438	26.5

[a] The "total" column for mortality is obviously the *average* death rate.

of the nurslings and regional differences in mortality are strikingly similar to the pattern found by Jacques Tenon a generation earlier in his analysis of 1,000 placements evenly distributed among four provinces from the wet-nursing bureau's register of 1786 (Table 6). Overall mortality was slightly lower before the Revolution (although first-year mortality and mortality of all nurslings are not strictly comparable). The range of mortality by location was wider before the Revolution. Before and after the Revolution mortality was higher in the southern and eastern areas (especially Champagne) than it was in the northern and western areas (especially Normandy). Whatever the explanation for the regional difference—whether it was the difference in the rural economy of the two regions, as Tenon suggested, or the different conditions of transport—the comparison between these two soundings from the books of the wet-nursing bureau supports the idea that the Revolution made little difference in the geographic pattern of wet-nursing around Paris. The transportation revolution of the next half-century had a greater impact.

Data concerning 826 children placed in the *arrondissement* of Évreux (almost all between 1814 and 1824) were recorded on computer punch cards for further analysis. The area around Évreux in Normandy was a major wet-nursing region for the city of Paris for more than two centuries. In 1690, eight of twenty-three *meneurs* serving the foundling hospital of Paris were residents of the future department of the Eure. The number of Parisian foundlings in the Eure probably reached a peak around 1820, when there were 974, then fell off quickly. The last offices of the foundling administra-

Table 6
First-year mortality of 1,000 babies placed in 1786

Province	First-year mortality (%)
Champagne	32.8
Burgundy	29.2
Picardy	23.6
Normandy	17.2
Average	25.7

Source. BN, NAF, 22,746, fol.3.

tion of Paris in the department of the Eure closed in the decade 1856–66.⁶ Alongside the foundlings, and before and after the foundlings came to the Eure, the region also supplied hundreds of nurses each year for Parisian babies placed by their parents, especially artisans and shopkeepers. The importance of this traffic is unmistakably indicated in the parish burial registers dating back to the seventeenth century, in the registers of the Parisian *recommandaresse* Delaunay (1732–35), and, on a diminished scale, in the records implementing the Roussel Law at the end of the nineteenth century.

The town of Évreux, seat of the department of the Eure, is located in Upper Normandy 106 kilometers to the west of Paris on the Iton River, a small tributary of the Eure, which, in turn, flows into the Seine. Before the railroad a national highway connected Paris with Évreux, and a coach covered this distance in seventeen hours. Wet nurses, however, would have traveled in slower vehicles and would probably have had to walk from Évreux to their villages.⁷

The *arrondissement* of Évreux, like the entire department of the Eure, was a populous region in the early nineteenth century but with no large cities. The 826 infants placed in the *arrondissement* in the years 1814–24 by the Direction des Nourrices were dispersed among at least 172 distinct communes. Only twenty-five communes received ten or more children from the municipal bureau over this eleven-year period, and only two communes received twenty or more (Vernon, 20, and Évreux, 29). Within the *arrondissement* of Évreux there were roughly two economic zones. In the east and south (the cantons of Vernon, Pacy, Saint André, Nonancourt, Damville, and Verneuil) the principal activity was agriculture, especially wheat and barley production associated with sheep-raising. Two-thirds of the wet nurses in the *arrondissement* came from these cantons. They likely belonged to the population of agricultural laborers who worked six or seven months a year for task wages or daily wages of 1 to 1.5 francs.⁸ The western parts of the *arrondissement* (the cantons of Évreux, Conches, Breteuil, and Rugles) had another resource in the state forests of the region and the small metallurgical and hardware industry that flourished around them. Most of the wet nurses from these western cantons probably came from the poorer families who lived a qua-

silegal existence around the forests as woodcutters, charcoal-burn-
ers, and scavengers of one sort or another. "What cultivable soil
there is in the area is worked by poor farmers," wrote an observer
of the forest population in 1838; "the other inhabitants are woodcutters or workers somehow involved with wood, and also a number of indigent people who live almost entirely off the forest or
who keep foundlings for the hospitals of Rouen or of Paris."[9]

The register of the Direction des Nourrices gives almost no
direct information about the wet nurses of the *arrondissement* of
Évreux. Only their names and communes appear, and for thirty-
one placements (3.8 percent of the total) the clerk noted that the
wet nurse was a "fille," unmarried. Each wet nurse received the
basic monthly wage of 10 francs, which was guaranteed by the
Direction, and usually 1–2 francs more depending on the contract
that she had made with the parents and the parents' readiness to
meet their obligations. The mean contracted wage for the wet
nurses of Évreux in the years 1814 to 1824 was 11.6 francs. If the
mean wage is compared for various smaller groups, it turns out
that there are no important differences in the wages contracted
by women from different cantons nor between unmarried women
and the sample as a whole. Nor does there appear to be any
relationship between the wage contracted and the treatment the
child received, which is measured by whether he or she survived.
The treatment might have varied in relationship to the wage paid,
but the information to assess that relationship is not available. The
mean contracted wage does appear to have fluctuated with the
month in which the contract was made: the lowest mean was 11.3
francs for children put out in May and the highest was 12.0 francs
for children put out in August. The availability of seasonal employment harvesting grain in August certainly accounts for the
relatively high prices the rural wet nurses received that month.[10]
Year-by-year fluctuations in the mean contracted wage show one
unusually low year, 1816, with a mean wage of 11.2 francs, and
a series of notably high years at the end of the period, 1821–24,
when the mean wage ranged from 11.9 to 12.3 francs. The low
figure for 1816 might be related to an abundance of nurses in a
year of high food prices and military occupation. The rise in the
mois de nourrice (the nurse's monthly wage) after 1821 is probably
related to the reorganization of the Direction that year. The *me-*

neurs, replaced by salaried employees of the bureau and hence operating on their own, offered the nurses higher wages and thereby raised the general price level.

Wet-nursing was an important source of supplementary income for many women, and many tried to make it a regular and enduring source of income as well, despite the unusual physiological demands it imposed. Assuming that where the nurse's surname and commune are identical, the nurse is the same, 274 of the 826 placements (one-third of the total) were with women who nursed more than one child for the bureau between 1814 and 1824. Eighty-six women nursed two Parisian children each, twenty-five nursed three, four nursed four each, one woman nursed five different children, and one woman nursed six children not her own in a period of eleven years (four of the babies survived).

There were three distinct patterns of placements with these repeating nurses. In some instances there was a long enough lapse of time between two placements with the same woman for her to have given birth to a child of her own, who may have died, been put out with another nurse, or been weaned before the mother took another commercial nursling. Then there were many cases of serial nursing with two Parisian infants—that is, when the lapse of time between the first child's death or return and the next child's placement with the same nurse is greater than zero and less than six months. A woman by the name of Bourgeois from the village of Mouettes took an infant on September 10, 1819, and returned him to Paris on June 7, 1820; took another child on July 16 and returned him on May 5, 1821; and took a third child on June 23 and returned him on March 3, 1823. In this example of serial nursing, three children were apparently on the same milk over a period of at least two years of nearly continuous nursing. A third possibility, which appears to violate the municipal bureau's rule against nursing more than one child at a time, occurred where the dates of two placements with one nurse overlapped. But the bureau seems to have permitted this situation rather often, either where the two babies were twins (César and Colas Lardi, both placed with a woman named Ste. Beuve on April 23, 1820, and both returned May 13, 1822) or where the first child had probably been weaned but still remained with the nurse (a woman named Malard from Pacy took one child March 31, 1818, then another nine months later on January 11, 1819, returning the first child in May 1819, and the second in December 1820). With the eighty-six women who nursed two children commercially, there were twenty-two instances where the two placements overlapped in time, thirty-three where the two placements were in series, and thirty-one where the two placements were separated by more than six months. Among all the women who nursed more than one child, there were fifty-nine instances of serial intervals between two placements and thirty-seven instances of overlapping placements. Both patterns, then, were not unusual.[11]

Of 826 Parisian babies placed by the municipal bureau in the *arrondissement* of Évreux during the first decade of the Restoration, 204 died, 598 were returned, sixteen were removed from the books, five were still with their nurses in 1825, and there is no information on three others (Table 7). The mortality rate on those for whom information is available was 24.8 percent, a quarter of the babies, a relatively low rate for the Direction des Nourrices in the nineteenth century.[12]

For those babies who died while they were out to nurse, the mean length of time elapsing between their placement and their death was 144 days, nearly five months. Working from the bureau's registers for 1770 to 1776, a half century earlier, Tenon computed the mean age at death to be five to seven months. The median age of death for the nineteenth-century sample from Évreux, the term by which half of the deaths had already occurred, was about ten weeks. Of all the babies placed, 21.4 percent died within one year of their placement. In general the age at death of nurslings in the *arrondissement* of Évreux around 1820 was somewhat younger (i.e., a higher proportion of deaths occurred under one month, under six months, and under one year) than with other samples of nurslings whom historical demographers have identified in seventeenth- and eighteenth-century parish registers (Table 8).[13] The probable explanation for this contrast is that in the eighteenth century babies were generally left in the country for a longer period of time so that a higher proportion of deaths occurred at older ages.

In arranging the fatalities of the nurslings of the Eure by the month in which they occurred, a startling pattern appears (Table 9). In every one of the first six months of the year but January

Table 7

Age of infants at time of death in or return from the *arrondissement* of ÉVREUX, 1814–25

Age	Death			Return		
	Number	Percent of Column	Percent of Table	Number	Percent of Column	Percent of Table
1st week	11	5.8	1.4	3	0.5	0.4
2nd week	22	11.6	2.8	0	0	0
3rd week	26	13.8	3.3	0	0	0
4th week	5	2.6	0.6	1	0.2	0.2
2nd month	27	14.3	3.4	4	0.7	0.5
3rd month	13	6.9	1.6	4	0.7	0.5
4th month	10	5.3	1.3	4	0.7	0.5
5th month	10	5.3	1.3	16	2.7	2.0
6th month	11	5.8	1.4	21	3.6	2.7
7th month	4	2.1	0.5	24	4.1	3.0
8th month	4	2.1	0.5	25	4.3	3.2
9th month	6	3.2	0.8	35	6.0	4.4
10th month	5	2.6	0.6	40	6.8	5.1
11th month	7	3.7	0.9	20	3.4	2.5
12th month	8	4.2	1.0	45	7.7	5.7
2nd year/1st quarter	8	4.2	1.0	95	16.3	12.0
2nd year/2nd quarter	6	3.2	0.8	58	9.9	7.3
2nd year/3rd quarter	2	1.1	0.3	52	8.9	6.6
2nd year/4th quarter	2	1.1	0.3	45	7.7	5.8
3rd year	2	1.1	0.3	64	10.9	8.1
4th year	0	0	0	17	2.9	2.2
Over 4 years	0	0	0	12	2.1	1.5
Total	189		23.9	585		74.1

Table 8
Age distributions of nurslings at death

Sample Group	Number of deaths	Percent of deaths occurring		
		under 1 month	under 6 months	under 1 year
Arrondissement of Évreux, 1814–24	189	33.8	71.4	89.3
Three villages of Beauvaisis, 1740–99	259	20.0	—	70.0
Meulan, 1670–1869	529	16.8	42.8	61.8
Parishes around Thoissey-en-Dombes, 1740–1814	249	33.7	67.1	88.0
Southern *banlieue* of Paris, nurslings only, 1774–94	795	17.4	38.7	58.0

Note. The percentages were calculated from tables in the references of note 13. Dash = not available.

Table 9
Percentage distribution of deaths by month and season

	Jan.	Feb.	Mar.	Apr.	May	June	July	Aug.	Sept.	Oct.	Nov.	Dec.
Arrondissement of Évreux, 1814–24 (189 deaths)	8.5	2.6	7.9	6.9	4.2	6.9	11.1	9.5	11.1	9.5	9.5	12.2
	1st quarter 19.0			2nd quarter 18.0			3rd quarter 31.7			4th quarter 31.2		
Banlieue sud of Paris, natives and nurslings, 1774–94 (2,224 deaths)	7.8	6.9	8.0	7.8	6.7	7.2	8.8	12.9	12.0	7.6	7.1	7.1
	1st quarter 22.8			2nd quarter 21.7			3rd quarter 33.7			4th quarter 21.8		

Source. Galliano, "La mortalité infantile," 161–64.

there were fewer fatalities than the mean, and January had exactly the mean. The lowest mortality occurred in February, followed by May. Altogether, 19.0 percent of the year's fatalities occurred in the first quarter (winter) and 18.0 percent in the second quarter (spring)—37.0 percent of these babies died in the first half of the year. Sixty-three percent of the deaths occurred in the second half of the year, and these fatalities were about evenly divided between the third quarter (summer), with 31.7 percent of the annual mortality, and the fourth quarter (autumn), with 31.2 percent. The highest monthly mortality was in December, followed by July and September. Every month of the second half contributed more than the monthly mean to the total mortality.

The seasonal pattern of mortality for the infants being nursed in the Eure only partially resembles the pattern that Paul Galliano found for native infants and nurslings in the southern *banlieue* of Paris. There the three summer months were even more deadly, accounting for 33.7 percent of the year's fatalities, but the three autumn months were about on a level with the winter and spring months (autumn, 21.8 percent; winter, 22.8 percent; and spring, 21.7 percent). Galliano found the highest infant mortality in August, followed by September, and the lowest in May, followed by February. For Galliano the explanation for the high summer mortality among infants was the preoccupation of the women—nursing mothers and commercial wet nurses—with outdoor work in the harvest months, resulting in neglect and premature weaning. This explanation would be more valid for the country around Évreux than for the suburban area that Galliano studied. Did women's outdoor labor in the Eure carry further into the autumn than outdoor labor in the Seine—perhaps gathering fuel or shearing sheep—or is there another explanation for the high mortality of the nurslings in the Eure in the last quarter of the year?

The seasonal distribution of mortality does not appear to have any relationship to the seasonal distribution of placements, unless it is inverse. The month-by-month fluctuations in the percentage of placements are smaller than those for mortality, partly because there is a larger number of placements (813 placements for which the month is known) than of deaths (189) (Table 10). Whereas mortality was concentrated in the third and fourth quarters of the year, placements are concentrated in the first quarter (winter),

Table 10

Month and season of placement of nurslings in the Eure, 1814–24

	Jan.	Feb.	Mar.	Apr.	May	June	July	Aug.	Sept.	Oct.	Nov.	Dec.
No. (total 813)	81	87	76	60	68	66	57	54	76	54	59	75
Percentage	10.0	10.7	9.3	7.4	8.4	8.1	7.0	6.6	9.3	6.6	7.3	9.2
Percentage by quarters	1st quarter 30.0			2nd quarter 23.9			3rd quarter 23.0			4th quarter 23.1		

Source. George D. Sussman, "Parisian Infants and Norman Wet Nurses in the Early Nineteenth Century: A Statistical Study," *Journal of Interdisciplinary History*, 7 (Spring 1977), 648.

when 30.0 percent of all placements occurred. Among the other seasons the distribution is more or less equal. The winter peak of placements began in December and extended through March. In addition to those four months only September had above-average placements. The lowest number of placements occurred in July, August, and October. This pattern points to the seasonal character of wet-nursing as a supplementary occupation for rural women. The women journeyed to Paris to collect babies in greater numbers in the winter months, when there was little work to be done in the fields, than in the summer months, when work was abundant.[14] The mortality figures suggest that the women may also have taken better care of their charges in the winter months when they were not occupied with outdoor work.

Three out of four infants placed through the municipal Bureau of Wet Nurses in the *arrondissement* of Évreux in the years 1814 to 1824 returned to their parents' home in Paris. The normal pattern appears to have been for the child to be restored to his parents soon after his first birthday (Table 7). The median length of stay in the country, for those who survived, was 406 days or about 13.5 months. The number of babies returned before the end of the fourth month was insignificant, only 2.8 percent of the eventual returnees. From the fifth through the twelfth month there was a slow, mounting movement of returns, from 2.7 percent of all returns occurring in the fifth month to a peak of 7.7 percent in the twelfth. By the end of the first year 41.4 percent of all returns had occurred. Another 16.3 percent of returns occurred in the first quarter of the second year (compared to 17.9 percent in the fourth quarter of the first year); then, the rate began to taper off: 9.9 percent in the second quarter of the second year, 8.9 percent in the third quarter, and 7.7 percent in the fourth quarter. By the second birthday 84.2 percent of all returns had taken place. Most of the remainder (10.9 percent) returned in the third year. Considering the total population put out to nurse in the country, at the end of one year 21.4 percent of the nurslings had died, and 30.6 percent had been returned to their parents; at the end of two years 23.7 percent had died, and 62.2 percent had been returned. Most of the deaths occurred early in the first year; the returns were about evenly divided between the latter part of the first year and the second year.

An important influence on the length of time that Parisian babies placed by the Direction des Nourrices spent in the country was the duration of the bureau's guarantee of wages to wet nurses. Around 1820 the bureau paid the nurses 10 francs a month, whether or not the parents paid the bureau the amount they had agreed upon with the nurse. If the parents failed to pay, the baby was only returned at a certain age, after the guarantee had run out. It is difficult to determine what the duration of the guarantee was before 1821. One administrator who was involved in straightening out the bureau's books from this period stated that the bureau would advance up to three months' wages when the parents did not pay, but rarely more. After the reorganization of the municipal bureau in 1821 the duration of the guarantee was ten months, which would mean that children whose parents did not pay would be returned after eleven months, since all parents paid the first month directly to the nurse in advance. Does this mean that the bureau regarded eleven months as a suitable age for a baby to be weaned? Probably it was expected that the child would have been weaned a month or two before his return. The nurse's own child was expected to be suckled at least seven months, for if her most recent child were alive, no woman was accepted as a nurse until that child was seven months old.[15]

The mean length of placements for those who returned was 493 days, about 16.5 months. By comparison Tenon calculated that the mean length of placement for all infants placed by the Bureau of Wet Nurses in the years 1770 to 1776 and returned to their parents' home ranged between nineteen and twenty-one months.

By an indirect calculation Galliano came to the conclusion that most of the children placed with wet nurses in the southern *banlieue* of Paris in the years 1774 to 1794 were placed during the second fortnight of their lives and that those who survived were brought home after nearly two years.[16]

The evidence once again points to a longer average stay with the wet nurse in the late eighteenth century than in the early nineteenth. The explanation for the shortening of the length of stay is probably the increasing size of Paris and the growing competition for the services of good wet nurses within reasonable proximity to the capital. This competition drove the cost of wet-nursing up so high as to put it out of the reach of the urban poor for either any period longer than absolutely necessary to suckle the child or any period longer than the period when the municipal bureau guaranteed the wet nurse's wages. The opening of new roads and railroads relieved the pressure for a few decades by extending the area of recruitment. But finally wet-nursing became too expensive and gave way to bottle-feeding.

The communal archives of the department of the Eure provide a different view of wet-nursing activity in the region during the nineteenth century. The village mayors' files indicate that wet-nursing appears to have operated on two different levels. Officially, it was an activity closely regulated by the authorities, modulated by major administrative and legislative changes in Paris. Unofficially, it was a business with its own logic, operating in a climate of poverty and ignorance, a business never adequately described or controlled by Parisian legislation.

From the beginning of the century until 1820 the mayors of the Eure received a steady stream of communications from the administrators of the Bureau of Wet Nurses of Paris. These letters generally treated the same subjects—indeed, they often consisted of printed letter formats with blanks for individual information filled in by hand. The bureau asked for reports on the health of a baby or the care it received because an anxious parent had heard nothing from the *meneur* or because a baby was returned in very poor condition. The bureau responded to the nurses' claims that they were owed wages. And the bureau asked the mayor to compel the nurses to return babies whose parents had asked for them (nurses were reluctant to return the babies until they were paid in full). In responding to these letters mayors struggled with all the circumstances not foreseen in regulation: payments allegedly made directly rather than through the bureau; parents who sent for their babies directly; babies transferred by the *meneur* from one nurse to another and from one village to another without any notification of the bureau or the mayor; accidents and negligence; half-truths and lies.[17]

After 1820 the letters from the Bureau of Wet Nurses to the mayors in the Eure cease. In the reorganization of the wet-nursing services of Paris the *arrondissement* of Évreux was designated to serve foundlings only. In January 1825, J. P. Lecomte of Évreux sent a printed letter to the mayors of the area announcing that he was the appointed officer of the hospital administration of Paris in the *arrondissement* for the recruitment and payment of wet nurses for the foundlings. Lecomte asked for the mayors' help in recruiting nurses, as the number of placements in the *arrondissement* was down. Over the next few months additional letters from Lecomte announced when quarterly wages were available for payment at his house in Évreux and the schedule of semi-monthly trips via "suspended wagon" from Évreux to the Maternity Hospital in Paris (each nurse would get four pounds of bread and six francs per trip, as well as room and board at the hospital in Paris).[18] But the nurses of the Eure did not flock to the foundling hospital when the Bureau of Wet Nurses stopped recruiting in the area. They stayed with the *meneurs*, who maintained their contacts with the artisan and shopkeeping families in Paris.

Until 1830 this private placement was free of any surveillance whatsoever. Then the mayors began to receive a new set of communications from the Prefecture of Police of Paris enforcing the police ordinance of August 9, 1828. Unlike the Bureau of Wet Nurses, the Prefecture of Police was not involved in the financial arrangements between nurses and parents, nor did it evince any direct interest in the babies' condition or the treatment they received. The letters from the Prefecture to the mayors of the nursing villages were confined to the requirements of registration and certification, which were indirectly related to the babies' well-being: did the nurse, on coming to Paris, deposit at the Prefecture a certificate from her mayor before taking a baby? Did the nurse, on returning to her village with a baby, deposit a copy of the baby's birth certificate with the mayor?[19]

Finally, in the late 1870s and early 1880s, in implementing the Roussel Law, the mayors began to keep registers of all infants under two years of age being nursed for pay outside their parents' home within their communes. The number of declarations by the wet nurses recorded in these registers is generally small, whether because wet-nursing activity was disappearing in this area or because it continued to evade official surveillance. In the commune of Caillouet-Orgeville, which had a population of 291 in 1892, only one or two wet nurses were listed per year during the period from 1879 to 1908, and in many years there was none. The nurses of Caillouet-Orgeville were generally married to day laborers or shepherds, they had two or three children of their own, and their nurslings usually came from artisan and shopkeeping families in Paris and (at this date) were mostly being bottle-fed by the nurses. The register of wet nurses' declarations in the industrial town of Corneville-sur-Risle, which had a population of about 1,000, showed a newer kind of wet-nursing. In Corneville, where the nurses usually had four or five children of their own, the nurslings were mostly the children of the workers in the local spinning mills, and they were all bottle-fed.[20]

The department of the Eure exemplifies the earlier pattern of a nursing region serving the city of Paris. The wet-nursing business of the Eure was based in the country. The wages derived from it were a supplement to inadequate agricultural incomes, a resource for the marginal population of the country (landless laborers, charcoal burners) and for the slow seasons in the agricultural cycle. The business was closely tied to a particular segment of the Parisian population—foundlings and the class of artisans and shopkeepers—through a network of *meneurs* who made frequent trips back and forth over the 100 kilometers between village and metropolis. In the nineteenth century the supply of wet nurses in the Eure began to decrease, as rural incomes increased, population stabilized and began to decline, and industry came to Normandy. Wet nurses' wages rose, the term of wet-nursing contracted, and the *meneurs* found it more difficult to recruit nurses or to make a living. The wet-nursing business was not in decline. It was merely shifting to poorer, more remote regions and different patterns of organization.

The Morvan in the Late Nineteenth Century

Table 11 shows dramatically both the diminished importance of the department of the Eure in the wet-nursing business of Paris in the late nineteenth century and the prominence of the Morvan, located between the four departments of Burgundy, as well as some of the structural changes that accompanied this geographical shift.

In 1872 the department of the Eure contributed only 1 percent of the wet nurses placed by the twelve private bureaus of Paris. The four departments of Burgundy (effectively, the region of the Morvan located within those four departments) contributed 28 percent of the wet nurses. The wet nurses placed in 1872 by the private bureaus were divided nearly equally between rural nurses, who carried their nurslings back to their cottages in the country, and live-in nurses, who moved into the urban homes of their nurslings' parents for the nursing period. The nurses of the Eure were almost all rural nurses. Those of the Morvan were predominantly hired as live-in nurses and constituted, in fact, about half of the live-in nurses placed by the private bureaus in 1872. The wet nurses of the Morvan have already been mentioned in the discussion of the very hostile and influential book published by Dr. Charles Monot of Montsauche in 1867. Dr. E. Bailly, a Parisian obstetrician, presented a more sympathetic view of the subject in a published series of letters written during a ten-day vacation in the Morvan in October 1881. "The women of the Morvan,"

Table 11

Wet nurses from the Eure and the Morvan placed by the private bureaus of Paris, 1872

Region of origin	Rural nurses		Live-in nurses		Total	
	Number	Per-cent	Number	Per-cent	Number	Per-cent
Department of the Eure	83	2	7	0	90	1
The Morvan[a]	403	10	1,742	49	2,145	28
All departments	4,073	100	3,570	100	7,643	100

[a] Includes the departments of the Côte-d'Or, Nièvre, Saône-et-Loire, and Yonne.

Source. Roussel, *Rapport fait*, 153.

wrote Bailly, "are fruitful and most often make admirable nurses. The long tradition of nursing their own children has developed their nursing capacities to a high degree, and there is no contradicting the fact that the best wet nurses come to us from the Morvan. Since the region offers few resources for women, a great number of them take advantage of their milk in coming to practice the trade of live-in nurse for the wealthy families of Paris."[21]

The Morvan is a mountainous region at the northeast corner of the Massif Central. Measuring roughly 90 kilometers from north to south and 60 kilometers from east to west, the Morvan was described by Bailly as an area of heavy rains, half-covered by forests and wasteland, half-cultivated with poor crops of rye, oats, buckwheat, and potatos. The population was dispersed among hamlets and small villages. Most of the cottages were low, ill-lit structures built into the sides of hills. The economy was poor, with no significant trade or industry. But the local roads were very good.[22]

Transport was the key that unlocked the most significant business in the Morvan during the nineteenth century—wet-nursing. A study of the region published in 1909 observed, "Raising children [*l'élevage humain*] has been for a long time, since the opening of the road network, the largest industry of the Morvan, larger perhaps than the cutting and floating of wood." It was during the July Monarchy that the first good roads were built through the Morvan. The few roads that existed before then were of such poor quality that they were turned into quagmires by heavy rains through most of the year. In 1847 the first coach from Nevers to Dijon passed through Montsauche. The road network was completed in the 1850s. That part of the Morvan in the department of Nevers had 156 kilometers of roads in 1830 and 1,564 in 1889. At the same time the railroad reached the towns on the periphery of the Morvan. In 1909 the trip from Paris to Avallon, the gateway to the Morvan, took five hours by train and cost about 18 francs in second class.[23]

The wet nurses of the Morvan were especially sought after by the wealthy families of Paris and distinguished among the women who looked for places as live-in nurses not only because of their physical qualities but also because of their moral qualities. They were generally married women, in contrast to the unmarried mothers from Paris or from the coalfields of Artois and Flanders who competed for the same places, and the nurses from the Morvan had generally raised one or several babies already.[24] Virtually all the women of the Morvan made the trip to Paris for two or three stints as a live-in nurse, just as the men of this poor region periodically left home for a stint (*une campagne*) of unskilled labor in the mines, foundries, forests, or fields of adjacent provinces. "A rooted prejudice treats it as cowardice on the part of a woman to be faithful to her home and compels her, so to speak, to do at least one stint away from home as a wet nurse [*une campagne de nourrissage*]." Once past the age to nurse themselves, like the "veteran of the army of wet nurses" who invited Bailly to lunch at her home in Planchez, they looked for advantageous placements for their daughters as the latter began to bear children.[25]

In 1884, according to the Prefecture of Police of Paris, there were seventy-two registered *meneuses* who specialized in recruiting live-in nurses, sixty of them from the two departments of the Nièvre and Saône-et-Loire in Burgundy. The business was highly competitive. Each *meneuse* might come to Paris only five or six times a year with one nurse each time. The *meneuse* brought the prospective nurse to the bureau with which she was associated in Paris, waited there with the nurse until she was hired, and then took the nurse's own baby back to the country to the person already selected to raise the baby. Deducting her expenses from the fees she earned from the nurse, the bureau, and the family hiring the nurse, the *meneuse* might clear about 25 francs on each trip. Only a minority of live-in nurses relied on a *meneuse*, however. "The greater part of the wet nurses from Burgundy come accompanied by a female relative, their mother, their sister, a neighbor, sometimes even their baby's future nurse. This person acts as the *meneuse* and brings the child back as soon as the mother is hired."[26]

The prospective live-in nurses came to Paris as soon after giving birth as possible, because their clientele preferred the "youngest" possible milk for their newborn babies. Ninety-six percent of a sample of 2,000 women who registered as live-in nurses in 1895 had given birth within the past seven months; the average age of the milk of this group was two months and twelve days. The law required that if a wet nurse had a living child of her own under seven months of age, she had to arrange for the baby to be nursed by another woman. Nevertheless, the police discovered that of the

1,901 live-in nurses in this survey with living children under seven months of age, only 491 or 26 percent had arranged to place their babies with wet nurses, while 1,174 or 62 percent had arranged for their babies to be bottle-fed, and 237 or 12 percent had not yet made any arrangements for their babies. The 1,174 live-in nurses who had arranged bottle-feeding for their babies were in violation of the law but had nevertheless been certified by their mayors. Seventy-five percent of the bottle-fed babies would be raised by relatives, usually the baby's grandmother, sometimes an aunt or a cousin.[27] Considering the general prevalence of bottle-feeding by the mid-1890s, the fate of the babies of the Morvan left behind by their mothers to become live-in nurses for the wealthy families of Paris does not appear to have been nearly so bad as it was represented thirty years earlier by Monot.

J. Levainville, author of the 1909 study of the Morvan, argued that the wet-nursing business depressed the birth rate in the region and temporarily increased the death rate. "Natality begins to decline at the moment (1842) when the region's fortune prospers thanks to the money earned by the wet nurses. A profession whose *raison d'être* is procreation thus causes a decline in natality. After two or three nursing stints, the wet nurses come back to settle in the country. They are rich, they have no more children." Mortality, still according to Levainville, increased in the period from 1846 to 1872, the period in which Monot wrote, after falling somewhat in the preceding two decades. Levainville attributed the mid-century surge in mortality in the Morvan to neglect of the wet nurses' children and to the death of the Parisian foundlings, who, ironically, were beginning to be placed in the Morvan in large numbers just when the region's best wet nurses were setting off for Paris. Mortality declined again in the first two decades of the Third Republic, which Levainville ascribed primarily to the Roussel Law and secondarily to the spread of education and hygiene (an indirect effect of prosperity and wet-nursing).[28]

The career of a live-in wet nurse could lead in either of two directions for the nurse and her family. For many of the nurses several stints in Paris were the means of building up a little capital, which made life more comfortable in the Morvan. A live-in nurse could expect to bring home 1,200 to 1,800 francs from each campaign. "With the first contribution they began to construct a house;

they finished it with the second and furnished it with the third."[29] The Parisian earnings of a wet nurse in the village of Saint-Léger were invested in an inn, from which she and her husband, a former mason, derived a comfortable living. The returning wet nurses brought home more than capital: after eighteen months or two years in Paris, they returned with new habits of cleanliness, new styles of dress, "more correctness in their speech," and "a certain polish of education lacking in the village woman who never set foot outside the hamlet." The most enterprising of the former live-in nurses opened placement bureaus in Paris and lived very comfortably in the Morvan. Dr. Bailly visited the home of one bureau *directrice* in Lormes, "one of the most charming properties in the region," where he found "elegant carriages, a pair of beautiful carriage-horses, a poultry yard amply stocked with choice fowl, a kennel well arranged for the master's pleasures, etc."[30]

But the career of live-in wet nurses did not necessarily lead back to a more prosperous and more sophisticated Morvan. For many families the mother's stint as a live-in nurse in Paris was the first step in a permanent migration to the capital. While the mother was away, the father rented out the family's small landholding and looked for temporary work elsewhere, particularly in Paris. "At present," wrote Levainville in 1909, "the dream of every Morvandeau is to be a domestic servant in Paris or to find a little job there." Like so many immigrant groups, once one member found work in a large enterprise, he recruited other natives of his region or village. The Noisiel chocolate factory was said to employ over 200 natives of the Morvan who were brought in successively by a wet nurse's husband employed there. The street sweepers of Paris recruited one another from three specific villages of the Morvan. Overall, emigration was a major factor in the 10 percent population decline of the Morvan between 1851 and 1901, from 135,000 to 122,000.[31]

The live-in nurse in Paris made the reputation of the Morvan in the wet-nursing business. But numerically just as significant, perhaps more significant, were the babies placed with wet nurses or dry nurses in the Morvan, including the live-in nurses' babies and a large number of "Petits-Paris." Dr. Monot claimed in the mid-1860s that most of the "Petits-Paris" in the Morvan were placed there either through the agency of a live-in wet nurse from the region (who might place the babies of other servants working in the same household or bring a nursling home with her at the end of her stint) or through an unregistered *meneur* or *meneuse*, who procured babies from the private bureaus or directly from midwives. Many of the babies were illegitimate. Their fathers were unknown, and their mothers stopped paying the wet nurse after a few months. The rural nurses of the Morvan, Monot contended, eschewed the municipal Bureau of Wet Nurses and the Administration of Public Assistance (abandoned children), despite the greater security of payment from those agencies, because the nurses wanted to avoid any supervision.[32]

According to Levainville, however, the "Petits-Paris" in the Morvan were primarily abandoned children placed by the Administration of Public Assistance. The first placements, he wrote, went back to the beginning of the nineteenth century, but the traffic really developed about 1850. "[Live-in] nurses returning to the country usually brought back a nursling. Later the *conducteurs d'enfants* became more numerous." In 1903 the administration sent 1,074 abandoned babies from Paris to the Morvan. Mortality had once been very high, but it declined with increasing supervision under the Roussel Law. Many of the children grew up and settled in the Morvan. Some were adopted by the wet nurse and her husband, especially when the child reached age thirteen and had to be paid for his work.[33] In 1906 there were nearly 22,000 wards of the Administration of Public Assistance of the Seine in the four departments of the Côte-d'Or, Nièvre, Saône-et-Loire, and Yonne. The four departments of Burgundy accounted for 41 percent of the total population of abandoned children from the department of the Seine.[34]

In the wet-nursing business of late nineteenth-century Paris, the Morvan served the extremes of wealth and poverty. While the recently delivered mothers of the Morvan flocked to the capital to nurse the children of the wealthy in their homes, illegitimate and abandoned Parisian children were shipped out by the hundreds into the cottages of the Morvan. Wet-nursing in the Morvan was rooted in the tradition of long-distance labor migrations from a remote and poor region. Like the word that indicated a period of work away from home—*campagne*—the tradition was transposed from men to women, from masonry, forestry, and harvesting to wet-nursing, by the development of communications with Paris in the mid-nineteenth century and the capital's insatiable demand for cheap, safe, and reliable infant care and feeding. The Morvan never did, however, become a wet-nursing center for the Parisian group that was traditionally the most important consumer, artisan and shopkeeping families. Perhaps its distance from Paris, over 250 kilometers, precluded any possibility of parental supervision or visits. Another explanation is the difference between the two traditions of rural labor represented by the Norman district around Évreux and the Morvan, the difference between wet-nursing as a seasonal cottage industry, a small and steady supplement to agricultural income, and wet-nursing as a long-distance labor migration, an intermittent source of significant, personal capital in a region that had almost no natural resources of its own.

Notes

1. AAP, 283.
2. Figures aggregated from the table in Roussel, *Rapport fait*, 153.
3. Dom Bénigne Defarges, "L'industrie des nourrices morvandelles au XIXe siècle," *Pays de Bourgogne*, 20 (1974), 979.
4. Dupoux, *Sur les pas de Monsieur Vincent*, 261–76.
5. AAP, 224. Manuscript register entitled "Administration générale des hôpitaux, hospices et secours de la Ville de Paris. Direction des Nourrices. Service extérieur. Payement des mois de nourrices et dépenses accessoires. Contrôle du Bureau."
6. Dupoux, *Sur les pas de Monsieur Vincent*, 261–76.
7. Jean Vidalenc, *Le département de l'Eure sous la monarchie constitutionnelle, 1814–1848* (Paris: Librairie Marcel Rivière et Cie., 1952), 522–23.
8. *Ibid.*, 437–39.
9. Quoted, *ibid.*, 486.
10. In parts of the Parisian Basin in the eighteenth century the price of a wet nurse doubled in August. Marcel Lachiver, "Tarif des mois de nourrice dans le Bassin parisien en 1771," *Annales de démographie historique, 1968* (Paris: Éditions Sirey, 1968), 383–84.
11. Both patterns were also found to be common in a small sample of women who nursed foundlings from Reims in the late eighteenth century. See Chamoux, "L'enfance abandonnée à Reims," 274–76.
12. The annual mortality among all the infants placed by the Direction of Wet Nurses, that is, the number who died each year as a per-

centage of the number placed the same year, ranged between 25.2 percent and 34.8 percent in the years 1813 to 1822. Over the whole ten-year period mortality was 29.8 percent. See Table 4.

13. Ganiage, *Trois villages*, 75; Lachiver, *La population de Meulan*, 126–28; Galliano, "La mortalité infantile," 159; Alain Bideau, "L'envoi des jeunes enfants en nourrice. L'exemple d'une petite ville: Thoissey-en-Dombes, 1740–1840," in *Hommage à Marcel Reinhard. Sur la population française au XVIIIe et au XIXe siècles* (Paris: Société de démographie historique, 1973), 49–58.

14. The seasonal distribution of placements is not related to the seasonal distribution of births in Paris. The latter, as reported by Louis-René Villermé for the department of the Seine over the years 1807–16, shows very little month-by-month fluctuation, at least in comparison to the fluctuation of placements in the Eure. The monthly percentage of births ranged from a low of 7.7 percent in June to a high of 9.2 percent in March. By seasons the distribution of Parisian births was 26.0 percent in the winter, 25.0 percent in the spring, 24.6 percent in the summer, and 24.4 percent in the autumn. Villermé, "De la distribution par mois des conceptions et des naissances de l'homme," *Annales d'hygiène publique et de médecine légale*, 5, pt. 1 (1831), 55–155. I calculated the percentages from the table on pp. 128–29.

15. AAP, 592[6] and 709[2], various documents of the Direction des Nourrices.

16. Galliano, "La mortalité infantile," 159–61.

17. AD Eure, AC Beaubray, 5 Q 4; AC Houlbec-Cocherel, 1 Q 1; AC Verneuil, 5 Q 7.

18. Ad Eure, AC Louversey, 5 Q 2.

19. Ad Eure, AC Beaubray, 5 Q 4.

20. AD Eure, AC Caillouet-Orgeville, 5 Q 2, and AC Corneville-sur-Risle, 5 Q 2.

21. E. Bailly, *Les vacances d'un accoucheur. Voyage au pays des nourrices. Dix jours d'automne dans le Morvan en 1881* (Paris: Imprimerie de A. Hennayer, 1882), 89.

22. *Ibid.*, 85–89.

23. Capitaine J. Levainville, *Le Morvan: étude de géographie humaine* (Paris: Librairie Armand Colin, 1909), 211–18. I am grateful to Nancy Fitch for bringing this source to my attention.

24. APP, D B/65, Report for 1887, pp. 74–75.

25. Bailly, *Les vacances d'un accoucheur*, 90, 36–37.

26. APP, D B/65, Report for 1884, pp. 83–85.

27. APP, D B/66, Report for 1895, pp. 108–9.

28. Levainville, *Le Morvan*, 269–70.

29. *Ibid.*, 277.
30. Bailly, *Les vacances d'un accoucheur*, 22, 89–90, 94.
31. Levainville, *Le Morvan*, 277–79.
32. Monot, *De l'industrie des nourrices*, 75–113.
33. Levainville, *Le Morvan*, 280–81.
34. Dupoux, *Sur les pas de Monsieur Vincent*, 272–75.

7

The End of the Wet-Nursing Business

A NEW PERIOD IN THE HISTORY of French wet-nursing began with the demise of the Bureau of Wet Nurses of the City of Paris in 1876 and the passage of the Roussel Law in 1874. Aided by the railroad and the improvement of local roads, the wet-nursing business had expanded from an exchange of cities with their rural hinterlands into vast regional markets, sometimes reaching across international borders, as into Luxemburg and Piedmont, and covering, in the case of the Parisian market, perhaps one-fifth to one-fourth of the national territory. In 1874 the law caught up with this fact. Under the Roussel Law, for the first time supervision of wet-nursing became a national rather than a municipal responsibility. With the law's full implementation, some ten to twenty years after its passage, good data on the extent and character of wet-nursing finally became available on a national scale. These data recorded the great shifts in wet-nursing and infant-feeding that also characterized the period that began in the mid-1870s: the adoption of bottle-feeding and then later, the vulgarization of the Pasteurian techniques of infant-feeding and, finally, the end of the wet-nursing business.

Late as they may appear to come in the history of French wet-nursing, the data collected under the Roussel Law nevertheless provide the means of testing the three explanations of the wet-nursing phenomenon sketched in Chapter 1. Each of the three explanations—the cultural, socioeconomic, and technological—implies a different pattern for how and when the practice ended.

The cultural explanation for the end of the practice of wet-nursing views wet-nursing as part of a "traditional" or "pre-industrial" pattern of parental indifference or hostility toward children. These attitudes were rooted in the demographic patterns of high natality and high infant mortality, an economy of scarcity, and a communal social organization. Wet-nursing thus disappeared when parents began to view their children, even their babies, with affection and to see their babies' lives as precious and capable of being preserved. That change of attitude toward children occurred first among the urban elite in the late eighteenth century (for example, in the Roland and Bombelles families), then filtered down through the social ranks with the related attitudes associated with urban life—the isolated nuclear family, birth control, and reduced infant mortality in the course of the nineteenth century. The cultural explanation, then, implies a gradual decline in wet-nursing beginning in the late eighteenth century and in the most urbanized and industrialized social groups. Edward Shorter is the principal recent exponent of this view.[1]

According to the socioeconomic explanation, rural wet-nursing was not a "traditional" practice, but one associated with the transition from traditional to modern, with the early stages of industrialization and urbanization. It reached its widest extent in the eighteenth and nineteenth centuries. The principal consumers were urban artisans and shopkeepers, whose numbers multiplied in this period while their economic circumstances deteriorated. The reason that this class in particular resorted to rural wet-nursing for its children was the active participation of the mother in the family's economic enterprise. Rural wet-nursing, cheap and readily available, freed the mother from the trouble and expense of infant care in the city and allowed her to contribute all her time to bolstering the insecure income of the family enterprise at a time when the birth rate remained high, urban rents were soaring, and artificial infant-feeding was expensive and difficult, especially in the cities.

The proportion of all females employed in the market economy in the nineteenth century was high, perhaps 43 to 44 percent in France in the latter half of the century if census figures are adjusted to include a realistic estimate of agricultural employment. During the twentieth century the proportion of French women who were employed fell, descending to 33 percent in 1954. For the study of wet-nursing the significant fact is not so much the high incidence of overall female employment in the nineteenth century as the growing numbers of women employed outside the home, in the workshop, retail store, or factory rather than on the farm or in the cottage. Female nonagricultural employment in France rose between 1856 and 1906 from 2.3 million to 4.6 million. Male nonagricultural employment was, of course, also rising in this period, from 4.4 million to 7.1 million. But from 1906 to 1954, while the French population rose slowly, from 40.7 million to 42.8 million, and male nonagricultural employment continued to rise, from 7.1 million to 8.7 million, female nonagricultural employment remained stationary (4.6 million in 1906 and 4.7 million in 1954).

A proportionate decline in female employment appears to have occurred between 1906 and 1926. For French women aged fifteen to sixty-four, the number working in the nonagricultural population fell by about 10 percent in those two decades (from 44.8 percent), then remained steady at about 40 to 41 percent for the next three decades. In other words, between 1906 and 1926 about 10 percent of the women in France who had been working outside of the agricultural sector dropped out of the work force. The evidence suggests that most of these dropouts were married women and women between the ages of twenty-five and forty-four—most likely mothers of young children.[2]

The movement of young married women out of the work force in the early twentieth century may be explained by the contraction of the artisan and shopkeeping sector, the increasing real wages of men (if family economic necessity had been the primary reason for young wives working), and declining employment opportunities in the industries traditionally reserved for women, particularly the garment and textile industries. Whatever the explanation, the implications for wet-nursing are the same. If it was the fact of mothers working in urban settings that explains the practice, the incidence of wet-nursing should have been expanding in the nineteenth century with the growth of the urban working class and the high incidence of working women. The socioeconomic explanation would place the end of the wet-nursing business in the twentieth century, when the proportion of women in the labor force declined—for whatever reason.

The socioeconomic explanation has a bearing on the problem of the unique development of wet-nursing in France as well as on the historical timing of the practice. Much has been written about the alleged slowness of France to industrialize in the eighteenth and nineteenth centuries, despite the country's advanced government and educational system, and about the persistence of small-scale family enterprise in France, whether it be the farm, the workshop, or the small retail store.[3] The puzzle is that France had a relatively advanced economy in the early eighteenth century, with large cities and an active colonial trade, but it failed to convert these advantages during the late eighteenth and early nineteenth centuries into a large-scale industrial sector as rapidly as England and, later, Germany did. The transitional state between pre-industrial and industrial society, that is, the period of large cities and small-scale enterprise, was, according to this argument, particularly prolonged in France.

This transitional economy was associated with a relatively high level of female employment. Around 1900 France ranked second among seventeen European and North American countries in the proportion of the female population that was employed. Sharing the top of this list with France were small or semideveloped countries (Austria, Denmark, and Italy), while the most industrialized and the most backward had the lowest proportion of women in the work force (Great Britian, the United States, Spain, and Russia).[4] Wet-nursing registers of various kinds from the eighteenth to the twentieth centuries show the connection between small-scale urban enterprise and wet-nursing. Macroeconomic analysis and labor-force statistics suggest how this connection explains the unique development of wet-nursing in France. Small-scale urban enterprise, the social basis of wet-nursing, was more extensive and lasted longer in France than in any other western country.

The technological explanation of wet-nursing associates the demise of the practice in the late nineteenth century with the advent of a safe alternative to breast-feeding, including the provision of an abundant and sanitary supply of cows' milk to the cities and the development of an effective feeding bottle and artificial nipple. Until well past the middle of the nineteenth century French medical manuals on infant care peremptorily rejected artificial feeding for newborns, especially in the cities, as far too dangerous to contemplate.[5] Nevertheless, the marketing of fresh cows' milk in the major European cities, including Paris, developed rapidly from the beginning of the nineteenth century, primarily in response to the demands of adults for milk to mix in their morning coffee, tea, or chocolate. In the late eighteenth and early nineteenth centuries the milk cows were brought into urban and suburban dairies, where they were kept in stables year round and fed on the new fodder crops. In addition, even before the railroads, rural milk was collected from as far as 60 kilometers away and delivered in Paris when it was still less than twelve hours old. Finally, with the completion of the railroads, farm milk began to take over the urban market. In 1855 more than one-half of the milk consumed in Paris came to the city on the railroad. Throughout the early and mid-nineteenth century dairy farmers and merchants made efforts to keep the milk from spoiling by cooling, boiling, or adding substances to it, but neither farmers, merchants, nor consumers paid any particular attention to its cleanliness.[6]

In the last quarter of the nineteenth century, as doctors began to understand the connection between microorganisms and gastrointestinal disorders in infants, companies began to market evaporated or condensed milk in sealed cans, sterilized milk in sealed bottles, and dried milk a little later. Meanwhile, the modern feeding bottle was being developed, and the adaptation of rubber nipples made this method a reliable alternative to breast-feeding.[7] The first mention of sterilized milk in the annual reports of medical inspectors for wet nurses in the department of the Seine occurred in 1892. At that time some doctors were still uncertain about its benefits, especially in light of the high price of commercially sterilized milk, but others thought nurses could be taught to sterilize milk at home to reduce the cost. By 1896 municipal authorities in several *arrondissements* of Paris and suburban communes lent nurses sterilizing equipment free of charge. By 1899 nearly 20 percent of infants being raised for pay outside their parents' homes on bottled milk were reportedly fed on sterilized milk, which had generally been sterilized by the nurse.[8]

Parallel to the scientific and technological innovations in infant-feeding was the effort to propagate the good news at all levels of society. France was an early focus of the international infant welfare movement, undoubtedly because of the acute concern there with the falling birth rate and slowing rate of population growth. In 1892 the obstetrician Pierre Budin founded his *consultation des nourrissons* at the Charité Hospital in Paris. Mothers who participated were to bring their babies to the hospital for weekly weighings and examinations and to receive medical advice and supplies of sterilized milk, free, in the absence of breast-feeding. Within a few years many other infant dispensaries had opened on the model of Budin's *consultation* or of the very similar private charitable institution called the Goutte de Lait, founded by Dr. Léon Dufour in Fécamp in 1894.[9]

Thus in the mid-1890s all the elements needed for safe, economical, and convenient bottle-feeding of urban babies were present—the bottle, the milk supply, and the advice on how to use them. If the reasons for wet-nursing were solely material or technological, the business should have collapsed in the last decade of the nineteenth century.

Data Collected under the Roussel Law

The data by which these three explanations of the wet-nursing business and its demise are tested were collected as a result of the Roussel Law, adopted by the National Assembly on December 23, 1874. Article I declared that all children under the age of two who were placed with paid nurses or guardians outside their parents' homes were subject to the surveillance of the state, "with the goal of protecting their lives and health." This surveillance was to be exercised by the prefect of police in Paris and by departmental prefects elsewhere, both assisted by medical inspectors to be designated by a central committee appointed by the minister of the interior. The law required both the parents who placed their children and the nurses who took them to register these facts with the local authorities. The central committee was to collect registration data from all the localities in France and publish annually the statistics on infant mortality, particularly for nurslings.[10] Théophile Roussel regarded the system of registration and accounting in infant lives as the principal safeguard created by the law.[11] When finally implemented nationwide, it provided the historian with the first comprehensive view of French wet-nursing, just as the practice was about to disappear.

The picture presented here of French wet-nursing during its final period derives for the most part from two series of reports prepared in execution of the Roussel Law. The first is the remarkable series of annual reports issued by the Prefecture of Police of Paris, concerning all aspects of the law within the department of the Seine (Paris and its suburbs) and stretching from 1880 into the 1930s.[12] These reports cover all infants placed with wet nurses within the department (usually in suburban communes), the police supervision of Parisian placement bureaus for wet nurses, registration and medical inspection of wet nurses brought to Paris by those bureaus, declarations of placements by Parisian parents, and other topics. What makes these reports particularly valuable, in addition to the Prefecture's insatiable appetite for quantitative data, is the remarkable length of the series—over fifty years of unbroken reporting on infant care during a period of crucial changes.

Many parts of the nation, less involved with the wet-nursing business than Paris, were slower than the capital in implementing the Roussel Law.[13] As a result, a fairly complete national accounting of the wet-nursing business and the associated infant mortality was not possible until 1897, twenty-three years after the law prescribed the annual reports. Reports for the years 1897 to 1907 offer valuable information concerning the geographic distribution of infants placed with wet nurses, regional variations in infant-feeding methods, and infant mortality.[14]

Patterns and Trends in the Recourse to Wet-Nursing

In the decade 1897-1907 the total number of infants under two years of age placed with paid nurses or guardians each year in France (that is, the total number admitted each year to state supervision, not the total number under supervision) was declining, from about 88,000 in the beginning of the decade to 79,000 in the end. But the actual number of live births in France was also declining at an alarming rate, so that the new placements each year over this decade constituted a fairly constant proportion of newborns, slightly over 10 percent. Of the approximately 80,000 infants placed with wet nurses each year in France around the turn of the century, about 70 percent were of legitimate birth, placed by their parents. The other 30 percent were illegitimate, generally placed by their unmarried mothers, often with financial assistance from local authorities. Since illegitimate births accounted for only about 9 percent of all births in France at this time, illegitimate infants were proportionately overrepresented among infants placed with wet nurses.

Under the Roussel Law parents were required to register with their mayor the fact that they were placing their infant with a wet nurse. Had this provision of the law been scrupulously observed all over France, it would be possible to map areas in which parents sent their babies away to be nursed and areas in which parents did not. Unfortunately, parental declarations were generally neglected, except in the department of the Seine. There, from 1881 until 1913, declarations of placements by parents amounted to a fairly steady 26 to 29 percent of live births in the department. The infants from the Seine placed with nurses, somewhat over 20,000 a year, constituted about one-quarter of the total number of French infants placed each year, although only one-tenth of French births occurred in the department. After the war, from 1919 to 1928, declarations ran at about 15 percent of live births. See Figure 1.

Within the department of the Seine the differences between the percentages of newborns placed from urban and suburban areas and the differences among the various *arrondissements* of Paris are wide and instructive. In 1889, when parental declarations of placement in the department of the Seine were 29 percent of live births, only 20 percent of infants born in the suburban communes were sent away to be nursed, compared to 31 percent of infants born in Paris proper. Within the city limits the percentage of newborns placed with nurses was as low as 15 percent in peripheral, industrial *arrondissements* (the 19th and 20th) and as high as 45 to 67 percent in the high-rent *arrondissements* of western and especially central Paris (in ascending order, the 16th, 3rd, 7th, 9th, 4th, 2nd, and 1st), where the predominant occupations were in retail trade, artisanal crafts, office work, and domestic service. See Figure 2.

More direct evidence on the occupations of parents who placed their infants with wet nurses is available from several surviving registers in which parental declarations of placement were recorded in the 1880s. The registers come from the 1st, 3rd, and 10th *arrondissements*, which placed between one-third and two-thirds of their newborn infants with paid wet nurses outside the home in these years (Table 12).[15] The fathers, whose names appeared in two-thirds of the entries sampled, were, in the overwhelming

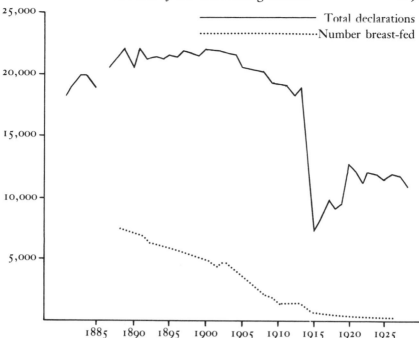

Figure 1.   Declarations of placements from the department of the Seine, 1881–1928.

majority, in lower middle-class occupations. One-third of them worked in miscellaneous skilled crafts, which were usually organized in small shops that both fabricated and sold products directly to the public (hat-makers, jewellers, engravers, but also house painters and sculptors). One-quarter of the fathers were *employés*— office workers and diverse other lower-level salaried employees of government or business (e.g., accountants, a mailman, a meter reader for the gas company). The other major occupational categories for the fathers were retail trade (one-fifth) and personal service and service trades (barbers, valets, waiters—one-tenth). The common features that linked these occupations in late nineteenth-century Paris were the modest income they provided and their location in the older, central quarters of the city, where rents were high and space was scarce. In addition, as many as half of the fathers (craftsmen, retailers, barbers) may have been self-employed. These conditions combined to encourage wives to work,

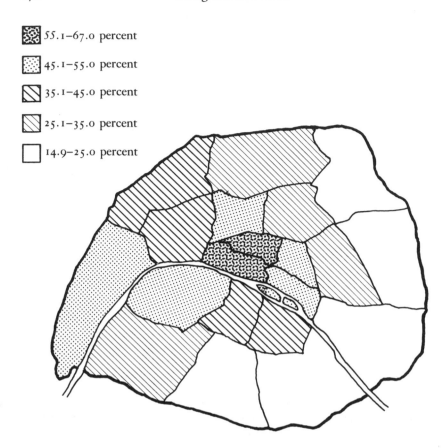

55.1–67.0 percent

45.1–55.0 percent

35.1–45.0 percent

25.1–35.0 percent

14.9–25.0 percent

Figure 2. Proportion of newborns placed from each *arrondissement* of Paris, 1889.

often alongside their husbands, and to send their infants away to be nursed.

About one-third of the sample were unmarried mothers, who worked predominantly in the small workshops of the garment industry, in domestic service, and in various crafts, especially fabricating the luxury or novelty items for which Paris is noted. Because of their low pay and also because they often lived with their employers, these women could not afford to keep their infants at home; the state gave them financial assistance to pay a wet nurse's wages, lest they abandon the infants altogether. Married women also worked in the garment trades and other skilled oc-

Table 12

Occupations of Parisian parents who placed their infants with nurses in the 1880s

Father's Occupations	Number	Percent
Miscellaneous skilled crafts	59	32
Employés	45	24
Retail trade	33	18
Personal service and service trades	19	10
Laborers	8	4
Industrial workers	7	4
Business and finance	7	4
Construction	4	2
Transport	3	2
Total	185	

Mother's Occupations	Number			Percent of total
	Married	Unmarried	Total	
Garment trades	15	26	41	34
Domestic service	7	21	28	23
Miscellaneous skilled crafts	12	11	23	19
Laundering	4	7	11	9
Unspecified day work	2	6	8	7
Employées	2	5	7	6
Industrial workers	1	3	4	3
Total	43	79	122	

Source. George D. Sussman, "The End of the Wet-Nursing Business in France, 1874–1914," *Journal of Family History*, 2 (Fall 1977), 237–58.

cupations, providing an essential supplement to their husbands' incomes. No doubt many other mothers, whose occupations were not recorded, worked beside their husbands, particularly in the retail trades.

Outside of the department of the Seine the origins of infants placed with wet nurses are much more difficult to determine because parents generally neglected the article of the Roussel Law that required them to declare placements of their children. However, at least three urban centers in France, besides Paris, supported significant organized wet-nursing activity around the turn of the century, as indicated by the presence of registered placement

bureaus. The department of the Seine-inférieure, including Rouen,
Le Havre, and smaller textile centers, had five authorized bureaus
in 1892, when some 7,714 infants from the department were reported under state supervision with nurses within the department.
Other infants from the Seine-inférieure were undoubtedly placed
in other departments.[16] In Lyon in 1906 there was a single authorized wet-nursing bureau, which registered 1,940 nurses. Other
infants from Lyon were certainly placed without the intermediary
of the bureau.[17] In 1883, 5,208 or 30.5 percent of the 17,088
infants born in the entire department of the Rhône were placed
with paid nurses outside their homes, and three-quarters of them
were placed outside their native department.[18] The department of
the Bouches-du-Rhône had no fewer than twenty-one authorized
wet-nursing bureaus in 1897, sixteen in Marseille, and five in Aix.
In 1883, when there were 10,758 live births in the city of Marseille,
2,236 infants (20.8 percent of births) were registered as having
been placed with paid nurses outside their homes; 55.1 percent
of these placements were within the department of the Bouches-
du-Rhône. Many placements from Marseille, especially of infants
who were nursed across the border in Piedmont, went unrecorded.[19]

The newer industrial regions of France, like the outlying industrial *arrondissements* of Paris, followed a different pattern from
that of the old urban centers. In a textile town of the Seine-
inférieure a medical inspector appointed under the Roussel Law
wrote, "Here the grandmother raises the children because the
mother works." In another district of the same department the
mill hands placed their small children with retired fellow workers:
"All the infants placed with nurses belong to workers in the spinning mills. The woman only stops working and stays home when
the number of her children is rather high. Necessarily these are
the women who take nurslings, often for modest wages."[20] This
description seems to refer to a day-care arrangement in which
infants were undoubtedly bottle-fed, since it also appears that each
woman looked after several children, her own and outsiders. In
the industrial Pas-de-Calais one fairly typical observation noted
that infants under two years of age were "almost all placed either
with relatives or with friends." In these places, as well as in the
Nord and Vosges, the doctors often expressed regret that such
day-care and unpaid familial arrangements for watching infant

children were not subject to their supervision under the Roussel Law, despite the unhygienic conditions and artificial feeding prevalent in these areas.[21]

It appears, then, that there was no organized wet-nursing in the industrial districts of Normandy, in northern and eastern France, just as there was none in the English industrial districts,[22] despite the extensive employment of women outside the home. Edward Shorter also notes this fact and the reliance of working mothers in the factory districts upon day nurses and hand-feeding. He offers a cultural explanation: "If despite the direst poverty and the sorest temptations to fail in the 'sacrifice test' [that is, to put their own happiness above their children's safety and welfare], proletarian women kept their infants at home, it must have been because their attitudes were already 'modern.' "[23]

Other reasons may be offered for the absence of wet-nursing in the industrial areas. In the first place, these areas only now open to female labor did not inherit a tradition and the institutions of rural wet-nursing, including placement bureaus and the kind of enduring commercial relationship with specific districts in the country that was embodied in the *meneurs* and *meneuses*. Nor did the social and economic arrangements of the new industrial areas give reason for such institutions to develop. In the small family shops so common in older French cities the wife's long unpaid labor was essential to the very operation of the enterprise on which the family income depended. It was difficult or impossible for her to perform both her economic role in the household and her maternal role in the family. In the newly industrialized areas the wife's work was no longer essential to the family income in the same way. The numerous women who did not work in the textile mills were for the most part young and unmarried. They looked upon their work in the mills as peasants' daughters had traditionally looked upon their period of domestic service in other people's homes or farms, as an apprenticeship for marriage and an opportunity to accumulate a dowry.[24] Upon marriage or shortly thereafter, they usually retired from the mills to mind their households and their children. But their households, unlike the traditional working households in such cities as Paris or Lyon, were not units of production for the market and sources of the family's income. Consequently, the wife in these industrial regions—occupying her traditional "place" in the home, but in a home stripped of its productive functions—was not prevented from nursing and caring for her young children.[25]

The Wet Nurses

The infants most commonly placed with wet nurses, then, were born in the central wards of older cities. Their nurses lived in poor, rural, often mountainous or swampy regions, usually at such a distance that their parents could rarely have visited their babies during the year or more they were away. Of 22,000 placements declared by parents from the department of the Seine in 1889, 20,000 were placed outside the department. When an infant was placed outside the parental home for pay, the nurse was required to notify her mayor: this declaration was at the heart of the accounting required by the Roussel Law. These declarations by the nurses enable us to estimate how many infants were placed in each of the eighty-seven departments of France each year. Relating new placements in a department during a specific period to live births in the same department during the same period provides a kind of index of nursing density. Assuming that all wet nurses were really breast-feeding their nurslings—an inaccurate assumption—the theoretical maximal nursing density would be 100 percent, where every recently delivered mother took a nursling for pay. (Wet nurses were not permitted to take more than one infant at a time.) In fact, around the turn of the century the ratio of new placements to births in the various departments ranged from 1 to 50 percent. The major nursing departments—e.g., the twelve departments where new placements with wet nurses numbered over 25 percent of births—were rural departments, with no major cities, no significant industries or mineral resources, generally located at distances of 50 to 200 miles from the great cities of the Seine and Rhône corridors. There were no major nursing departments in either the industrial northern tier of France nor in the agricultural southwest. See Figure 3.

The major series of reports generated by the Roussel Law provide little information about most of the wet nurses other than their department of origin. Wet nurses who were brought to Paris by placement bureaus and a small number who lived in the department of the Seine were required to register with the Prefecture

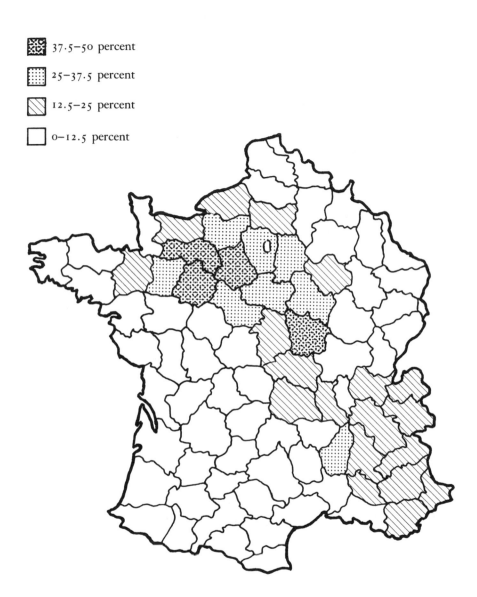

37.5–50 percent

25–37.5 percent

12.5–25 percent

0–12.5 percent

Figure 3. Nursing densities by department in France, 1897–1907, based on an average of data available for 1897, 1898, and 1907.

of Police, so more facts are available about them. There were about twelve placement bureaus in Paris during this period. In the 1880s they provided wet nurses for about half of the Parisian infants placed in the country. The other half of the rural placements were made directly by the parents through personal contacts. The wet-nursing bureaus, all privately owned at this time, also provided live-in nurses for the wealthy, a service that was the most profitable side of the business. From the 1880s until World War I the number of nurses provided annually by the placement bureaus declined steadily, partly because the number of Parisian births was falling and partly because an increasing proportion of placements was being made directly. In the early 1880s about 15,000 wet nurses registered each year with the Prefecture of Police (one-third as live-in nurses, two-thirds as rural nurses). The number of registrants fell to about 7,000 a year in 1913, stabilized at about 3,000 a year through the 1920s, and then trailed off in the Depression, falling below 1,000 in 1936.

The Prefecture of Police attributed this decline to the intensive competition among the bureaus. To attract business the bureaus offered higher and higher fees to doctors and midwives who directed clients their way. But this drove up their costs and, consequently, the fees they charged parents. This effort to attract parents ended up by driving them away, as the parents more and more procured unregistered wet nurses directly to avoid the high fees charged by the bureaus.[26] But this is not the whole story. The earlier history of the wet-nursing business offers parallel trends, where cost was not a factor, which suggest recurring efforts by the nurses to escape administrative supervision.

It is possible to draw a somewhat sketchy profile of the wet nurses registered with the Prefecture of Police of Paris in the late nineteenth and early twentieth centuries. Twenty-four percent of the wet nurses were unmarried mothers, and most of them became live-in nurses in bourgeois homes, where they were often preferred because they were free of family encumbrances (except, of course, for their infants, who were easily placed in the country with poorer nurses).[27] In a survey of 2,000 women who registered as live-in nurses in Paris during the first half of 1895, 62 percent were unmarried. The overwhelming majority of rural wet nurses, however, were married. In 1899, 90 percent of the nurses in Eure-et-

Loir, a major nursing department for the infants of Paris, were married.[28] As for their age, 66 percent of the nurses registered in Paris in 1888 were less than thirty, 24 percent were thirty to thirty-nine, and 9 percent were over thirty-nine. Wet nurses were generally younger than dry nurses, who bottle-fed the infants.

Increasing Incidence of Bottle-Feeding

In the thirty-five to forty years before World War I the proportion of newborn infants placed with wet nurses was unchanged, despite the crucial changes in the knowledge about and the technology of infant-feeding that characterized this period. However, while medical and technological changes did not immediately affect the reliance on wet nurses, they did alter the nature of nursing services that babies received. The reports on the application of the Roussel Law show that increasingly the so-called wet nurses were not breast-feeding but bottle-feeding the infants placed with them. Over the short space of six years, from 1901 to 1907, the proportion of newly placed babies in France reported to be exclusively breast-fed fell from 35 percent to 28 percent. The movement away from breast-feeding was occurring in all parts of France, but the southern half of the country was significantly behind the northern part, in that the highest proportions of breast-fed infants were always reported in the Midi.[29] In 1898 there were thirty-five departments in France that reported over 50 percent of newly placed babies being breast-fed; all but two (both on the Breton peninsula) were located south of the Loire River. In 1907 the number of departments reporting over 50 percent of newly placed babies being breast-fed had fallen to twenty-eight, all but one (in Brittany) in the South. See Figures 4 and 5.

The proportions and timing of the decline in breast-feeding are best observed in the long series of reports from the department of the Seine. Nearly all the infants from the Seine were placed in the northern half of France, where the shift to bottle-feeding occurred earliest. The graph of declarations of placements from the department of the Seine, 1881-1928 (Figure 1), shows a steady erosion dating from at least 1889 of the number of placements with nurses who breast-fed, although the total number of placements changed little before 1914. Already in 1889, when these

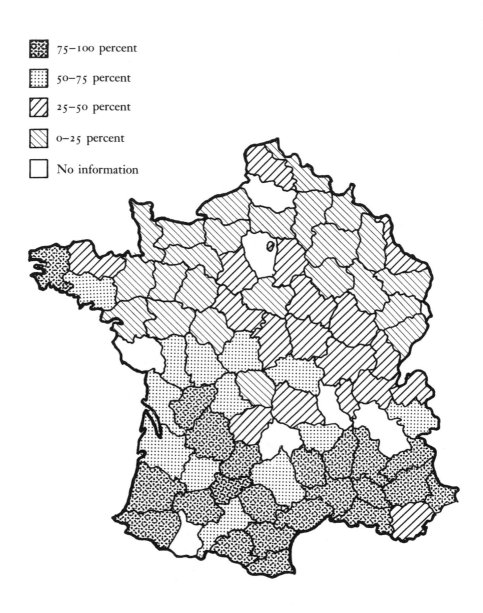

Figure 4.   Proportion of nurslings breast-fed, by department in France, 1898.

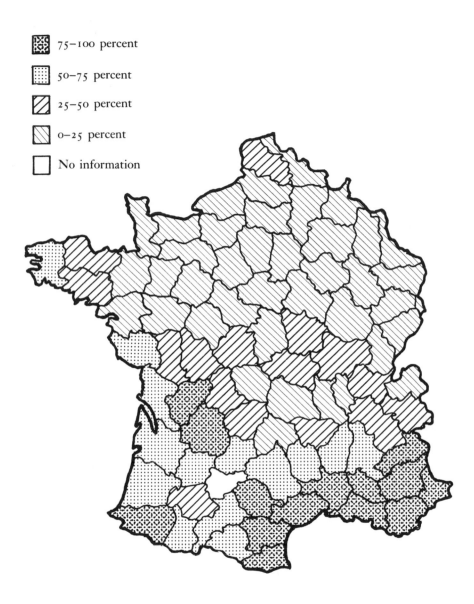

Figure 5. Proportion of nurslings breast-fed, by department in France, 1907.

data began to be collected, only about 34 percent of infants from the Seine placed with wet nurses were being breast-fed. This proportion declined steadily to 7.5 percent in 1913. The volume of the wet-nursing business in this period was unaffected by the change in feeding method. After the war, when the proportion of the newborns placed with wet nurses had fallen, the proportion of nurslings being breast-fed had declined still further to 2 percent or less. The decline in breast-feeding was already significantly advanced and probably irreversible by the mid-1890s, when sterilization technology was first introduced.

In the mid-1880s a medical inspector in the Jura suggested an explanation for the shift from breast-feeding to bottle-feeding in the wet-nursing business. "The pecuniary conditions of placement with a breast-feeding nurse are very onerous for families: thus, a breast-feeding nurse was content a few years ago with 25 or 30 francs a month; and today they easily obtain 60 to 70 francs. That is why families prefer to confide their children to bottle-feeding nurses."[30]

If, indeed, the resort to bottle-feeding was initially an economic necessity for some families, this was no longer the case by the 1890s, at least in Paris. In 1889 the annual report of the Prefecture of Police noted with regret that "not only does artificial feeding continue to be held in esteem, but breast-feeding, putting aside the question of price, is still, on the part of certain people, the object of absurd prejudices." And several local inspectors in the department of the Seine noted in 1893 and 1896 that the cost of breast-feeding nurses had fallen to the level of bottle-feeding nurses, yet the former found it more difficult to find infants than the latter. A change of attitude had occurred, and it was not confined to parents who placed their infants with nurses. The annual report on the application of the Roussel Law in the department of the Seine in 1898 observed that "it is unfortunately certain that this rapid and considerable decline in breast-feeding observed among infants placed with nurses is occurring equally among infants raised in their families." Noting the higher mortality associated with artificial feeding, the report concluded that its spread was "one of the evident causes of the country's depopulation."[31]

Infant Mortality and Wet-Nursing

The framers of the Roussel Law were anxious to discover how the mortality of infants placed with wet nurses compared with the mortality of infants raised at home. This comparison was difficult to make, however, because of the different ages at which infants were placed with or withdrawn from their wet nurses. It would be needlessly complex to follow here the various mathematical operations employed by the French administration to arrive at a measure of mortality that permitted such comparisons. A few statistics suggest a rough idea of the mortality of infants placed with wet nurses in this period and of some conditions affecting that mortality. Of the 173,372 infants placed with wet nurses all over France during the two years 1897 and 1898, 26,105 or 15.1 percent of them died during the period when they were under state supervision, that is, between the time they were placed (at whatever age) and the time they either returned to their parents or reached two years of age. This level of mortality was higher than the general infant mortality in France at this time, even though most infants were placed with nurses only after a few days of life—the most dangerous days—and most returned well before their second birthday.

A significant factor affecting the mortality of the infants placed with wet nurses was the legitimacy or illegitimacy of birth. Whereas 13.0 percent of the legitimate infants placed during 1897 and 1898 died while with their nurses, the mortality of the illegitimate infants was 19.7 percent. This difference may be due to the fact that a slightly higher proportion of legitimate infants was breast-fed. It is also possible that the better paid nurses of legitimate infants provided better care, or that the illegitimate infants were more likely affected by congenital infections, notably syphilis. Another factor affecting mortality was the feeding method employed. The difference between the mortality of breast-fed and bottle-fed infants was diminishing in the latter part of this period and had virtually disappeared by 1905 for infants placed with wet nurses in the department of the Seine and a few years later for infants placed in the provinces. The reason for this development was the declining mortality among bottle-fed infants, which is explained by improvements in the supply of uncontaminated cows' milk and the influence of the infant welfare movement, for which the medical inspectors appointed under the Roussel Law were fervent apostles.

Conclusion

In the period between the passage of the Roussel Law and World War I approximately 80,000 infants a year, or 10 percent of the children born in France, were placed with nurses outside their parents' homes. Thirty percent of the nurslings were illegitimate. Most of the infants came from cities (about 25 percent from the department of the Seine), particularly from the central districts of older cities, where the predominant occupations were retail trade, artisanal crafts, office work, and domestic service. They were placed with nurses in poor, rural departments at substantial distances from home. The total volume of the wet-nursing business remained fairly steady throughout the period from 1874 to 1914, although the role of commercial placement bureaus was declining. Among the infants placed with nurses, and probably among all French infants, breast-feeding was disappearing in all parts of the country, but first in the northern half, even before sterilization of cows' milk began to reduce the mortality of bottle-fed infants.

How, then, did the wet-nursing business end, and what is the explanation for the practice in the first place? It is easy enough to explain its short-run collapse during World War I, when the fighting on French soil interrupted normal commerce between city and country and created acute shortages of transport. The problem is to explain why, after the war, a fairly large proportion of Parisian parents of the working and lower middle class did not resume their prewar pattern of infant-feeding, as they had after an earlier interruption in the wet-nursing business during the siege and revolt of 1870-71. The appropriate historical parallel might be the permanent abandonment of rural wet-nursing by the Parisian bourgeoisie in the midst of the French Revolution.

Three explanations of wet-nursing have been considered in this book, and the one that best describes the end of the wet-nursing business is the one that relies on socioeconomic changes. The practice of rural wet-nursing did not trail off gradually over the eighteenth and nineteenth centuries, as the cultural explanation suggested it should have. In Paris at least it appears to have declined in two major steps, first during the French Revolution and then during World War I. Nor did the incidence of wet-nursing fall abruptly in the 1890s, when the technological explanation suggested it should have. The time when the great decline in wet-nursing did occur—in the immediate aftermath of World War I—was also the time of a significant decline in female employment, particularly of mothers of young children.

If the socioeconomic hypothesis seems best suited to explain the pattern and timing of the end of the wet-nursing business in France, the cultural and technological hypotheses cannot be totally discarded. Here is how I understand the popular phase in the history of wet-nursing. French cities grew rapidly in the late eighteenth and early nineteenth centuries because of the rural population explosion. Industrialization, however, occurred more slowly in France than in other West European nations. This combination of rapid urbanization and slow industrialization produced the special conditions existing in many French cities: high rents and low incomes for the working class and the persistence of, indeed the expansion of, the traditional household, which was a small unit of production for the market as well as the setting of family life. These conditions, in turn, imposed work roles on wives, and increasing numbers of women were unable to suckle and care for their very young children. Since this pre-industrial urban growth occurred before the development of safe methods of artificial infant-feeding and, for the most part, before the decline of popular fertility, it was responsible for a crisis in infant-feeding that inevitably took its toll in infant lives. Wet-nursing, then, was the particular solution to the problem of feeding the infant children of working mothers living in older French cities. In adopting wet-nursing, these working families were merely following the example of first the nobility and then the professional and skilled artisan classes, who, for a century or more and for different reasons, had put their children out to nurse.

There were always difficulties with wet-nursing as a solution to the problem of infant-feeding for working mothers in the nineteenth century, and these difficulties undoubtedly contributed to its eventual demise. In the first place, human milk being a scarce commodity, wet-nursing was expensive and became ever more so as the cities grew and the rural population declined. Even among rural nurses, cost was the initial reason for the replacement of breast-feeding by bottle-feeding, which was well advanced before the appearance of sterilized cows' milk. The new technology did not cause a change in the method of infant-feeding; rather, it saved infant lives from the deadly effects of a preexisting, economically and socially determined feeding pattern. The second difficulty with wet-nursing was the developing hostility on the part of opinion-makers since the late eighteenth century to the idea of sending infants away from home to be raised for their first year or more by unknown, poor, ignorant peasant women. From the 1860s, for humanitarian and nationalistic reasons, the middle and upper classes began to impose these feelings on the urban populace through such efforts as the Sociétés protectrices de l'enfance, the Roussel Law, and the infant welfare movement.[32] However, neither the scarcity and mounting cost of obtaining wet nurses who would breast-feed infants nor the hostility of opinion-leaders toward wet-nursing ended the wet-nursing business. Popular wet-nursing adapted to bottle-feeding and administrative regulation and survived until 1914.

World War I, by interrupting the wet-nursing business temporarily, undoubtedly demonstrated to some working families how unnecessary distant rural wet-nursing was, since abundant and healthful supplies of infant food had become available in the cities. After the war, too, fewer mothers of young children were working. And economic and cultural changes affected the supply of wet nurses, just as they affected the supply of women willing to be domestic servants in other people's houses: there were simply fewer peasant women desiring to undertake either task.

By the early twentieth century the wet-nursing business had become an insoluble substance in French society. World War I was the precipitant. The chemical reaction registered in the columns of data from the Roussel Law during the war years was, in fact, prepared over two centuries. The cultural, social, and technological changes responsible for the end of the wet-nursing business began to develop in the eighteenth century almost simultaneously with the emergence of wet-nursing as a general practice of urban society. Neither traditional nor modern, wet-nursing was part of the transition that French society passed through on its way to becoming industrialized.

Notes

1. Shorter, *Modern Family*, ch. 5.
2. H. Nolleau, "Les femmes dans la population active de 1856 à 1954," *Économie et politique* (Paris), 75 (Oct. 1960), 2–21.
3. A few of the principal articles are Rondo Cameron, "Economic Growth and Stagnation in France, 1815–1914," *Journal of Modern History*, 30 (Mar. 1958), 1–13; S. B. Clough, "Retardative Factors in French Economic Development in the Nineteenth and Twentieth Centuries," *Journal of Economic History*, 6 (1946), Supplement, 91–102; François Crouzet, "England and France in the Eighteenth Century: A Comparative Analysis of Two Economic Growths," in *Revolutions, 1775–1830*, ed. by Merryn Williams (Baltimore: Penguin, 1971), 131–66; François Crouzet, "French Economic Growth in the Nineteenth Century," *History*, 59 (June 1974), 167–79; David S. Landes, "French Entrepreneurship and Industrial Growth in the Nineteenth Century," *Journal of Economic History*, 9 (1949), 45–61.
4. Evelyne Sullerot, *Histoire et sociologie du travail féminin, essai* (N.p.: Éditions Gonthier, 1968), 133. Sullerot uses census figures unadjusted for the undercounting of female workers in the agricultural sector. On this basis she came up with the list of Western countries, in declining order of female workers as a proportion of the total female population: Austria, France, Denmark, Italy, Germany, Norway, Belgium, Switzerland, Sweden, Hungary, Scotland, England, Ireland, Netherlands, the United States, Spain, and Russia.
5. See, for example, Donné, *Conseils aux mères*, ch. 4, and Eugène Bouchut, *Hygiène de la première enfance, comprenant les lois organiques du mariage, les soins de la grossesse, l'allaitement maternel, le choix des nourrices, le sevrage, le régime, l'exercice et la mortalité de la première enfance* (Paris: J.-B. Baillière & fils, 1862), bk. 9.
6. Barruel, "Considérations sur le lait vendu à Paris comme substance alimentaire," *Annales d'hygiène publique et de médecine légale*, 1 (1829), 404–5; Beaver, "Population, Infant Mortality and Milk," 245–46; Armand Husson, *Les consommations de Paris* (Paris, 1856), 274–95; T. A. Quevenne, "Mémoire sur le lait," *Annales d'hygiène publique et de médecine légale*, 26 (1841), 92–99; E. H. Whetham, "The London Milk Trade, 1860–1900," *Economic History Review*, 2nd ser., 17 (1964), 369–75.

7. Ian G. Wickes, "A History of Infant Feeding," *Archives of Disease in Childhood*, 28 (1953), 419–21.

8. APP, D B/66, Préfecture de Police, *Protection des enfants du bas âge*, reports of 1892, 1896, 1899.

9. G. F. McCleary, *The Early History of the Infant Welfare Movement* (London: H. K. Lewis & Co., 1933), ch. 3. See also the suggestive insights on the infant welfare movement in France in Boltanski, *Prime éducation et morale de classe*, and Donzelot, *La police des familles*, especially 33–34.

10. Duvergier and Duvergier, *Collection complète des lois*, 461–66.

11. Théophile Roussel, *Rapport concernant l'application de la loi du 23 décembre 1874, présenté à M. le Ministre de l'intérieur, au nom du Comité supérieur de protection des enfants du premier âge* (Paris: Imprimerie du Journal officiel, 1882), 12.

12. APP, D B/65–68. Préfecture de Police, *Protection des enfants du premier âge, rapports annuels, années 1881–1936.*

13. Théophile Roussel, *Rapport concernant l'application de la loi du 23 décembre 1874, présenté à Monsieur le Ministre de l'intérieur, au nom du Comité* . . . (Paris: A. Wittersheim, 1880); Roussel, *Rapport* (1882); [Waldeck-Rousseau], *Rapport adressé au Président de la République sur l'exécution de la loi du 23 décembre 1874 relative à la protection du premier âge* (Paris: Imprimerie des Journaux officiels, 1886); Paul Bucquet, *Rapport concernant l'application de la loi du 23 décembre 1874, présenté à M. le Ministre de l'intérieur, au nom du Comité supérieur de protection des enfants du premier âge* (Paris: Imprimerie des Journaux officiels, 1888).

14. AN, AD XIX[1] 156, Ministère de l'Intérieur, Bureau des Services de l'Enfance, *Statistique du Service de la Protection des Enfants du Premier Age* (1897–1907). The data presented in the remainder of this chapter derive from these reports of the ministry of the interior or the annual reports of the Prefecture of Police, cited in note 12, unless any other source is specifically cited.

15. AD Paris, [x]V bis 1 Q[7], [x]V bis 3 Q[7], [x]V bis 10 Q[7], Registres des déclarations de placement des enfants en nourrice, en sevrage ou en garde. I collected information from a sample of 289 entries divided approximately equally among three registers: no. 5 from the 1st *arrondissement* (1884–85), no. 4 from the 3rd *arrondissement* (1883–84), and no. 1 from the 10th *arrondissement* (1879–80). I designed the occupational classifications that I employ in Table 12 for these specific data. For a useful discussion of occupational classification for Paris in the late nineteenth century, see Jacques Rougerie, "Belle-

ville," in *Les élections de 1869, études*, ed. by Louis Girard (Paris: Librairie Marcel Rivière et Cie., 1960), 3–36.

16. Département de la Seine-inférieure, *Rapport sur le service de la Protection des enfants du premier âge pendant l'année 1892 présenté à M. le Préfet* (Rouen: Imprimerie de Esperance Cagniard, 1893), 4, 28.

17. AN, AD XIX^I 152 bis, Département du Rhône, *Protection des enfants du premier âge, exercice 1906* (Lyon, 1907), 82–83.

18. [Waldeck-Rousseau], *Rapport adressé au Président*, 94.

19. *Ibid.*, 44, and Dr. Mazade, *Département des Bouches-du-Rhône. Assistance Publique . . . 2e. Protection du premier âge . . . rapport . . . (Année 1897)* (Marseille: Imprimerie meridionale, 1898), 101, 210.

20. AN, AD XIX^I 152, Département de la Seine-inférieure, *Rapport sur le service de la protection des enfants du premier âge pendant l'année 1905, présenté à M. le Préfet par l'Inspecteur départemental* (Rouen: Imprimerie Cagniard, 1906), 61, 66.

21. [Waldeck-Rousseau], *Rapport adressé au Président*, 88, 91, 130.

22. Margaret Hewitt, *Wives and Mothers in Victorian Industry* (London: Rockliff, 1958), and Michael Anderson, *Family Structure in Nineteenth Century Lancashire* (Cambridge: Cambridge University Press, 1971), 71–74.

23. Shorter, *Modern Family*, 177.

24. Hufton, *The Poor in Eighteenth-Century France*, 25–33, and Scott and Tilly, "Women's Work and the Family in Nineteenth-Century Europe," 36–64.

25. Neil J. Smelser, "Sociological History: The Industrial Revolution and the British Working-Class Family," *Journal of Social History*, 1 (1967), 17–35, and Sullerot, *Histoire et sociologie du travail féminin*, ch. 1.

26. APP, D B/65, Préfecture de Police, *Protection des enfants du bas âge*, report of 1887, pp. 80, 82.

27. Donné, *Conseils aux mères*, 81–83.

28. Dr. Barthès, *Protection des enfants du premier âge en Eure-et-Loir pendant l'année 1899* (Paris: Imprimerie nationale, 1901), 6.

29. For further discussion of regional differences in infant-feeding customs, see Cathérine Rollet, "Allaitement, mise en nourrice et mortalité infantile en France à la fin du XIXe siècle," *Population*, 33 (1978), 1189–1203, and J. Knodel and E. van de Walle, "Breast feeding, fertility and infant mortality," *Population Studies*, 21 (Sept. 1967), 109–31.

30. Quoted in [Waldeck-Rousseau]. *Rapport adressé au Président*, 67.

31. APP, D B/65–66, Préfecture de Police, *Protection des enfants du premier*

âge, report of 1889, p. 53; report of 1893, p. 103; report of 1896, p. 100; report of 1898, p. 102.

32. André Armengaud, "L'attitude de la société à l'égard de l'enfant au XIXe siècle," *Annales de démographie historique, 1973* (Paris-The Hague: Mouton, 1973), 303–12.

List of Sources

ARCHIVAL MATERIAL

Archives de l'Assistance publique, Paris.
   224. Administration générale des hôpitaux, hospices et secours de
      la Ville de Paris. Direction des Nourrices. Service extérieur.
      Payement des mois de nourrices et dépenses accessoires. Contrôle
      du Bureau.
   283. Registre pour Anne Françoise Yon Delaunay, l'une des quatres
      Recommandaresses de la Ville et fauxbourgs de Paris, juillet
      1732–mai 1735.
   592. Direction des Nourrices.
   709. Direction des Nourrices.
Archives communales de Strasbourg.
      Fonds de Police, 85-478. Proposal to create a wet-nursing bureau
      in Strasbourg, 1822–25.
Archives départementales de l'Eure.
      E 3234. Livre de raison de Claude Le Doulx, conseiller au Parlement
      de Paris (1665–1712).
      II F 4097. Certificats de renvoi pour les nourrices, 1729–93, and
      other documents related to wet-nursing.
Archives départementales de l'Eure, Archives communales de Beaubray.
      5 Q 4. Direction générale des nourrices, 1807–35.
Archives départementales de l'Eure, Archives communales d'Houlbec-
Cocherel.
      1 Q 1. Nourrices: correspondance de la direction du bureau des
      nourrices avec le maire d'Houlbec; certificat de renvoi pour les
      nourrices.
Archives départementales de l'Eure, Archives communales de Verneuil.
      5 Q 7. Direction générale des nourrices: correspondance concernant
      les enfants décédés chez les nourrices, la surveillance des en-
      fants, an VII-1807.
      5 Q 9. Certificats de renvoi pour les nourrices, an VI-1807.

Archives départementales de l'Oise, Archives communales de Milly-sur-Thérain.

    13 Q 1. Protection du premier âge et de l'enfance, nourrices, enfants assistés, 1798–1879.

Archives départementales de Paris.

    3 AZ 140. Letter from Bailly to Pastoret, June 1, 1791.

    ^{x}V bis 1 Q^7, ^{x}V bis 3 Q^7, ^{x}V bis 10 Q^7. Registres des déclarations de placement des enfants en nourrice, en sevrage ou en garde, 1er, 3e, et 10e arrondissements, 1878–94.

Archives départementales de Seine-et-Oise.

    E 432, E 434. Lettres d'Angélique-Charlotte de Mackau à son mari, le marquis de Bombelles, 1777–83.

    E 2644. Lettres addressées à Nicod, horloger, 1781–86.

Archives nationales, Paris.

    F^{4*} 32. État général des débiteurs de mois de nourrices, dont les enfants leur ont été rendus ou sont décédés chez leurs nourrices, avant l'époque du 15 septembre 1791, et contre lesquels il y a des contraintes par corps décernées.

    F^{15} 1937. Bureau des nourrices, an IX-1820.

    H 1461. Projets divers: bureaux des nourrices, 1753.

    Y 9510–9511. Minutes de sentences contre les parents qui ne payaient pas les mois de nourrices de leurs enfants, 1723–1775.

    Y 13,359–13,401^A. Papers of Grimperel (Michel-Martin), Commissaire au Châtelet, 1730–74.

    Y 14,045–14,075. Papers of Aubert (Joseph), Commissaire au Châtelet, 1708–49.

    Y 14,787–14,838. Papers of Mouricault (Thomas), Commissaire au Châtelet, 1739–89.

    AD XIV 9. Nourrices, 1789–1815.

    AD XIX^I 152. Département de la Seine-inférieure. *Rapport sur le service de la protection des enfants du premier âge pendant l'année 1905, présenté à M. le Préfet par l'inspecteur départemental.* Rouen: Imprimerie Cagniard, 1906.

    AD XIX^I 152 bis. Département du Rhône. *Protection des enfants du premier âge, exercice 1906.* Lyon: Imprimeries réunies, 1907.

    AD XIX^I 156. Ministre de l'Intérieur, Bureau des Services de l'Enfance. Statistique du Service de la Protecction des Enfants du Premier Age, 1897–1907.

Archives de la Préfecture de Police, Paris.

    D B/61. Protection des enfants du premier âge, réglementation.

    D B/63. Protection des enfants du premier âge. Documents parlementaires.

D B/65–68. Préfecture de Police. Protection des enfants du premier âge. Rapports annuels. Années 1881–1936.

Bibliothèque de l'Arsenal, Paris. Archives de la Bastille.

    11,064. Dossier Morel (Blaise), 1729.

    11,070. Dossier Royer (Marie), 1729.

    11,149. Dossier Housseau (Michelle), 1731.

    11,322. Dossier Gabreuse & Macré, 1736.

Bibliothèque nationale, Paris.

    Imprimés, B 2298. Collection of printed diocesan statutes.

    Collection Joly de Fleury, 1304. Prisonniers pour dettes, Compagnie pour leur délivrance.

    Collection Joly de Fleury, 2425. Nourrices, Code des nourrices, recueil de déclarations, d'arrêts et d'ordonnances, formé en 1781, correspondance administrative.

    Manuscrits français, 14,300. Extraits des lettres écrites par les curés de l'arrondissement des nourrices à M. de Sartine, Conseiller d'État Lieutenant général de Police de la Ville de Paris à l'occasion de son nouvel établissement concernant les nourrices et observations des directeurs aux reflexions contenues aux dits extraits.

    Manuscrits français, 21,800, fols. 64–116. Police ordinances, court judgments, etc., related to wet-nursing in Paris, early eighteenth century.

    Nouvelles acquisitions françaises, 22,746. Papiers du chirurgien Jacques Tenon (1724–1816).

PRINTED PRIMARY SOURCES

Albis de Belbèze, Le conseiller et la comtesse d'. *Une famille de parlementaires toulousains à la fin de l'Ancien Régime, correspondance du Conseiller et de la Comtesse d'Albis de Belbèze (1783–1785)*. Edited by Auguste Puis. Paris: Edouard Champion, 1913.

Bailly, E. *Les vacances d'un accoucheur. Voyage au pays des nourrices. Dix jours d'automne dans le Morvan en 1881*. Paris: Imprimerie de A. Hennayer, 1882.

Balzac, Honoré de. *Le curé de village. La comédie humaine*. Bibliothèque de la Pléiade. Vol. 8. Paris: Éditions Gallimard, 1949.

Barruel. "Considérations sur le lait vendu à Paris comme substance alimentaire." *Annales d'hygiène publique et de médecine légale*, 1 (1829), 404–19.

Barthès, Dr. *Protection des enfants du premier âge en Eure-et-Loir pendant l'année 1899*. Paris: Imprimerie nationale, 1901.

Bermingham, Michael. *Manière de bien nourrir et soigner les enfans nouveaux-nés.* Paris: Barrois, 1750.

Bertillon, [Louis-Adolphe]. *La démographie figurée de la France.* Paris: Masson, 1874.

Bloch, Camille, and Tuetey, Alexandre, eds. *Procès-verbaux et rapports du Comité de Mendicité de la Constituante, 1790–1791.* Paris: Imprimerie nationale, 1911.

Bouchut, Eugène. *Hygiène de la première enfance, comprenant les lois organiques du mariage, les soins de la grossesse, l'allaitement maternel, le choix des nourrices, le sevrage, le régime, l'exercice et la mortalité de la première enfance* (Paris: J.-B. Baillière & fils, 1862), bk. 9.

Boudet, Félix-Henri. *Coup d'oeil sur l'origine et les oeuvres de la Société protectrice de l'enfance.* Paris: Imprimerie de F. Malteste, 1869.

Boys de Loury, Dr. "Mémoire sur les modifications à apporter dans le service de l'administration des nourrices." *Annales d'hygiène publique et de médecine légale,* 27 (1842), 5–35.

Bringuier. "Étude sur l'hygiène de l'enfance dans le département de l'Hérault suivie d'une statistique médicale des mort-nés." In Académie de Médecine, *Recueil de mémoires publiées par la Commission permanente de l'hygiène de l'enfance,* Vol. 1, 1st fascicule (1875), 17–32.

Brochard, André-Théodore. *De la mortalité des nourrissons en France, spécialement dans l'arrondissement de Nogent-le-Retrou (Eure-et-Loir).* Paris: J.-B. Baillière et fils, 1866.

———. *De l'industrie des nourrices dans la ville de Bordeaux, conseils aux jeunes mères.* Bordeaux: Féret, 1867.

Bucquet, Paul. *Rapport concernant l'application de la loi du 23 décembre 1874, présenté à M. le ministre de l'intérieur, au nom du Comité supérieur de protection des enfants du premier âge.* Paris: Imprimerie des Journaux officiels, 1888.

Bulletin de l'Académie impériale de médecine, Vols. 31–35 (1865–70).

"Une circulaire sur les nourrices (XVIIIᵉ siècle)." *Bulletin de la Société française d'histoire de la médecine,* 18 (1924), 405–6.

[Clinton, Elizabeth]. *The Countesse of Lincolnes Nurserie.* Oxford: John Lichfield & James Short, 1622.

Le Code des nourrices, ou recueil des Déclarations du Roi, Arrêts du Parlement, Ordonnances et Sentences de Police concernant les nourrices, les recommandaresses et les meneurs. Paris: P. D. Pierres, 1781.

Couillard. "Résumé d'une étude statistique et géologique sur le canton d'Issoire (Puy-de-Dôme)." In Académie de Médecine, *Recueil de mémoires publiées par la Commission permanente de l'hygiène de l'enfance,* Vol. 1, 1st fascicule (1875), 79–83.

Decrusy, Isambert, and Jourdan. *Recueil général des anciennes lois françaises.* Vol. 4. Paris: Belin-le-Prieur & Verdière, n.d.

Delore. "Nourrice" and "Nourrissons." *Dictionnaire encyclopédique des sciences médicales.* Edited by A. Dechambre. 2nd ser. Vol. 13.

Deparcieux, [Antoine]. *Essai sur les probabilités de la durée de la vie humaine.* Paris, 1746.

Desgenettes, René Nicolas Dufriche, Baron. *Souvenirs de la fin du XVIIIe siècle et du commencement du XIXe, ou mémoires de R. D. G.* Vol. 1. Paris: Firmin Didot Frères, 1835–36.

Devilliers, Charles. *Rapport de la commission de l'hygiène de l'enfance.* Paris: Imprimerie de E. Martinet, 1872.

Dionis, P. *Traité général des accounchemens . . .* Paris, 1718.

Donné, Alfred. *Conseils aux mères sur la manière d'élever les enfans nouveau-nés, ou de l'éducation physique des enfans du premier âge.* Paris: J.-B. Baillière, 1842.

Duvergier, J. B., and Duvergier, J. *Collection complète des lois, décrets, ordonnances, règlements et avis du Conseil d'État.* Vol. 74. Paris, 1874.

Flaubert, Gustave. *Madame Bovary.* Translated by Max Aveling. New York: Universal Library, n.d.

Framboisier de Beaunay. *Instructions utiles à MM. les curés, vicaires ou desservans des villes, bourgs et paroisses où il y a des nourrissons de Paris, ainsi qu'à MM. les médecins ou chirurgiens inspecteurs, et aux meneurs et meneuses.* Paris, 1776.

Froissard-Broissia. "Livre de raison de la famille de Froissard-Broissia de 1532 à 1701." *Mémoires de la Société d'émulation du Jura,* 4th ser., 2 (1886), 33–105.

Gardane, J. J. *Détail de la nouvelle direction du Bureau des Nourrices de Paris.* Paris, 1775.

Gédéon. *Les nourrices.* Paris: A. de Vresse [1866?].

Genlis, Madame la comtesse de. "Allaitement." *Dictionnaire critique et raisonné des étiquettes de la Cour . . .* Vol. 1. Paris, 1818.

Gérando, J.-M. de. *De la bienfaisance publique.* Paris: Renouard, 1839.

Gibert. "Étude de statistique sur la mortalité des jeunes enfants à Marseille et questions relatives à la conservation des nouveau-nés." In Académie de Médecine, *Recueil de mémoires publiées par la Commission permanente de l'hygiène de l'enfance,* Vol. 1, 1st fascicule (1875), 51–77.

[Gilibert, Jean-Emmanuel]. "Dissertation sur la dépopulation causée par les vices, les préjugés et les erreurs des nourrices mercenaires . . ." *Les chefs d'oeuvres de Monsieur de Sauvages.* Edited by J. E. G. Vol. 2. Lyon, 1770.

Hamp, Pierre. "Nounou." *Gens.* Paris: Éditions de la nouvelle revue française, 1917.

Héroard, Jean. *Journal de Jean Héroard sur l'enfance et la jeunesse de Louis XIII (1601–1628), extrait des manuscrits originaux.* Edited by Eud. Soulié and Ed. de Barthélemy. Paris: Firmin-Didot frères, fils et Cie., 1868.

Hugo, Victor. *Oeuvres complètes.* Edited by Jean Massin. Tome II, vol. 2. Paris: Le Club français du livre, 1970.

Husson, Armand. *Les consommations de Paris.* Paris, 1856.

Imbert, F. *Des crèches et de l'allaitement maternel, lettre au docteur Barrier.* Paris and Lyon, 1847.

Lagneau, Gustave. *Mortalité des enfants nés dans le département de la Seine.* Paris: G. Masson, 1873.

Lefort, Léon. "La mortalité des enfants et de l'industrie des nourrices en France." *Revue des deux mondes*, 86 (Mar. 15, 1870), 363–91.

LeNoir, [Jean-Charles-Pierre]. *Détail sur quelques établissemens de la ville de Paris, demandé par sa majesté impériale la reine de Hongrie . . . .* Paris, 1780.

Le Rebours, Marie Angélique (Anel). *Avis aux mères qui veulent nourrir leurs enfans.* 2nd ed. Paris: P. F. Didot, le jeune, 1770.

Levainville, Capitaine J. *Le Morvan: étude de géographie humaine.* Paris: Librairie Armand Colin, 1909.

L'Oisel, Antoine. *Memoires des pays, villes, comté et comtes, evesché et evesques, pairrie, commune et personnes de renom de Beauvais et Beauvaisis.* Paris, 1617.

Marlet. *Nouvaux tableaux de Paris.* Paris, 1821 (?).

Martange, Le Général-Major de. *Correspondance inédite du Général-Major de Martange, aide de camp du Prince Xavier de Saxe, Lieutenant Général des Armées (1756–1782).* [Edited by Charles Bréard]. Paris: A. Picard et fils, 1898.

Mayer, Alexandre. *De la création d'une société protectrice de l'enfance pour l'amélioration de l'espèce humaine par l'éducation du premier âge.* Paris: Librairie des sciences sociales, 1865.

————. *De la mortalité excessive du premier âge en France considérée comme cause de dépopulation et des moyens d'y remédier.* Paris: J.-B. Baillière, 1873.

————. *Des moyens pratiques de ramener à ses limites naturelles la mortalité du premier âge en France, mémoire.* Paris: Imprimerie de F. Malteste, 1869.

————. *Projet de loi et de règlement concernant la protection des enfants placés en nourrice.* Paris: Imprimerie de F. Malteste, 1870.

Mazade, Dr. *Département des Bouches-du-Rhône. Assistance publique. . . 2ᶜ.*

Protection du premier âge . . . rapport . . . Année 1897. Marseille: Imprimerie méridionale, 1898.

Mercier, Charles. *Les Petits-Paris, considérations sociologiques relatives à l'hygiène infantile.* Paris: G. Steinheil, 1894.

[Mercier, Louis-Sébastien]. *Tableau de Paris.* 8 vols. New edition. Amsterdam, 1782–83.

Miranda, M. *Paris.—Scènes de moeurs.—À la porte d'un bureau de nourrices. Le monde illustré, journal hebdomadaire* (November 7, 1874), p. 300.

Monot, Charles. *De l'industrie des nourrices et de la mortalité des petits enfants.* Paris: A. Faure, 1867.

Ordonnances synodales du diocèse de Soissons. Soissons, 1769.

Piarron de Chamousset, [Claude-Humbert]. *Deux Mémoires: le premier, sur la conservation des enfans, et une destination avantageuse des enfans trouvés . . .* Paris, 1756.

Prost de Royer, Antoine-François. *Mémoire sur la conservation des enfants.* Lyon: Aimé Delaroche, 1778.

Quevenne, T. A. "Mémoire sur le lait," "Deuxième mémoire sur le lait," and "Falsifications du lait." *Annales d'hygiène publique et de médecine légale,* 26 (1841), 5–125 and 257–380, and 27, 1st Part (1842), 241–86.

Ramazzini, Bernardino. *Diseases of Workers.* Translated by Wilmer Cave Wright. New York: Hafner Publishing Co., 1964.

"Rapport sur le Bureau de la Location et de la Direction des Nourrices." In *Rapports au Conseil général des Hospices, sur les hôpitaux et hospices, les secours à domicile, la Direction des Nourrices.* Paris, fructidor an XI.

Règlemens de la compagnie de messieurs qui travaillent à la délivrance des pauvres prisonniers pour dettes dans toutes les prisons. Paris: de Butard, 1774.

[Rétif de la Bretonne]. *Les contemporaines, ou avantures des plus jolies femmes de l'âge présent.* Volume 6. Leipzig, 1780.

Rhône, Département du. *Recueil des actes administratifs du Département du Rhône, année 1853.* Lyon, 1853.

Roland, Jeanne-Marie Phlipon de. "Avis à ma fille, en âge et dans le cas de devenir mère." *Oeuvres de J. M. Ph. Roland, femme de l'ex-ministre de l'intérieur.* Edited by L. A. Champagneux. Volume I. Paris: Bidault, an VIII.

———. *Lettres de Madame Roland. 1780–1787.* Edited by Claude Perroud. Vol. 1. Paris: Imprimerie nationale, 1900–15.

———. *Mémoires de Madame Roland.* Edited by Berville and Barrière. 2nd ed. Paris, 1821.

Rousseau, Jean Jacques. *Émile.* Translated by Barbara Foxley. Everyman's Library. New York: Dutton, 1911.

Roussel, Jean-Baptiste-Victor-Théophile. *Assemblée nationale. Année 1874. Annexe du procès-verbal de la séance du 9 juin 1874. Rapport fait, au nom de la commission chargée d'examiner la proposition de loi de M. Théophile Roussel, relative à la protection des enfants du premier âge et en particulier des nourrissons.* Versailles: Imprimerie de Cerf et fils, 1874.

————. *Candidature à l'Académie de médecine. Titres et travaux scientifiques du Dr. Théophile Roussel.* Paris: Imprimerie de E. Martinet, 1868.

————. *Rapport concernant l'application de la loi du 23 décembre 1874, présenté à M. le Ministre de l'intérieur, au nom du Comité supérieur de protection des enfants du premier âge.* Paris: Imprimerie du Journal officiel, 1882.

————. *Rapport concernant l'application de la loi du 23 décembre 1874, présenté à M. le Ministre de l'intérieur, au nom du Comité . . .* Paris: A. Wittersheim, 1880.

Roze de l'Épinoy, Dr. *Avis aux mères qui veulent allaiter . . .* Paris: P. F. Didot, 1785.

Seine, Département de la. *Recherches statistiques sur la ville de Paris et le département de la Seine, Année 1823.* 2nd ed. Paris: Imprimerie royale, 1834.

Seine-inférieure, Département de la. *Rapport sur le service de la Protection des enfants du premier âge pendant l'année 1892 présenté à M. le Préfet.* Rouen: Imprimerie de Esperance Cagniard, 1893.

Stahl, P.-J. *Mon petit frère, ou une visite à la nourrice.* Illustrated by E. Valton. Paris: J. Hetzel et Cie., [1876?].

Talleyrand. *Mémoires du Prince de Talleyrand.* Edited by the duc de Broglie. Paris, 1891.

Tortat, Gaston, ed. *Un livre de raison au XVIIe siècle: journal de Samuel Robert, lieutenant particulier en l'élection de Saintes, 1639–1668.* Pons: Imprimerie de Noel Texier, 1883.

Villermé, Louis-René. "De la distribution par mois des conceptions et des naissances de l'homme." *Annales d'hygiène publique et de médecine légale,* 5, Part I (1831), 55–155.

————. *Tableau de l'état physique et moral des ouvriers employés dans les manufactures de coton, de laine et de soie.* Vol. 1. Paris: J. Renouard, 1840.

[Waldeck-Rousseau.] *Rapport adressé au Président de la République sur l'exécution de la loi du 23 décembre 1874 relative à la protection du premier âge.* Paris: Imprimerie des Journaux officiels, 1886.

Zola, Émile. *Les quatre évangiles, Fécondité.* Paris, 1899.

SECONDARY WORKS

Anderson, Michael. *Family Structure in Nineteenth Century Lancashire.* Cambridge: Cambridge University Press, 1971.

Ariès, Philippe. *L'enfant et la vie familiale sous l'ancien régime*. Paris: Librairie Plon, 1960.

Armengaud, André. "L'attitude de la société à l'égard de l'enfant au XIXe siècle." *Annales de démographie historique, 1973*. Paris-The Hague: Mouton, 1973.

———. "Les nourrices du Morvan au XIXe siècle." *Études et chroniques de démographie historique, 1964*. Paris, 1965.

Balandra, Pierre-Louis-Paul. *Les nourrices des rois dans l'ancienne France*. Paris: Librairie médicale Marcel Vigné, 1936.

Bardet, Jean-Pierre. "Enfants abandonnés et enfants assistés à Rouen dans la seconde moîtié du XVIIIe siècle." *Hommage à Marcel Reinhard. Sur la population française au XVIIIe et au XIXe siècles*. Paris: Société de démographie historique, 1973.

Beaver, M. W. "Population, Infant Mortality and Milk." *Population Studies*, 27 (July 1973), 243–54.

Bezucha, Robert J. *The Lyon Uprising of 1834: Social and Political Conflict in the Early July Monarchy*. Cambridge, Mass.: Harvard University Press, 1974.

Bideau, Alain. "L'envoi des jeunes enfants en nourrice. L'exemple d'une petite ville: Thoissey-en-Dombes, 1740–1840." *Hommage à Marcel Reinhard. Sur la population française au XVIIIe et au XIXe siècles*. Paris: Société de démographie historique, 1973.

Biraben, J.-N. "Le médecin et l'enfant au XVIIIe siècle (aperçu sur la pédiatrie au XVIIIe siècle)." *Annales de démographie historique, 1973*. Paris-The Hague: Mouton, 1973.

Bloch, Camille. *L'assistance et l'état en France à la veille de la Révolution. Généralités de Paris, Rouen, Alençon, Orléans, Châlons, Soissons, Amiens. 1764–1790*. Paris: Librairie Alphonse Picard et Fils, 1908.

Boltanski, Luc. *Prime éducation et morale de classe*. Paris-The Hague: Mouton, 1969.

Braudel, Fernand. "History and the Social Sciences." *Economy and Society in Early Modern Europe, Essays from Annales*. Edited by Peter Burke. New York: Harper and Row, 1972.

Brinton, Crane. *The Jacobins: An Essay in the New History*. New York: Macmillan Co., 1930.

Brookner, Anita. *Greuze: The Rise and Fall of an Eighteenth-Century Phenomenon*. Greenwich, Conn.: New York Graphic Society, Ltd., 1972.

Cameron, Rondo. "Economic Growth and Stagnation in France, 1815–1914." *Journal of Modern History*, 30 (Mar. 1958), 1–13.

Chamoux, Antoinette. "L'enfance abandonnée à Reims à la fin du XVIIIe siècle." *Annales de démographie historique, 1973.* Paris-The Hague: Mouton, 1973.

———, ed. "Mise en nourrice et mortalité des enfants légitimes." *Annales de démographie historique, 1973.* Paris-The Hague: Mouton, 1973.

Clough, S. B. "Retardative Factors in French Economic Development in the Nineteenth and Twentieth Centuries." *Journal of Economic History,* 6 (1946), Supplement, 91–102.

Crouzet, François. "England and France in the Eighteenth Century: A Comparative Analysis of Two Economic Growths." *Revolutions 1775–1830.* Edited by Merryn Williams. Baltimore: Penguin, 1971.

———. "French Economic Growth in the Nineteenth Century." *History,* 59 (June 1974), 167–79.

Defarges, Dom Bénigne. "L'industrie des nourrices morvandelles au XIXᵉ siècle." *Pays de Bourgogne,* 20 (1974), 979–83, and 21 (1974), 18–22.

Delasselle, Claude. "Les enfants abandonnés à Paris au XVIIIᵉ siècle." *Annales: économies, sociétés, civilisations,* 30 (Jan.–Feb. 1975), 187–218.

DeMause, Lloyd. "The Evolution of Childhood." *The History of Childhood.* Edited by Lloyd DeMause. New York: Harper & Row, 1974.

Dinet, Dominique. "Statistiques de mortalité infantile sous le Consulat et l'Empire." *Hommage à Marcel Reinhard. Sur la population francaise au XVIIIᵉ et au XIXᵉ siècles.* Paris: Société de démographie historique, 1973.

Donzelot, Jacques. *La police des familles.* Paris: Éditions de Minuit, 1977.

Dupoux, Albert. *Sur les pas de Monsieur Vincent: Trois cents ans d'histoire parisienne de l'enfance abandonnée.* Paris: Revue de l'assistance publique, 1958.

Flandrin, Jean-Louis. "L'attitude à l'égard du petit enfant et les conduites sexuelles dans la civilisation occidentale: structures anciennes et évolution." *Annales de démographie historique, 1973.* Paris-The Hague: Mouton, 1973.

———. *Familles. Parenté, maison, sexualité dans l'ancienne société.* Paris: Hachette, 1976.

Fleury, Michel, and Valmary, Pierre. "Les progrès de l'instruction élémentaire de Louis XIV à Napoléon III d'après l'enquête de Louis Maggiolo (1877–1879)." *Population,* 12 (1957), 71–92.

Fosseyeux, Marcel. "L'assistance aux prisonniers à Paris sous l'ancien régime." *Mémoires de la Société de l'histoire de Paris et de l'Ile-de-France,* 48 (1925), 110–29.

———. "Sages-femmes et nourrices à Paris au XVIIᵉ siècle." *Revue de Paris* (October 1, 1921), 535–54.

Franklin, Alfred. *La vie privée d'autrefois: arts et métiers, modes, moeurs, usages des parisiens du XIIᵉ au XVIIIᵉ siècle.* Vol. 19, *L'enfant.* Paris: Librairie Plon, 1896.

Galliano, Paul. "La mortalité infantile (indigènes et nourrissons) dans la banlieue sud de Paris à la fin du XVIIIᵉ siècle (1774–1794)." *Annales de démographie historique, 1966.* Paris: Éditions Sirey, 1967.

―――. "Le fonctionnement du bureau parisien des nourrices à la fin du XVIIIᵉ siècle." *Actes du 93ᵉ Congrès national des sociétés savantes. Tours. 1968.* Section d'histoire moderne et contemporaine, Vol. 2. Paris: Bibliothèque nationale, 1971.

Ganiage, Jean. "Nourrissons parisiens en Beauvaisis." *Hommage à Marcel Reinhard. Sur la population française au XVIIIᵉ et au XIXᵉ siècles.* Paris: Société de démographie historique, 1973.

―――. *Trois villages d'Ile-de-France au XVIIIᵉ siècle. Étude démographique.* Institut National d'Études Démographiques, Travaux et Documents, Cahier no. 40. Paris: Presses universitaires de France, 1963.

Garden, Maurice. *Lyon et les lyonnais au XVIIIᵉ siècle.* Paris: Les Belles Lettres, 1970.

Gautier, Étienne, and Henry, Louis. *La population de Crulai, paroisse normande. Étude historique.* Paris: Presses universitaires de France, 1958.

Goubert, A. "Le placement et la mortalité des enfants de Paris dans les paroisses du Vieux-Rouen et de Bouafles, de 1686 à 1824." *Bulletin de la société des études locales dans l'enseignement public. Groupe de la Seine-inférieure* (May 1935–May 1936), 61–85.

Greenbaum, Louis S. " 'Measure of Civilization': The Hospital Thought of Jacques Tenon on the Eve of the French Revolution." *Bulletin of the History of Medicine,* 49 (Spring 1975), 43–56.

Guillaume, Pr. Pierre. *La population de Bordeaux au XIXᵉ siècle, essai d'histoire sociale.* Paris: Librairie Armand Colin, 1972.

Henry, Louis. "The Population of France in the Eighteenth Century." *Population in History: Essays in Historical Demography.* Edited by D. V. Glass and D. E. C. Eversley. London: Edward Arnold, 1965.

Hewitt, Margaret. *Wives and Mothers in Victorian Industry.* London: Rockliff, 1958.

Hufton, Olwen H. *The Poor in Eighteenth-Century France, 1750–1789.* Oxford: Clarendon Press, 1974.

Hunt, David. *Parents and Children in History: The Psychology of Family Life in Early Modern France.* New York: Harper & Row, 1972.

Kaplow, Jeffry. *The Names of Kings: Parisian Laboring Poor in the Eighteenth Century.* New York: Basic Books, 1972.

Knodel, J., and van de Walle, E. "Breast feeding, fertility and infant mortality." *Population Studies,* 21 (Sept. 1967), 109–31.

Lachiver, Marcel. *La population de Meulan du XVIIe au XIXe siècle (vers 1600–1870). Étude de démographie historique.* Paris: S.E.V.P.E.N., 1969.

———. "Tarif des mois de nourrice dans le Bassin parisien en 1771." *Annales de démographie historique, 1968.* Paris: Éditions Sircy, 1968.

Landes, David S. "French Entrepreneurship and Industrial Growth in the Nineteenth Century." *Journal of Economic History,* 9 (1949), 45–61.

Le Pesant, Michel. "Les nourrissons parisiens dans les campagnes de l'Eure sous l'Ancien Régime." *Cahiers Léopold Delisle,* 6 (1957), 137–45.

Loux, Françoise, and Morel, Marie-France. "L'enfance et les savoirs sur le corps: pratiques médicales et pratiques populaires dans la France traditionelle." *Ethnologie française,* 6 (1976), 309–24.

May, Gita. *Madame Roland and the Age of Revolution.* New York: Columbia University Press, 1970.

McCleary, G. F. *The Early History of the Infant Welfare Movement.* London: H. K. Lewis and Co., 1933.

Mercier, Roger. *L'enfant dans la société du XVIIIe siècle (avant L'ÉMILE).* Paris, 1961.

Morel, Marie-France. "Théories et pratiques de l'allaitement en France au XVIIIème siècle." *Annales de démographie historique, 1976.* Paris-The Hague: Mouton, 1977.

———. "Ville et campagne dans le discours médical sur la petite enfance au XVIIIe siècle." *Annales: économies, sociétés, civilisations,* 32 (Sept.–Oct. 1977), 1007–24.

———, and Loux, F. "Prime éducation, savoirs populaires et pouvoir médical: XVIIIe–XXe siècles." *Politique aujourd'hui* (May–June 1976), 87–103.

Nolleau, H. "Les femmes dans la population active de 1856 à 1954." *Économie et politique* (Paris), 75 (Oct. 1960), 2–21.

Plumb, J. H. "The New World of Children in Eighteenth-Century England." *Past and Present,* 67 (May 1975), 64–95.

Rambaud, Pierre. *Les nourrices d'autrefois en Poitou.* Poitiers: G. Roy, 1915.

Renault, Jules, and Labeaume, G. "L'évolution de la Protection de l'enfance." *Bulletin de l'Académie de Médecine,* Series III, 117 (1937), 763–77.

Risler, Dominique. "Nourrices et meneurs de Paris au XVIIIe siècle." Unpublished Mémoire de maîtrise d'histoire, lettres et sciences humaines, Nanterre, June 1971.

Rollet, Catherine. "Allaitement, mise en nourrice et mortalité infantile en France à la fin du XIXe siècle." *Population,* 33 (1978), 1189–1203.

Rougerie, Jacques. "Belleville." *Les élections de 1869, études.* Edited by Louis Girard. Paris: Librairie Marcel Rivière et Cie., 1960.

Rudé, George. *The Crowd in the French Revolution.* New York: Oxford University Press, 1959.

Scott, Joan W., and Tilly, Louise A. "Women's Work and the Family in Nineteenth-Century Europe." *Comparative Studies in Society and History,* 17 (Jan. 1975), 36–64.

Shorter, Edward. *The Making of the Modern Family.* New York: Basic Books, 1975.

Smelser, Neil J. "Sociological History: The Industrial Revolution and the British Working-Class Family." *Journal of Social History,* 1 (1967), 17–35.

Soboul, Albert. *Les sans-culottes parisiens en l'an II. Mouvement populaire et gouvernement révolutionnaire, 2 juin 1973–9 thermidor an II.* Paris: Librairie Clavreuil, 1958.

Stearns, Peter N. "Working-Class Women in Britain, 1890–1914." *Suffer and Be Still: Women in the Victorian Age.* Edited by Martha Vicinus. Bloomington: Indiana University Press, 1972.

Sullerot, Evelyne. *Histoire et sociologie du travail féminin, essai.* N.p.: Éditions Gonthier, 1968.

Sussman, George D. "Carriers of Cholera and Poison Rumors in France in 1832." *Societas—A Review of Social History,* 3 (Summer 1973), 233–51.

———. "The End of the Wet-Nursing Business in France, 1874–1914." *Journal of Family History,* 2 (Fall 1977), 237–58.

———. "Parisian Infants and Norman Wet Nurses in the Early Nineteenth Century: A Statistical Study." *Journal of Interdisciplinary History,* 7 (Spring 1977), 637–53.

———. "The Wet-Nursing Business in Nineteenth-Century France." *French Historical Studies,* 9 (Fall 1975), 304–28.

———. "The Wet-Nursing Business in Paris, 1769–1876." *Proceedings of the First Annual Meeting of the Western Society for French History, March 14–15, 1974.* Edited by Edgar Leon Newman. Las Cruces: New Mexico State University Press, 1974.

van de Walle, Étienne. *The Female Population of France in the Nineteenth Century: A Reconstruction of 82 Départements.* Princeton: Princeton University Press, 1974.

———, and Preston, Samuel H. "Mortalité de l'enfance au XIXᵉ siècle à Paris et dans le département de la Seine." *Population,* 29 (Jan.–Feb. 1974), 89–107.

———, and van de Walle, Francine. "Allaitement, stérilité et contraception: les opinions jusqu'au XIXᵉ siècle." *Population,* 27 (July–Oct. 1972), 685–701.

Vidalenc, Jean. *Le département de l'Eure sous la monarchie constitutionnelle, 1814–1848.* Paris: Librairie Marcel Rivière et Cie., 1952.

Whetham, E. H. "The London Milk Trade, 1860–1900." *Economic History Review*, 2nd ser. 17 (1964), 369–80.

Wickes, Ian G. "A History of Infant Feeding." *Archives of Disease in Childhood*, 28 (1953), 151–58, 232–40, 332–40, 416–22, and 495–502.

Index

A Note on the Author

GEORGE D. SUSSMAN is assistant commissioner for Postsecondary Education Policy Analysis in the New York State Education Department at Albany. Prior to working for the State of New York, Mr. Sussman taught history at Tuskegee Institute, C. W. Post College, and Vanderbilt University. He received his M.A. (1966) and Ph.D. (1971) from Yale University. He has numerous publications in such journals as the *Bulletin of the History of Medicine*, the *Journal of Family History*, *French Historical Studies*, and the *Journal of Interdisciplinary History*.